THE GAME CHANGERS

THE
GAME CHANGERS

ABNER HAYNES, LEON KING, AND
THE FALL OF MAJOR COLLEGE
FOOTBALL'S COLOR BARRIER IN TEXAS

JEFF MILLER

FOREWORD BY JOE GREENE

**SPORTS
PUBLISHING**

Sports Publishing books may be purchased in bulk at special discounts for sales promotion, corporate gifts, fund-raising, or educational purposes. Special editions can also be created to specifications. For details, contact the Special Sales Department, Sports Publishing, 307 West 36th Street, 11th Floor, New York, NY 10018 or sportspubbooks@skyhorsepublishing.com.

Sports Publishing® is a registered trademark of Skyhorse Publishing, Inc.®, a Delaware corporation.

Visit our website at www.sportspubbooks.com.

10 9 8 7 6 5 4 3 2 1

Library of Congress Cataloging-in-Publication Data is available on file.

Cover design by Tom Lau
Cover photo credit: University of North Texas

ISBN: 978-1-61321-937-9
Ebook ISBN: 978-1-61321-942-3

Printed in the United States of America

CONTENTS

FOREWORD
Joe Greene

I HAD A WONDERFUL EXPERIENCE at North Texas. I met my wife, Agnes, there. My two sons—Major and DeLon—played football for North Texas. To say that North Texas had an influence on my life and my career is an understatement.

People like Abner Haynes, Leon King, and others who preceded me, softened the experience for me. I was probably naïve. Growing up in Temple, Texas in the early 1960s, I didn't have an opportunity to play for the University of Texas, which was only seventy miles away. Same for Baylor, which was only thirty-five miles away. But integration in football was not a pressing interest for me at the time. I was interested in studying accounting, and I read about North Texas's business department in a college catalog in the library of my high school, Dunbar High. That was my first encounter with North Texas.

I turned the pages in that catalog, and there was a picture of Abner Haynes. And it mentioned their Sun Bowl team from 1959. I read more and more, and then I investigated North Texas. I had a couple of scholarship offers—from Texas A&I down in Kingsville, New Mexico State, and the University of Houston. I thought Kingsville was too far. I was going to visit Houston, but the visit coincided with my school prom. Well, the prom was going to win over that.

I sent a letter to North Texas, and they invited me up to visit. I met with head coach Odus Mitchell and assistant coach Fred McCain. I was only 6-foot-3 and 235, maybe 240 pounds. It turns out they saw some game film on me. They offered me a scholarship. After that, I got a visit every other week from Coach McCain and coach Bob Way. I decided that was where I wanted to go.

Coach Mitchell really cared about his players. He was easy to talk to. You could visit with him anytime. He was a very nice man—and a very good football coach. Going to North Texas, playing football, and learning from them and from coach Herb Ferrill for three years taught me things that helped me through my entire pro career. I played with some great players and great individuals at North Texas. There was my roommate, Chuck Beatty—he became the mayor of Waxahachie; we call him "Hatchet"—and Cedrick Hardman, Ron Shanklin, Steve Ramsey. We only lost five games through all of my three varsity seasons.

I met Leon King a couple of times. I've been in the company of Abner frequently after meeting him in 1968 or '69. I saw him a couple of years ago when we both attended a meeting of the North Texas Super Bowl Committee, before the Super Bowl game between the Steelers and the Packers at Cowboys Stadium in 2011. Abner was asked to speak about his experiences at North Texas. It was the first time I heard him talk about that, and the very same things that I'd heard from one of Abner's teammates, Bill Carrico, about the great togetherness of those North Texas teams. I eventually also had the opportunity to talk to Jerry LeVias about what he went through at SMU, only thirty miles away from Denton, when I was at North Texas.

I'm proud of my time at North Texas, and proud of what the school accomplished in the years before me that changed the face of college football in the state of Texas.

Joe Greene did not remain at 235-240 pounds much longer. He became a three-year starter for North Texas when freshmen were still prohibited from participating in varsity competition. He was a three-time All-Missouri Valley Conference performer, and the school's first consensus All-American selection as a senior defensive tackle in 1968.

Greene was selected fourth overall in the 1969 pro football draft by the National Football League's Pittsburgh Steelers, earned a starting position before the season began, and was named the NFL's Rookie of the Year that season. Within a few years, Greene and fellow 1969 Pittsburgh draftee L.C. Greenwood were joined by defensive linemen Ernie Holmes and Dwight White to form the famed "Steel Curtain." In his thirteen-year NFL career, the 275-pound Greene was named to the All-Pro team five times, selected to the Pro Bowl team ten times, chosen as the league's Defensive Player of the Year twice, and played for four Super Bowl champions.

Greene was inducted into the College Football Hall of Fame in 1984, the Texas Sports Hall of Fame in 1985, and the Pro Football Hall of Fame in 1987. He was one of the six charter members of the University of North Texas Athletic Hall of Fame in 1981. In April 2013, Greene and Abner Haynes were among the North Texas gridiron standouts selected to the school's All-Century football team. Away from the playing field, Greene in 1983 became the first black appointed to North Texas's Board of Regents.

INTRODUCTION

"How do you act?"

THE FIRST DAY OF SEPTEMBER 1956 dawned bright and seasonably warm across northern Texas on a Saturday. But in a region of the country that was still morphing fitfully, and to a great degree unwillingly, from the Confederate bloodlines of almost 100 years earlier to a post-World War II American society of inclusion, the racial climate of the day displayed itself through contrasting scenes across the area.

Just south of Fort Worth in the Tarrant County farming community of Mansfield, that Saturday morning found attorneys for the town's school district meeting to plan their latest attempt to prevent a handful of black students from integrating Mansfield High School with the might of the federal judiciary behind them. In front of the students and their families earlier that week, though, stood literally hundreds of angry white citizens who had done whatever they deemed necessary to prevent the students from enrolling. By the time the school district's attorneys gathered quietly that Saturday morning, the hunting dogs from days earlier no longer guarded the school property, and the effigies that had been hung on the school's main flagpole and across Main Street downtown had been removed.

That Saturday afternoon on Fort Worth's east side, Lloyd Austin was busy moving his family into a house on North Judkins Street. Maybe

Austin was unrealistically optimistic that a black family would be welcomed onto an otherwise all-white block, since there were black families living in the same neighborhood only a few streets away. Maybe he feared brief trouble but thought it would blow over, that it wouldn't be so bad. Austin surely knew otherwise that night, when his new home was surrounded by an estimated 150 whites, some of whom yelled, "Get those niggers!" Some carried signs, such as "I ain't no jungle monkey lover, send 'um back to the dark Congo;" some threw rocks; some hung an effigy in his front yard. It wouldn't be his front yard for long. Before the weekend was out, front windows were broken out, screens were ripped, and Austin—who armed himself and fired toward at least one menacing car that drove by—abandoned his efforts to move his family into the neighborhood.

About forty miles northeast of Fort Worth that Saturday morning, a cabbie pulled over in Denton toward the east end of Hickory Street, on the black side of town, to take in two passengers. "Where you going?" the cabbie cheerfully asked. One of the two young men who entered replied, "Fouts Field." "What's going on there?" the cabbie continued. "We're reporting to football practice." The cabbie would have had good reason to be intrigued by two blacks heading to Fouts Field, home of North Texas State College's all-white football team. The school had only first allowed blacks to enroll as undergraduates during the previous full semester, in February 1956, with the admission of a middle-aged Fort Worth woman named Irma Sephas. More blacks took advantage of the new opportunity in September 1956 (though it's difficult now to determine how many, since North Texas wasn't in the practice of asking each of its students to officially identify his or her race).

Two of the new black students that fall—two of the black freshmen—sat in the back of that cab as it headed west across town to Fouts Field on the western edge of the North Texas State campus. Those two young black men, Abner Haynes and Leon King, had both graduated from Dallas's Lincoln High School the previous spring. They weren't sure what to expect as the cab pulled into the parking lot next to North Texas's football stadium. That's why Haynes and King held hands during part of the ride. That's why each carried a pocketknife, a common safeguard back home in south Dallas that they'd agreed to bring only at the last minute, before leaving the house in east Denton and walking a few blocks to catch a cab on the relatively busy Hickory Street.

The cabbie parked in a lot next to Fouts Field. Haynes, his mind and heart racing, tried to remember what his father—Bishop Fred Haynes of the Church of God in Christ—had advised him. "How do you act?" King and Haynes exited the cab in the gravel parking lot, dozens of white football players standing on the other side of the lot—each apparently looking directly at them. Haynes and King said nothing, and weren't sure if they should make the first move, literally, and walk toward their new teammates. That wasn't necessary; three of the white players began to walk slowly toward them. The three whites finally reached the two apprehensive blacks, and one of the whites—Garland Warren, a junior center from right there in Denton—extended his right hand and said, "Welcome to the team."

By all accounts, that handshake—and those that immediately followed from the other two white players who walked across that parking lot, Charlie and Vernon Cole from nearby Pilot Point—ushered in the era of racially integrated football at four-year schools in the state of Texas. Leon King and Abner Haynes played that 1956 season on North Texas's freshman team, and saw their first varsity action a year later. Nevertheless, some sports authors and athletics historians through the years have hedged on citing North Texas as breaking the color line for so-called major college football among four-year schools across the state.

In 1956, North Texas was transitioning from membership in the Gulf Coast Conference to full membership in the Missouri Valley Conference beginning with the 1957-'58 academic year. During that era's classification of college programs, the Missouri Valley was in the equivalent of today's Football Bowl Subdivision, but wasn't akin to a power conference. Still, there could be no denying that North Texas fielded a "big-league" football program in 1959, when Haynes was a senior on the football team, and after King had left the program and temporarily dropped out of school. The Eagles appeared in the Associated Press's Top 20 poll of the best football squads in the country for two weeks in November '59 after running their record to 8-0. Dreams of an undefeated season ended soon after, on a 25-degree day at Tulsa. North Texas thought its dream of playing in a bowl game ended that frigid day, too, but the Eagles were invited to play in the 1959 Sun Bowl in El Paso, Texas.

It would be reasonable to conclude that North Texas entered college football's upper echelon—albeit far from the top of that strata—in 1957, the year the Eagles first competed for the Missouri Valley Conference championship. That year, six state football programs played in the Southwest Conference (alphabetically Baylor, Rice, SMU, Texas, Texas A&M, and TCU). One was transitioning from the Border Conference up toward football membership in the SWC beginning in 1960 (Texas Tech), one was also playing in the MVC (Houston), and three were members of the Border Conference (Hardin-Simmons, Texas Western, and West Texas State). It would be years before the names that are most commonly associated with racial integration of college football in Texas first stepped on campus: Warren McVea at the University of Houston in 1964, and Jerry LeVias at SMU in 1965.

The Latin phrase *bonum arduum* means "a difficult good," and maybe that's what happened when North Texas succeeded in integrating its football program years before its SWC neighbors. The school's first black student at any level was a forty-one-year-old educator named A. Tennyson Miller, who was able to enroll in a doctorate class at North Texas during the summer 1954 session because the class wasn't offered at any of the state's black colleges. In an interview for UNT's oral history collection in 1992, Miller described his face-to-face encounter with school president J.C. Matthews as one of reasonable discourse lacking in edge or confrontation of any kind: "Since we're both plowing new ground, we can both guarantee each other that we plow it in the most gentle way possible."

Just as the school had integrated its student body well before the state's better-known institutions, North Texas did so via a school's most visible ambassadors—its athletes—with a minimum of strife, and the wisdom not to boast or preen over a perceived victory of sorts. Matthews held his alma mater's top office from 1951-'68. He grew up amid segregated north Texas towns, but in early adulthood recognized and empathized with the plight of the state's blacks in a society that denied them the best education. Under Matthews's leadership, North Texas welcomed Miller as its first black student at any level in 1954, and its first black undergraduate during the second semester of the 1955-'56 school year (the forty-one-year-old Sephas, who commuted from Fort Worth). The arrival of Sephas and every other subsequent black undergrad was made possible by a 1955 lawsuit brought against the school by the family of a young man from Dallas named Joe Atkins, who was a few years ahead of King and Haynes at Lincoln High. The court victory in December 1955 came too late for Atkins to personally benefit, since he'd already enrolled elsewhere for the '55-'56 school year.

Abner Haynes went on to become North Texas's greatest athletic hero to that point, arguably surpassed since then by only 1960s defensive tackle Joe Greene, a member of the Pro Football Hall of Fame. Haynes became an immediate pro football star after leaving North Texas, winning not only the Rookie of the Year award for 1960 in the new American Football League, but also its inaugural Most Valuable Player honor that same year. He helped the Dallas Texans win the third AFL championship in 1962, was a three-time all-star during his seven-year pro career, and went on to build a successful business career. Leon King didn't possess the same level of football talent as his high school friend. King played football at North Texas into the 1958 season, then left the team. He withdrew from school to support a young wife and family, but returned to the Denton campus in the early 1960s to earn not only his bachelor's degree but also a master's degree—to which he eventually added a doctorate. He became a fixture in the Dallas school district from which he'd graduated, serving as a teacher, coach, and administrator, as the district went through its own contentious desegregation.

In the opinion of this writer, this story deserves a thorough telling decades later to recognize the contributions of those involved. That includes King and Haynes themselves. It includes such North Texas officials as president Matthews, head football coach Odus Mitchell, and his staff. It also includes white teammates who went beyond the initial welcoming handshakes, some of whom refused to be seated at restaurants during out-of-town game trips when service was denied to their new black peers, and who formed emotional bonds that have lasted into another century. The contributions include those made by other new black students at North Texas beyond those on the football team, who simply sought an education that was previously afforded exclusively to their white counterparts, and it includes faculty members who believed augmentation of a new age of racial acceptance at North Texas should be accompanied by similar changes just a few blocks from campus, where hostility and resentment still ran rampant.

This book attempts to recount the events, introduce the people, and provide a better understanding of a unique era at North Texas, detailing what happened before then to help make that time possible and what has happened since.

Abner Haynes has been deservedly recognized for his exploits on the football field, having had his North Texas jersey number retired, inducted into the Texas Sports Hall of Fame, and named to North Texas's All-Century football team in 2013. Leon King didn't amass the same kinds of football statistics in his time as a North Texas player, and never played pro ball. But King suffered the same kinds of indignities as Haynes during that 1956 season as a freshman football player, and again the following year as a member of the North Texas varsity, almost a decade before any other black football player went through a similar experience at a predominantly white four-year school in the state of Texas. That surely would qualify him for consideration to join his old friend from North Texas, from Dallas's Lincoln High—from one end of south Dallas's Pine Street to the other—for inclusion in the Texas Sports Hall of Fame.

CHAPTER 1

"When the rabble hiss, well may the patriots tremble"

THE COUNTY AND TOWN OF Denton are named after John Bunyan Denton, a native Tennessean who came to Texas from Arkansas in 1837. Denton was orphaned as a child, taken in by a neighboring family, but took leave of their hospitality at the age of twelve, when he was greatly dissatisfied with his treatment at home. In his late teens, Denton took up a career in the ministry and married a school teacher by the name of Mary Greenlee Stewart. By the time he arrived in the Lone Star Republic, only months after the young nation's successful rebellion from Mexico, Denton's list of occupations had varied from preacher to lawyer to soldier. He's credited with delivering the first sermon on Denton County soil, in 1839, when he served as a volunteer accompanying a ranger force on an Indian campaign camped at Hackberry Creek.

Standing 5-foot-10 with blue eyes and curly black hair, Denton took up law when frontier preaching proved insufficient for supporting a wife and four children. Early in their marriage, he put his legal skills to the test in a murder case in which the defendant was none other than his wife. Mary Denton had briefly left her husband while they were living in Arkansas, and became a milliner—a hat maker. (According to the *Denton Record-Chronicle* account of the episode many years later, "a milliner's morals were often suspect.") A wealthy male merchant tried to enter her room one night, and Mrs. Denton refused. The undaunted gentleman then simply broke the door down, only to be halted by fatal gunfire.

Mrs. Denton faced an enormous obstacle in being cleared, considering the social status of the deceased compared to her own lowly standing. She was initially brought before a judge without any legal counsel. She told the court that she had no attorney, nor friends at all. It was then that John Denton, simply an out-of-town stranger to those in the courtroom, interrupted and said, "No, not without friends. If it pleases your honor, I will appear for the defendant, if acceptable to her and the court." He eventually revealed his standing as the defendant's husband in an emotional soliloquy: "Gentleman of the jury, look upon the defendant. Scan that face and behold something dearer to me than life and more precious to me than all things else under the blue canopy of heaven. Need I tell you that she is my wife. She never had an impure thought in her life." He then turned from the jury toward the defendant and said, "Behold, in me you have more than a friend—a husband." She jumped into his arms and broke into tears. The jury didn't even leave the jury box in returning a verdict of not guilty. Victorious counselor and defendant, reunited as husband and wife, left the courtroom arm in arm.

But the Dentons' days in Arkansas were over. They settled in Clarksville, Texas, about 140 miles northeast of what is now Denton, in Red River County. He partnered with Edward Tarrant, for whom Tarrant County is named. While Denton's fractured upbringing was greatly responsible for him not participating in formal schooling for terribly long, he made himself into a well-read man and boasted possibly the best personal library in Clarksville. In 1840, Denton attempted to add politician to his stable of avocations, but was defeated in his pursuit of a seat in Texas's 5th Congress by Robert Potter. It turned out Potter was killed in 1842 in an east Texas land battle called the Regulator-Moderator War. But he outlived Denton, who was felled by an Indian's arrow in May 1841 at the Battle of Village Creek, just east of the present-day Fort Worth. Denton's troops encountered the Indians on the opposite side of the creek. Gen. Tarrant urged a group to cross the creek, Denton among them. There was concern that Indians would exhume Denton's body in order to claim a scalp, so he was initially buried in an unmarked grave with squares of grass carefully placed back in their original places. He was later reburied, first in the yard of his home, and finally in the lawn of the county courthouse. In November 1856, the settlement of Denton—officially incorporated in 1866—was chosen as the county seat. The county's first jail, located just behind the courthouse, was a two-story structure made of logs and featured a creative design meant to bolster security. Prisoners were taken upstairs, and then lowered through a trap door into their accommodations.

The vote on Texas's secession from the Union on January 18, 1861, was 166-8 in favor of separation. One of the eight nay votes came courtesy of Denton's representative to the state legislature, Collin County resident James W. Throckmorton. While small in relative number, the eight were siding with Gov. Sam Houston. After Throckmorton delivered his simple "No," he wasn't booed or jeered—merely hissed. "When the rabble hiss," Throckmorton retorted in disdain, "well may the patriots tremble." It was weeks after the fall of Fort Sumter in South Carolina, and battles such as the first Bull Run in Virginia, that news of the ultimate escalation of tensions, an actual Civil War, reached the citizens of Denton County. Their sentiments were with the southern cause, but more so to enthusiastically carry the banner for states' rights than to prevent the Yankees' eradication of slavery. It was estimated there weren't even a dozen slaves present in the county at the time. While Texas was geographically on the fringe of Dixie's boundaries, there apparently was no lack of avidity to don the battle grays. So wrote Ed F. Bates in his 1918 *History and Reminiscences of Denton County*: "The hearts of our people were filled with human liberty as never before. ... The military spirit prevailed and young Denton County, sixteen years old, furnished eight companies of as brave, hardy, and fearless soldiers as could be found in the State, with many joining companies from other counties. Nearly one thousand men enlisted from the county and went to the front." (Bates previously served as a Denton councilman and mayor, and was credited with installing the city's first sewer system.)

Curiously, one of the county's fighting men was a native of Maine and a graduate of Yale. Otis G. Welch came south in 1852 to practice law, became legal advisor to the city of Denton, and helped plot and name its streets. In the Confederate army, he rose to the rank of colonel and indicated no conflicted feelings toward his former home in a letter written in August 1861: "The most of us are well and in fine spirits and anxious for a brush with the damned Union men of Missouri or anywhere else." Another officer from north Texas was none other than James Throckmorton. He put together a company of men from Collin and Denton counties and combined them with soldiers from Cooke County, which separated Denton County from Oklahoma to the north. The fighting force crossed the Red River and captured northern military installations at Fort Arbuckle, Fort Washita, and Fort Cobb.

The conflict had about reached its midpoint in 1863, though no one was aware that two more deplorable years of bloodshed lay ahead, when a black man living in Denton County learned justice could be relatively swift and not necessarily balanced. Pess White, age thirty, was accused by a white woman whose husband was fighting with the Confederate army of entering her home uninvited and attempting an assault. White was tried in a town on the east side of the county, Little Elm, which borders Lewisville Lake. The proceedings were run by Joel Clark, the justice of the peace. White "was given a speedy trial and condemned to death," Bates wrote. The woman's husband actually wasn't fighting on some far-off battlefield, but was relatively close by, serving in nearby Fannin County, just northeast of Collin County. Clark had the husband summoned to serve as executioner. White was provided fifteen minutes in which to pray. He was kneeling with his hands together in prayer when a bullet rendered him dead instantaneously.

Soon after, a Denton County slave named Nelse was suspected of trying to poison some of the soldiers' wives—"war widows"—though the description thankfully didn't accurately apply to all of them. Nelse was found guilty and hanged from a tree. And there was the case of the black man from north of Denton in Pilot Point who was found guilty of murder and hanged. Bates, after detailing the troika of incidents, wrote:

> These three cases are the only ones where the negro was involved in our county during the war, and are recorded to show not only the fact, but the method, of meting out justice by the white men or home guard. Quite a number of white men were hanged in like manner. The executions of these three negroes may seem unauthorized and barbarous, but when compared to the lynchings and the use of the torch of this age, which took place in our adjoining counties, we can but commend the wisdom, patience, and mercy of the home guards of 1861–65 in their effort to protect the women and children of Denton County. … Fifty-two years have passed [as of 1918]. People have made rapid progress in every other line, but the negro question is still unsettled in the matter of crimes against women. Lynchings are of frequent occurrence, and the wild passions of men seemingly cannot be controlled, either in the North or the South, when these horrible crimes are committed. Denton County has never yet burned a man at the stake.

It required almost a year following Gen. Robert E. Lee's begrudged visit to the Appomattox court house in April 1865 for the last of the Denton County militia to make it back to hearth and home. Like the defeated athlete who bemoaned that his team simply ran out of time, Bates depicted the soldiers' succumbing as a near inevitable consequence of the Confederacy's disadvantage in funding and materials. "Not conquered but disarmed," he wrote. "… heroes of the lost cause!" Texas's post-war politics were greatly shaped by Throckmorton, who was returned to Austin as the area's representative to the new constitutional convention. He was named the chairman of the convention, was instrumental in shaping the document and—in June 1866—was elected governor.

CHAPTER 2

The Green and White

THAT NORTH TEXAS WOULD LATER assume a leading role in desegregating its student enrollment in general, and its football team in particular, during the 1950s might have been traced to the school's roots. It was initially named Texas Normal College—normal as in the era's moniker for an institution of higher learning dedicated to the instruction of teachers. Texas Normal began educating students on the second floor of the B.J. Wilson hardware store at the northwest corner of the town's courthouse square in September 1890. Only weeks after the school opened, its enrollment became more diverse than most. Twenty-eight Creek Indians who lived in the territory located just beyond the Red River in what would become Oklahoma were admitted as students.

The institution's name was changed in 1894 to North Texas Normal College, and in 1901 to North Texas State Normal College. A more significant transformation took place in 1916, when the teaching certification was replaced as the ultimate didactic goal with a full-fledged bachelor's degree, which soon after led to another name change—North Texas State Teachers College, in 1923. Athletics had been introduced in 1902, when a group of boys informally started a football team and were outfitted in uniforms financed by town businessmen. What is recognized as North Texas's first intercollegiate sports competition took place in September 1903, when a baseball team representing the school defeated the team from a private school across town, John B. Denton College, by a score of 14–6.

During the next two months, a North Texas intercollegiate football team entered the fray and scored victories over an aggregation known as "the Denton boys" and Polytechnic College of Fort Worth. School colors of green and white were chosen, and the nickname Eagles came aboard through a student election in 1922.

That same year, North Texas became a charter member of the Texas Intercollegiate Athletic Association, whose members were primarily teachers' schools. Lest anyone fear North Texas would stray from its mission and make academic concessions for the benefit of its athletic program, the school's president from 1923 to '34—Robert Lincoln Marquis—wasn't interested in having a football team that would be proud of him. (Google "George Cross" and "Oklahoma" or "Gordon Gee" and "Ohio State" if that's unclear.) Marquis prohibited North Texas coaches from recruiting, essentially telling them to make do with whoever decided to enroll. He also bristled at the prospect of freshmen being eligible for varsity competition, a practice common at that time. Were those constraints not enough, Marquis also touted the idea that athletes should compete on the varsity for only one season, in order to allow more students the opportunity of benefitting from athletic participation.

During the 1927–'28 school year, a new male social fraternity unique to North Texas made its debut. It didn't have a name like the nationally affiliated Greek frats, such as Kappa Alpha or Beta Theta Pi. The "Geezles" were started by six students, one of whom—Tom Lawhorn—came up with the curious name, according to one of the other charter members, Cap Gilbreath, in his writing of a history of the Geezles in 1983. Just how Lawhorn concocted such a name Gilbreath failed to explain. As the Geezles caught on, a fair number of its members were North Texas athletes, particularly football players.

In 1931, North Texas and about half of the schools in the TIAA formed a new league, the Lone Star Conference, again populated primarily by teaching institutions. The Eagles dominated that conference into the late 1940s, primarily under the direction of coach Jack Sisco. Most of the defeats suffered during Sisco's thirteen seasons came while playing "up" against the more dominant Southwest Conference schools. Most of those games were competitive, but North Texas's 54-0 loss to SMU opening the 1941 season—Sisco's last campaign before retiring—revealed how unacceptable he found such a margin of defeat.

When the team returned from Dallas after that game, he steered the bus driver down a back alley and insisted the players enter a local restaurant that night through a back entrance, apparently to avoid the embarrassment of being seen. Sisco told his beleaguered troops that he initially considered ordering them back on the practice field the following day for a rare Sunday workout, but changed his mind. He instead suggested they all attend church, that they'd need some religion before hitting the field on Monday afternoon. Indeed, Sisco worked them that Monday well after sunset. When it was too dark to continue football-related activities, he had his charges end their day by doing leap-frog drills in pairs, lap after lap around the perimeter of the practice field. Deterrent or not, the Eagles followed their long, punitive session on the practice field by winning each of their remaining seven games that season.

Meanwhile, membership in the Geezles grew and began overlapping that of the school's male service organization known as the Talons. Attendance at one particular Talons meeting proved embarrassingly thin until those who were also Geezles belatedly arrived following the fraternity's meeting that same night. The sponsor of the Talons then essentially challenged those who were members of both groups to choose one or the other. All of the Geezles immediately rose to their feet and bid adieu. Such discord produced a rivalry between students who belonged exclusively to either the Geezles and Talons, even those who were North Texas football players. It reached the point that Sisco called a meeting of football-playing Talons and Geezles one afternoon in the locker room to negotiate a peace agreement.

As with the Greek frats, there was a Geezles house located at various points around campus through the years. It eventually sported a handsome statue of an eagle in the front yard. Also like the Greek frats, the Geezlers performed initiation rituals that weren't for the faint of heart. If a pledge couldn't swim, for instance, asking him to reach the shoreline of Lake Lewisville after being dumped well off into the briny deep could be a challenging assignment. There were other innovative exercises involving blindfolds and body parts that probably weren't all that different from what was asked of newcomers in the Greek houses across campus. Geezles initiations were scaled back in their creativity after one pledge's assignment resulted in hospitalization. What the other fraternities didn't have was *Spiriki* (pronounced SPEAR-a-kee), the greeting that Geezles used solely among themselves. The origin of Spiriki is as hazy as how the group was named, though one explanation offered is that it combined the word spirit with the "kee" cry of an eagle.

CHAPTER 3

"There was a colored boy in the lineup"

BE IT THE TEXAS INTERCOLLEGIATE Athletic Association, the Lone Star Conference, the Gulf Coast Conference—or the region's alpha dog of intercollegiate athletics for much of the twentieth century, the Southwest Conference—one aspect of competition never varied. The teams, like the student bodies that they represented, were white and were interested in exclusively facing white opponents.

Not that white schools located in Texas were any different from their brethren across the South. When schools in the region sought to play inter-sectional competition that happened to include blacks on their rosters, a custom euphemistically referred to as the gentlemen's agreement was employed. The mixed team, generally featuring only a small number of black players, would agree to field an all-white roster for the game in question. There sometimes were negotiations in which the all-white school tried to achieve some sort of competitive compromise if a star black player was being held out by volunteering to hold out its own player of near-equal athletic value.

The first Texas football program from what today would be called major college football to agree to face an opponent with one or more black players was Texas Tech. The school's athletic teams were known as the Matadors then, playing in Los Angeles in October 1934 against Loyola College (now known as Loyola Marymount). Tech opened in 1925 and fielded a football team that first fall. The trip to Los Angeles in 1934 was Tech's first to California and didn't feature a pushover opponent. The Loyola Lions were 4-0 and had outscored their opponents 104-0. They featured a black lineman named Al Duvall. In the *Lubbock Avalanche*'s write-up following the Friday night game that Loyola won 12-7, sports editor Collier Parris expressed neither surprise nor disdain regarding the presence of a black player in the Lions' lineup. To the contrary, Parris was complimentary of Duvall: "There was a colored boy in the pileups tonight who did much toward smothering Tech plays. His name is Al Duval [sic], and he plays tackle. They say here that he is the best tackle on the coast. He was there with the goods tonight, playing nearly all the game."

A trio of Southwest Conference football programs soon emulated Tech in agreeing to play integrated opponents to apparently satisfy the same desire—the opportunity to play in California. SMU played at UCLA in 1937 against a Bruins team whose two offensive stars were black: Kenny Washington and Woody Strode. TCU followed suit against UCLA in 1939, losing by the score of 6-2 to a squad that featured a new junior college transfer at running back named Jackie Robinson. Texas A&M had better luck with Robinson and the Bruins in 1940, winning 7-0.

Coach Matty Bell and SMU were also responsible for what appears to be the first instance of a major college football team featuring both whites and blacks playing within the confines of the Lone Star State. As the 1947 season was approaching its finish, the Mustangs clinched the Southwest Conference champion's host role in the Cotton Bowl Classic, to be played on New Year's Day 1948. When bowl invitations were being extended, SMU was ranked third in the nation behind top-rated Notre Dame (which voluntarily wasn't participating in bowls then) and No. 2 Michigan (as the Big Ten champion, tied to the Rose Bowl). The next highest ranked team—No. 4 Penn State, an eastern independent then—was therefore available for the Cotton and two other major bowls, New Orleans' Sugar and Miami's Orange. But none of those three bowls had ever invited a team with blacks, and the Nittany Lions' squad included two—juniors Wally Triplett, a two-way back, and Dennie Hoggard, an end. Penn State had made headlines in 1946 for taking a stand against segregation with its refusal to abide by the gentlemen's agreement and bench its black players for a scheduled game at Miami. The players voted to cancel the trip to Florida.

The mere presence of a black player in a college football game played in the South between predominantly white institutions had only happened for the first time in October 1947, when Harvard lineman Chester Pierce played at Virginia. SMU—namely Bell, who was also the Mustangs' athletic director—stepped forward after SMU clinched the Cotton Bowl berth and lobbied to play the best opponent possible. And if that opponent included one or more black players, Bell told *The Dallas Morning News*, "We have no objections ourselves. After all, we're supposed to live in a democracy." One of the players on that SMU team was Frank Payne Jr., a sophomore running back who served as understudy to All-American Doak Walker. Payne doesn't recall any issue among the Mustang players when they were collectively asked about facing an integrated opponent. "Nobody did," Payne says, "and that was the last I heard about it."

When the 1947 Nittany Lions were approached about accepting the bid, the players indicated they wouldn't again require the formality of a squad vote in determining whether they would acquiesce to playing without their two black members. Team captain Steve Suhey spoke to his fellow players and, according to teammate William "Rip" Scherer decades later, said, "Look. We're Penn State. We play as one, or we don't play at all." Which led to the popular *We are Penn State!* chant that is now standard fare at Nittany Lion athletic events. While SMU succeeded in opening the Cotton Bowl Classic to a mixed team, it couldn't achieve the same results when it came to housing the Penn State squad locally. With Dallas's hotels segregated, Bell and his staff helped arrange for the Nittany Lions to stay at the Dallas Naval Air Station located in suburban Grand Prairie, effectively cut off from the attractions of the big city. The blacks on the Penn State squad actually enjoyed a superior social experience during the team's time in Texas, squired off by local blacks to various engagements. The team's white players, many of whom were military veterans and not terribly accepting of confinement to their sleeping quarters, literally took matters into their own hands on occasion and hopped the fence to pursue personal entertainment. In the spirit of solidarity, SMU and Penn State played to a 13-13 tie.

By all appearances, North Texas's football team first played against a racially mixed opponent when the 1947 Eagles faced Nevada-Reno, featuring Sherman Howard and Alva Tabor, in the inaugural Salad Bowl in Phoenix. North Texas played at Nevada in 1948 and '49, and then hosted the Nevada Wolf Pack in 1950 in what appears to have been the first integrated visiting team to play at North Texas—if not the first at any major-college campus across the state, with Howard Barber, Al Barham, Lawrence "Nate" Hairston, and Howard Hartsfield. The account of that Eagles home game in the *Denton Record-Chronicle* didn't indicate any outcry among local football fans at North Texas hosting an opponent with blacks on its roster.

CHAPTER 4

"I came here to win"

JAMES CARL MATTHEWS BECAME NORTH Texas's eighth president in September 1951, having served on the school's faculty since soon after his graduation in 1925. His ascension to the office brought his North Texas experience full circle; on the autumn 1920 day when he got off a train in Denton upon first arriving at the school, he was personally greeted by North Texas president W.H. Bruce. Matthews, who went by J.C., was the first alumnus to occupy the position, and had toyed years earlier with becoming either a doctor or a druggist before honing in on a career as an educator. It was a career that he was already knee-deep into well before receiving his bachelor's degree in history. Matthews interrupted his student time at North Texas at age nineteen to take a teaching job in the three-teacher school in the little Foard County town of Rayland. A month into the job, the school had new plans for Matthews; he was named principal. He returned to North Texas soon after, only to leave prematurely again to teach at Weatherford High just southwest of Fort Worth. Matthews coached both of the sports offered there at the time (basketball and baseball), and was often the principal's right-hand man. He earned master's and doctoral degrees from George Peabody College for Teachers in Nashville, Tenn., before returning to Denton yet again.

Matthews was born in northwest Grayson County, which borders Oklahoma, and no blacks lived in that corner of the county. The largest town in that area was Whitesboro, where a black man was lynched and burned. To apparently avoid any further trouble after that, blacks weren't even allowed to get off a train there. As a ten-year-old, Matthews spent the summer with his grandparents and often traveled over to Sherman, the county seat, to sell apples. He and his grandfather were typically helped by a young black boy, with the two youngsters working opposite sides of a street. That was Matthews's first significant interaction with blacks, which became his first instance of befriending a black.

Matthews's educational career included a stint during the late 1930s as the state curriculum director, which included an overnight trip to Prairie View A&M near Houston for a review of the black colleges' offerings. White guests were quartered on campus in a loft in what was then the equivalent of the union building. Matthews found that arrangement uncomfortably similar to that of a plantation landlord and his slaves. As he traveled the country and visited more schools, both white and black, Matthews more readily recognized the significant academic hardships and disadvantages that blacks faced.

When the U.S. Supreme Court decided *Brown v. Board of Education* in May 1954 and desegregated public schools nationally, Matthews began informal discussions with North Texas's board of regents. To him, *Brown* was something of the extra point that was simply added to the similar *Sweatt v. Painter* decision of the high court in 1950 that emanated from Texas. Heman Sweatt was a black man from Houston, a graduate of Wiley College in the northeast Texas town of Marshall, who was denied entrance into the University of Texas law school in 1946 because of his race. Sweatt filed suit on the grounds that no other law school in the state was of the same quality as that at UT and was denied multiple times by the state legal system. He appealed his case to the U.S. Supreme Court and was victorious in 1950. After *Brown*, Matthews made sure each member of the North Texas board was aware of what he considered the inevitable: a black student was going to seek admission to North Texas, possibly in the near future. Matthews made it clear that he thought the school should avoid having to be dragged into court, the equivalent of moving into the era of desegregation kicking and screaming.

....

Odus Mitchell played in the first football game that he ever witnessed. That was for West Texas State, where he actually finished high school while growing up in the adjacent Texas Panhandle town of Canyon. Mitchell required some remedial football instruction before going in for his first play from scrimmage. For instance, one of the coaches mercifully asked another player to yank the helmet that Mitchell was wearing by 180 degrees since it was on backwards. (Understand that such a gaffe could more easily be made back then before helmets were fitted with facemasks.)

Mitchell began his schooling in the tiny nearby town of Antelope in its one-teacher facility. His original high school didn't field a football team, but there was a track team—he was it. In that first football game played for the West Texas State Buffaloes, Mitchell came away somewhat bloodied and definitely muddied, both of which he gladly wore as badges of honor in the aftermath of West Texas's season opening 30-0 loss to TCU. He rode back to campus in a friend's car—actually *on* a friend's car, standing on a bumper. Riding beyond the confines of the vehicle succeeded both in keeping the car's interior decidedly cleaner, and allowing young Mitchell to show off evidence of how he'd spent the afternoon.

Mitchell set a West Texas State athletic mark that will likely never be broken. In his four years of college there, he collected a total of eighteen varsity letters. He was twenty-five years old when he graduated and was planning to seek a career in coaching—really the only vocation that seemed to interest him—until he was offered a contract to play minor-league baseball for a team in Oklahoma City. But his coach at West Texas, Samuel Burton, recommended that, given his age, he forget dabbling in a prospective career as a ballplayer and enter the coaching job pool as soon as he could.

Mitchell landed the position of head football coach at the high school in Post, a small town located southeast of Lubbock. Only weeks before the season began, he took care of pertinent personal business by marrying Rowena Shields, whom he'd met at West Texas. Mitchell's coaching career got off to an inauspicious beginning when his team trotted out onto the field for the opening kickoff of the opening game and collectively realized their rookie coach had never taught them how to receive a kick. The 1925 Post Antelopes kicked off much more often than they received, winning that game by 40 points and claiming the district championship that season.

Mitchell moved on after only one season, to Childress High, located near the eastern base of the Texas Panhandle—for a raise of $10. His stay there also lasted only one season, though not of his own volition. Mitchell was fired, caught in the middle of a power struggle between the superintendent and school principal. Players who supported him went on strike, refusing to attend classes until he was rehired. Mitchell was prepared to take at least temporary leave of the coaching profession and go work for his father-in-law in the furniture business before he was offered the head coaching job at Slaton High, just outside of Lubbock. Some of the Childress players and their families were so devoted to Mitchell that the families rented properties in Slaton—almost 150 miles away—so the boys could continue playing for him. That was a development that a fair number of opposing coaches hardly considered within the residence rules of the state's governing body for high school athletics, the University Interscholastic League.

Those rental agreements were hopefully for only one year because Mitchell coached at Slaton for only one season (of course), an unbeaten one at that. He was hired away by Pampa High, located in the northeast corner of the Panhandle. Mitchell was able to lift Pampa to nearly the same level as the region's largest and toughest football programs, Amarillo High and Lubbock High. He managed to win three district titles coaching the Harvesters before taking on another Texas high school challenge 500 miles to the east in Marshall, only a few miles west of the Louisiana line.

Sophomore quarterback Y.A. Tittle, who would go on to star in the NFL, recalled the new coach's first meeting with his players. "I came here to win," Mitchell told the young men. "The world is full of good losers. I want good winners." Which is what the Marshall Mavericks immediately became, claiming district championships in each of Tittle's seasons under center. When Tittle was a senior, Marshall advanced to the state semifinals and lost to Waco High 6-0.

If Mitchell aspired to coach at any level above high school to that date, it didn't appear that he seriously pursued any such post. But when North Texas State resumed its football program in 1946 following the end of World War II, the owner of the daily newspaper in Marshall—who also owned the *Denton Record-Chronicle*—recommended Mitchell to Eagles athletic director Theron Fouts. Mitchell agreed to travel to Denton for an interview, most intrigued by how becoming a university employee would lessen the future burden of funding higher education for his four young children. Mitchell presented a persona in stark contrast to North Texas's previous coach, the combustible Sisco. His vocabulary in times of crisis didn't extend beyond "crap" or "cram's sake." When the tension of a game did require some form of emotional outlet, he would chew on blades of grass. Mitchell certainly must have been everything that North Texas expected and more. He was offered the job on his interview and accepted.

The 1946 schedule that Mitchell inherited didn't exactly provide him the opportunity to gently break in his new Eagles program. North Texas opened at Texas A&M, unbeaten in its ten previous non-conference games at home. The Eagles managed to keep the score close for a half (trailing 14-0) but could neither score nor finish with a plus number of rushing yards (-3). Mitchell's debut as a college coach was a 47-0 thumping. The "Teachers," as identified in *The Dallas Morning News* story, reached the Aggies' 6-yard line in the third quarter against A&M's fourth stringers. If anyone doubted that maintaining a shutout against the outmanned Eagles was important to Aggies coach Homer Norton, he hurried in a combination of first- and second-stringers to squelch the North Texas threat.

The defeat, though, proved to be the exception rather than the rule for the '46 Eagles. For one, they didn't face another Southwest Conference opponent for the balance of the season. North Texas closed the regular season with a 6-3-1 record and its seventh Lone Star Conference championship in twelve years as a member of that league. The Eagles were invited to play in their first post-season game, Houston's inaugural Optimist Bowl. The coaching matchup couldn't have been more contrasting. North Texas and Mitchell, finishing his first season as a college head man, were pitted against the College of the Pacific and its eighty-four-year-old leader in his fifty-seventh year of college coaching, Amos Alonzo Stagg. The college football legend had announced before the season that the 1946 campaign would be his last. Mitchell and the Eagles sent him off with a defeat, grabbing the lead with only nine seconds to play, and winning 14-13. North Texas was forced to play much of the game without starting sophomore quarterback Fred McCain, whose competitive spirit and combustible nature led him to get involved in a fight and be thrown out of the game.

Mitchell suffered no sophomore jinx; North Texas's 1947 squad won a school-record ten games during the season, losing only on the road to an Arkansas team that was the defending SWC co-champion. But the Eagles traveled to Florida the following week and stunned the Southeastern Conference's Gators 20-12 en route to another bowl invitation, the aforementioned Salad Bowl meeting with Nevada. *Morning News* sports columnist George White wrote following the victory at Florida that North Texas had supplanted Texas Tech as the state's most impressive college football program outside of the six SWC teams—and might be better than some of those schools, too: "Odus Mitchell has come up with an outfit that on the record looks like one of the strongest in this section."

The pre-game newspaper coverage for the '47 Salad Bowl didn't play up the fact that the Eagles would, for the first time, be playing an opponent with black players. Both of them were reserves playing for their second college with a stint in the military sandwiched between. Junior running back Sherman Howard previously played for Iowa, junior quarterback Alva Tabor for all-black Tuskegee Institute in Alabama. North Texas failed to make it two post-season victories in as many years, losing to the Wolf Pack, 13-6.

Mitchell's first four seasons with the Eagles all resulted in winning records. As the 1950s began, North Texas traded in membership in the Lone Star Conference for the new Gulf Coast Conference, which was also comprised of only Texas schools. But there was also literal moving for the football program. New Eagle Stadium was opened in 1952, seating 20,000. The facility was renamed in 1954 for the school's former football coach and athletic director, Theron Fouts.

CHAPTER 5

"Dear old North Texas—I just love it!"

MONDAY, JULY 19, 1954, BEGAN almost savagely warm in Denton. The overnight low temperature of 80 degrees was bookended that afternoon with a high of 105. Readers of the *Record-Chronicle* that afternoon could peruse a front-page story from the Associated Press, written from the Texas-Mexico border town of McAllen, which heralded: "An estimated 35,000 Mexican wetbacks have been rounded up or have voluntarily returned to Mexico in the Lower Rio Grande Valley drive to oust the illegally-entered aliens. The campaign today was in its fifth day." Aliens were bused from a detention camp in McAllen across to El Paso, where the Mexican government took them across the border and "deep into the interior."

That day, a forty-one-year-old high school principal began attending a doctoral-level class in public school law offered by North Texas State. What made Alfred Tennyson Miller's attendance in class that day front-page news was Miller being black. Since North Texas first opened its doors as Texas Normal College in 1890, a black person had never previously been offered the opportunity to enroll in a class—undergraduate or otherwise. Miller grew up in Fort Worth, the youngest of nine children born to a laborer and a domestic whose formal education in east Texas ended in the seventh grade. Miller graduated from I.M. Terrell High School, and then earned a bachelor's degree from Prairie View A&M in 1935. He went into education, interrupted by a couple of years serving in World War II. Miller received a master's degree from the University of Wisconsin in 1952 and, along the way, earned membership in the Phi Delta Kappa national honorary fraternity for graduate men in education. He spent eight years at Denton's secondary school for blacks, Fred Douglass High. Miller initially both taught and coached—his football players included Abner Haynes' brother, Samuel—and later became principal. The high school's football team was invited one year to play a popular regional post-season game for black high schools called the Chocolate Bowl. Miller himself had hurt a leg while attending high school, leaving him with a stiff-legged walk. He was immensely popular and respected by his students at the high school, which was renamed Fred Moore High in 1950 in honor of one of its previous principals. Some male students liked to mimic Miller's distinctively flawed gait and referred to him as "the black bear."

Miller in 1947 became principal at Lincoln High School in Port Arthur, Texas, in the state's southeast corner near the Louisiana line, while his wife remained behind to continue operating a beauty shop. He returned to Denton early in the summer of 1954 when he began to mull a suggestion made to him by one of his college professors; he should take the public school law course specifically at North Texas. Though the college had never previously admitted a black student, the professor told Miller that he would qualify for admission per the 1950 *Sweatt* legal decision, since none of the state colleges for blacks offered that class. On the day that Miller visited North Texas and stated his intention to enroll during the summer term scheduled to begin in mid-July, word was quickly relayed to the president's office. J.C. Matthews left campus that afternoon for the office of Ben Wooten, chairman of the board of regents and president of the First National Bank of Dallas. There, the two of them set up a telephone conference with the other regents. They collectively couldn't identify a means to prevent Miller from enrolling. The board instructed Matthews to consult with the state attorney general, who reached the same conclusion.

Soon after, Miller formalized his request in the form of a letter sent to Matthews. He addressed what his admission would mean well beyond his own personal career goals: "It is my conviction that my entrance now would contribute much to the successful, inevitable integration of Negroes into the school. My every effort would be toward the quality of deportment and performance that would dispel much of the apprehension that some may be harboring at this time." Matthews's reply was direct, indicating neither trepidation nor a sense of accomplishment for what admitting Miller would mean for North Texas: "Administrative approval meant necessity of checking with Board of Regents. Now seems possible for you to enter North Texas upon completion of health blank and graduate admission blanks provided you are planning to pursue doctorate program."

The *Record-Chronicle* apparently learned of Miller's presence as a prospective North Texas student the morning after Matthews had corresponded with Miller. A representative of the newsroom contacted Matthews in time for a follow-up story to appear in that afternoon's edition. Matthews told the paper that Miller's enrollment for doctoral study had no bearing on the school's policy to prohibit blacks from studies below the doctorate level: "Our policy on Negro undergraduates or Negro students working on master's degrees is not changed. They will not be admitted at this time."

Before Miller began his ground-breaking term at North Texas, he was escorted on a one-student campus tour by one of the deans that turned some heads. Miller attended only that one summer session, continuing his professional career that fall in Port Arthur. He was selected as the head of the state organization of black teachers in 1956. About a year before his death in 1993, Miller reflected on his experience of becoming North Texas's first black student in an interview with UNT oral historian Michele Glaze: "I think the administration wanted me not as a token but as the first to open the doors to other black students."

On June 13, 1955, Dallas NAACP official A. Maceo Smith announced that the organization would soon begin filing petitions across the state to get the wheels of desegregation moving forward in Texas public schools. One of the NAACP's national lawyers, Thurgood Marshall of Baltimore, further identified September 1956 as the group's deadline. That same day, the next milepost in North Texas's racial evolution took place. Joe Atkins, a 1954 graduate of Dallas's Lincoln High School, visited the North Texas registrar's office along with his mother and a woman named Juanita Craft, an activist on racial issues in Dallas and a member of the NAACP since the mid-1930s. The three of them approached the front desk and asked an astonished office employee for a registration packet.

Atkins was already a year out of high school, having spent his freshman year of college at the black Philander Smith College in Little Rock, Arkansas. Founded in 1877, Philander Smith was the first college located west of the Mississippi to offer higher education to freedmen—former slaves. Atkins earned an academic scholarship there and majored in English. A beanpole of a teenager, he and his family moved from east Texas to south Dallas in 1950 as Atkins entered the ninth grade at Lincoln. He wasn't terribly coordinated for his size and failed to make the Tigers' basketball team. Atkins was a member of Lincoln's photography club, was on the student council, and was very interested in social issues in light of the segregationist laws and practices that he encountered in Dallas; there had even been some homes in his neighborhood that were firebombed. His parents were involved in the NAACP, and he joined Craft's NAACP Youth Council. The council held periodic meetings during which she expounded on the racial issues of the day and offered ways to combat bigotry. One target was the annual State Fair of Texas. Blacks could only attend the fair on specially designated days, so Craft and the Youth Council protested the practice and urged the black students to boycott the event. (According to Atkins, students from Dallas's white Hillcrest High joined in their protests.)

When the NAACP held its national convention in Dallas in 1954, Atkins had the opportunity to meet Marshall and a black attorney working for the Dallas NAACP named U. Simpson Tate. The *Brown v. Board of Education* decision took place late in his senior year, when Abner Haynes and Leon King were Lincoln sophomores. According to Atkins, news of the monumental court decision was announced to the student body over the school's public address system. Teachers, he says, began telling Lincoln students that they could attend any college. After a year at Philander Smith, Atkins decided to act on that presumption and transfer to a college in his home state; he selected North Texas. He'd been on the campus a handful of times—occasionally with Craft's youth group—and liked the idea of attending a college relatively close to his home in Dallas. Atkins' parents approved of the idea and got Craft involved.

The response to Atkins's request at the front desk in the North Texas registrar's office was an awkward pause, followed by instructions that they would need to talk directly to the registrar, Alexander Dickie. The three visitors were led into a conference room, where they met with Dickie. He told them they would need to speak with the person who was overseeing the university during the summer term in Matthews's absence, vice-president Arthur Sampley. "They kept saying they didn't want a fight—'Don't want anybody to sue us'—so maybe they'd let me in," Atkins recalled in an interview three years before his death in 2015.

While the meeting was for the most part civil, Sampley stated the school was planning to begin a staggered approach to desegregating its undergraduate population over a four-year period beginning with the senior class and working its way to the freshmen. But until that happened, Sampley added, he was bound to uphold state law at that moment and deny Atkins entry to North Texas. Craft expressed her displeasure with Sampley's refusal to comply with *Brown v. Board of Education* and had Atkins take home an application packet. Atkins went through the formality of filling it out, mailing it back to North Texas, and arranging to have his academic transcript sent from Philander Smith. If Matthews had not been brought into the loop regarding Atkins's efforts by then, he was as soon as the completed application form arrived back on campus. Matthews gathered the regents, who expressed collective indignation with Atkins and Craft and dared them to sue. Sampley wrote back to Atkins in mid-July and assured him that he wasn't eligible to be admitted to North Texas.

The Atkins family took that letter to U. Simpson Tate, the regional NAACP lawyer. Tate told the Atkinses that they had no choice but to seek an injunction for Atkins to be admitted, and Willie Atkins, Joe's father, agreed. In the course of the discussions, Tate told the family that Texas Western College in El Paso (now named the University of Texas at El Paso, UTEP) had just desegregated for that fall term—the first integrated four-year college in the state—and could be an acceptable alternative pending the upcoming legal battle with North Texas. The petition was filed on August 11 by Willie, stating that his son met all the requirements for enrollment and was denied admission solely on the basis of his race. Matthews told the *Record-Chronicle* the rules for minority enrollment that Atkins pointed to in the lawsuit pertained only to doctoral students—as had been stated a little more than a year earlier when Tennyson Miller was admitted—and noted that two more black doctoral students had been allowed to enroll during the summer 1955 session.

Joe Atkins realized that, at best, his entry to North Texas would require a lengthy legal conflict and couldn't be achieved in time for him to enroll as a sophomore in autumn 1955. Following Tate's advice, he looked at Texas Western, which had just come through similar litigation brought forth by the family of a black El Paso high school valedictorian named Thelma White. El Paso's location on the Mexican border resulted in a more racially diverse environment that set it apart from the state's other major cities. The presence of nearby military installations also contributed to a more accepting community stance toward race relations. White's case was also handled by Tate. When U.S. district court judge R.E. Thomason refused to dismiss her family's lawsuit in mid-July 1955, Tate's remarks to the *El Paso Times* included, "Miss White and members of her race should know they are entitled to attend Texas Western College as a matter of right and not of graces." (When the court ruled in White's favor, the story on the front page of the following day's *Times* appeared near the bottom of the page, "below the fold" in industry lingo. That edition's main headline was reserved for a story about the local school board planning to build a new junior high.) White, similar to Atkins, had already chosen another college before her admission to Texas Western was allowed; she enrolled at New Mexico A&M, located a short drive north of El Paso just across the state line.

Atkins soon learned that El Paso had integrated public transportation and at least some restaurants that served racial minorities. With an in-state tuition that was much cheaper than what his family paid at Philander Smith, Atkins applied for admission to TWC, was accepted and enrolled. The one significant disappointment that he experienced upon moving to El Paso was learning that the school's dorms had not yet been integrated, and he was forced to find lodging off campus. Atkins was one of a dozen new black students at Texas Western, a handful of whom immediately became active in the school's chapter of the Baptist Student Union. Almost before he had time to unpack, Atkins was off with the BSU group for a weekend retreat in New Mexico.

He soon landed a part-time job at a recreation center and eventually met a promising young basketball player from El Paso's *Segundo Barrio* named Nolan Richardson, who would play for Texas Western and coach the University of Arkansas' basketball team to the national collegiate championship in 1993-'94. (Texas Western became well known among sports fans when its 1965-'66 basketball team became the first with an all-black starting lineup to win the national title, shocking Kentucky's all-white squad.)

On Sept. 2, 1955, Judge Joe Sheehy denied Atkins the temporary injunction that would allow him to be admitted to North Texas. The basis of Judge Sheehy's decision? The suit's defendants included all of the members of the school's board of regents. One of them, former North Texas football coach Jack Sisco, had been out of state and couldn't be served with a subpoena. Atkins was out of luck, at least for becoming a North Texas student during the fall '55 term. Sheehy then set November 14 as the date to begin the trial in Sherman. The only witness for the state was Matthews. His testimony included statements that indicated race wasn't the only reason for North Texas to prohibit Atkins from enrolling. Matthews stated the school was operating at 102-percent capacity. He further detailed a plan to integrate North Texas similar to what Sampley had mentioned to the Atkins party the previous summer, in which a staggered admission schedule would have blacks allowed into the senior class in 1956, into the junior class in 1957, the sophomore class in '58, and as freshmen in '59. Matthews also stated he was hopeful that a $5 million building appropriation in 1957 would alleviate the campus overcrowding. Tate, lead attorney for the plaintiff, argued that other colleges managed to admit blacks while facing overcrowding.

On December 2, Sheehy ruled in Atkins's favor, technically a permanent injunction that "forever enjoins" North Texas from denying black students admission from the school's undergraduate and graduate programs. Black students could enroll beginning with the next semester, scheduled to begin in early February 1956. "I have no doubt that the board of regents was acting in good faith when it proposed the plan," Sheehy told the court, "but the fact that a school might be crowded is not a basis for segregation." Attorneys for the defendants initially indicated they would appeal but that such a decision would be made by the state attorney general's office. But in a letter to Matthews dated December 7, 1955, North Texas regent Berl Godfrey, a Fort Worth attorney, advised, "While I have very little of the facts upon which to base a judgment, it would seem that the school would not be in good graces to appeal the Joe L. Atkins decision." The landmark decision was curiously given relatively muted play in the next edition of Dallas's black weekly, the *Dallas Express*—five paragraphs on the bottom half of the front page. (A much larger headline and story appeared a week earlier heralding the selection of Tennyson Miller as the president of the state association for black teachers.)

On the afternoon of Friday, February 3, 1956, North Texas and all of Denton struggled to deal with the worst winter weather of that season to date. An inch of freezing rain and sleet coating area roads had caused three traffic accidents in the city the previous night and a couple more that following morning. The office of North Texas registrar Alex Dickie was only minutes from closing for the weekend when a forty-one-year-old woman walked through the door and into school history. Irma Sephas operated two small businesses out of her home in Fort Worth: a bookkeeping service and piano lessons. But that's not what made history, of course. When Sephas registered late that Friday afternoon to continue her collegiate education as a sophomore in North Texas's School of Business beginning with the upcoming semester, she became the first black to take advantage of the racial portal at the school that had been pried open a little more than two months earlier with the Atkins legal decision. Having previously studied at Huston-Tillotson College in Austin, she specified that she would commute. With Sephas enrolling during the final minutes of business hours that day, the revelation of the event didn't reach the readers of the *Denton Record-Chronicle* until Sunday morning, since the paper didn't publish on Saturdays at the time. The following week's edition of *Campus Chat*, North Texas's student newspaper, stated the foul weather led to her eleventh-hour timing.

Sephas had yet to attend her first class at North Texas, but events that same day at the University of Alabama might have served as a harbinger for what could happen on the Denton campus. A black woman named Autherine Lucy—at age twenty-six, certainly younger than Sephas, but similarly a student who didn't come directly from high school—became the first black student in that school's 125-year history. Having already graduated from Miles College just outside Birmingham, Alabama., Lucy enrolled as a graduate student in library science. Like the sequence of events at North Texas, Lucy's enrollment had required legal coercion. In a geography class that first day, she was the only student to take a seat at a desk in the front row. On her way to a class in children's literature, she was struck by an egg.

Having the first day of Alabama's semester followed by a weekend provided ample opportunity for those opposed to Lucy's presence to express themselves. For the better part of three hours that Saturday, an estimated 1,000 exasperated men took to the streets of Tuscaloosa,

Alabama. They paraded. They sang *Dixie*. They chanted, "Keep Bama white!" And they weren't shy about identifying the offending party with a boisterous chorus of "To hell with Autherine." A burning cross became part of the spectacle as they descended upon the home of the university president, only to learn he was out of town.

Segregationists in Texas were busy that Saturday, too. The Association of Citizens Council started a drive to gain legislative support for "interposition," or contesting federal laws—in this case, those mandating desegregation of school systems. Thirty members of the association from across Texas met with state attorney general John Ben Sheppard, a native of east Texas and a staunch proponent of states' rights. "Interposition is the last line of defense that the state has, irregardless [sic] of the segregation issue," Sheppard told reporters following the meeting. "I'm for interposition down the line."

Lucy's semester at Alabama lasted two class days, which brought to four the number of total days that integration protesters essentially prevented the school from operating normally. That's precisely what university regents cited when they explained their unanimous vote to suspend her from school indefinitely as of Monday night; that stated Lucy had to leave for both her safety and that of everyone else connected with the university. Though she actually was removed from campus early in the afternoon with the help of security personnel, another mob gathered late that night and had to be dispersed with tear gas. Among their targets was any and all glass affixed to the car of the dean of women, which had been used to drive Lucy between classes in an attempt to ensure her safety.

The contrast in the proceedings that took place at Alabama and at North Texas provided a public relations opportunity for North Texas. Sephas herself agreed to do an interview with a Dallas-Fort Worth television station at her home in Fort Worth and stated, "Dear old North Texas—I just love it!" But Matthews said years later he didn't want North Texas to essentially beat its chest simply because Sephas's enrollment had not been accompanied by violence. When that same TV reporter requested access to also follow Sephas through a class day with a camera and microphone, Matthews steadfastly denied permission. "We would have been not doing what one ought to do in a classroom—not a good classroom situation," Matthews said in a 1977 UNT oral history interview. "We had yet to prove ourselves all the way. This was, I think, the attitude that most of us [within the school] were taking. But people outside were not as aware of the 'in-process' kind of thing, and they were wanting to say, 'Let's point this up. Let's tell the world about it. Let's brag a little,' and that type of thing. My counsel was, 'Let's be sure we do the thing as it should be done and stop at that.'"

Reaction to Sephas's inclusion into North Texas's student body arrived on Matthews's desk via the U.S. mail with regularity. One such letter was written by a Mrs. R. Snyder and was postmarked Binghamton, N.Y.: "I myself am a white person but I think it is wonderful that yours is the first college to let a negro student in your school without making trouble for her. You might know it would be the wonderful State of Texas to break the ice." And there was the following from a Fort Worth mother of two North Texas students, Mrs. R.M. Bennison: "I want to take this occasion to commend you and other N.T.S.C. personnel for the manner in which you have handled the entrance of a colored student … You people at N. Texas have showed great tact and judgment in seeing that it be made as commonplace as the entrance of a Japanese, Indian, or any other national into the college. Yes! I am very glad my son and daughter are enrolled at N.T.S.C. and not in the University of Alabama." Which earned a reply from the president's desk: "I was very pleased indeed to have your letter expressing confidence in the staff at North Texas State College. I should like to say that the students have had a hand in this matter in that they have conducted themselves in the same dignified manner in which the faculty has operated."

That didn't stop the *Record-Chronicle* from singing the school's praises and castigating North Texas's counterparts at Alabama on its editorial page on the Tuesday following Sephas' enrollment: "Students of North Texas State College are to be commended for their patience and understanding in the case of the enrollment of the first Negro undergraduate student at the college. The college's civilized, Christian treatment of a problem that is difficult for most Texans to solve certainly is a direct contrast to the mob violence being displayed at the University of Alabama. At the university a Negro woman student has been stoned, rotten eggs have been thrown at her, and she has been cursed and threatened. ... We should be thankful that North Texas students—at least a large majority of them—believe in the Golden Rule."

The next measured racial advancement in the North Texas community saw black students allowed to live in on-campus housing for the first time. During the summer 1956 session, two black women—Gwendolyn McDonald Jackson of Wichita Falls and Rosa Lee Thomas of Dallas—moved into the Terrill Hall dormitory. They were teachers working on masters degrees. According to Jim Neal's account in the *Record-Chronicle*, North Texas was believed to be the first institution of higher learning in the state that allowed white and black students to live beneath the same roof in a campus dorm. Enrollment for the summer term was expected to reach about 3,000—about half the amount for a semester during the standard academic year—including an estimated fifty to seventy-five blacks. As Matthews noted for the *Record-Chronicle*, the number was an estimate because the school's registration paperwork didn't at any point require a student to identify his or her race.

Near the summer session's midpoint a few weeks later, Jackson wrote to Matthews to express her delight with the reception that was afforded to her and Thomas at Terrill Hall, and also by the teaching staff during their classes: "I have witnessed a very successful half-term with unusual courtesies and kindness coming from both the instructors and students. My room has been very comfortable and convenient." She was ready to join anyone who wanted to congratulate Matthews for North Texas's handling of what could have been an incendiary occurrence. "Please allow me to thank you personally for my being another member of the dormitory family, and may I be some credit to your school for having attended. May you continue to have success in being a truly great, grand and humble President."

CHAPTER 6

"Butch" and "Bitty Bubba"

ABNER HAYNES WAS ONE OF eight children born to Fred L. and Ola Mae Haynes, growing up in Denton and later in Dallas, the son of a preacher and presuming his father had such a career in ministry planned for him. Haynes was glib, confident, and talented in the athletic arena even as an elementary school student. Early on, he was called "Butch," a nickname that he would carry on not only through high school but to North Texas. Neighborhood children gravitated toward "Butch," and he often referred to his ample group of young friends as "partners."

Fred L. Haynes was pastor of Denton's Church of God in Christ, a Pentecostal denomination whose members weren't shy about expressing their enthusiasm and absolute joy for following their faith. The Church of God in Christ was founded just before the start of the twentieth century in the United States, primarily by Baptists who sought something different from their faith lives, and most of the new religion's followers were black. A headquarters was established in Memphis, Tennessee, with a grand tabernacle and an adjoining auditorium that accommodated about 4,000 people. It was in that auditorium on the evening of Wednesday, April 3, 1968, that Dr. Martin Luther King Jr. gave his renowned "I've been to the mountaintop" speech that proved to be his last. The civil rights leader was gunned down the following day on the second floor walkway of Memphis's Lorraine Motel.

Pastor Haynes's ministerial work in Denton led to him becoming more than a preacher in the Church of God in Christ. He soon rose to the position of bishop of the church's territory encompassing north Texas. The duties of the bishop extended beyond tending to a single congregation; in secular terms, he was something of a regional supervisor, in charge of both staffing and strategy, including filling clergy vacancies at the other member churches in the region. Young Abner was fairly certain his father hoped and planned for his youngest son to follow him in such pastoral footsteps. But the youngest of Abner's siblings, James Neaul, offered a differing perspective during an interview conducted in his home two years before his death in 2015: "You made your own decisions in the family," he said. "Father would be proud and pleased for you to succeed him, but you did your own thinking."

The pastor's wife, the former Ola Mae Alexander, was similarly dedicated to the faith. She would fast for days, on her knees praying to the extent that the floor was left with bloodstains. There was no difficulty in identifying the head of the household at 713 Bailey Street on Denton's east side, though business often kept Fred L. Haynes away from his home. There simply were so many duties for the pastor to tend to and even more when he ascended to bishop. One of the aspects of family life that the bishop made clear to Ola Mae was that he wouldn't tolerate any physical punishment being doled out to the children. "Talk to them" was his constant message, though Abner and his siblings often tested their parents' adherence to that dictum. Like the episode in which Abner—desperate to watch a televised college football game when his father forbid the family to own a TV—followed the instructions in a department store's newspaper ad and simply called down to the store and had a set delivered on a trial basis. It was Abner who essentially stood trial with his father; still, no hitting took place. Pastor Haynes also made it clear to the youngsters that lying would not be tolerated.

The preacher was proficient at teaching by deed in addition to word. His congregation was made up primarily of poor blacks, many of whom were emotionally bolstered simply by a signal or sign of hope from their church. It could be a word of encouragement from the pulpit. It could just be having the sanctuary's lights on late at night, an indication that folks were involved and trying as best they could to live their lives as God wanted them to. Leading by example was sometimes accomplished by unanticipated and unwelcomed means, such as the occasion when local members of the Ku Klux Klan demonstrated in front of the church and greeted the clergyman with a pelting of eggs. When one of those eggs failed to break, Pastor Haynes took it home and cooked it. Call it a conversion of a different sort.

Abner's brothers were Fred Jr., Samuel, Timothy, and Neaul, his sisters Naomi, Maxine, and Melissa. All of his siblings graduated from Fred Moore High in Denton. Samuel was the first football player in the family and was named captain of the team at Prairie View A&M in 1945. Young Abner sensed excitement at home when Samuel, who earned the nickname of "Jitterbug," was getting prepared for a high school game. Neaul also played football for Fred Moore, was also proficient in tennis, and was his class valedictorian. While academics were important, and athletics had their place in home life, church was the axis on which family life rotated. That meant attending a service on Sunday morning, another that afternoon, meeting of the Young People Willing Workers and another service that night. If the children were reluctant to participate, they soon realized that the pastor's children would surely be in the pews if he expected all of the other families to do the same.

Abner was living in Denton, attending the seventh grade at Fred Moore, when his father was moved to Dallas to become bishop. The clergyman made the difficult commute for a time until the rest of the family, at least those who had not yet left the nest, could join him in south Dallas near what would become the Haynes Chapel Church of God in Christ on Ruskin Avenue. Haynes enrolled as an eighth grader at Lincoln, located only a few blocks from their new home.

The Haynes family settled on Pine Street near Lamar Avenue. Leon King and his family lived on Pine Street about six blocks away, across the street from Exeter Park. The middle child of five, Leon was nicknamed "Bitty Bubba" at a young age by his eldest sibling, sister Vivian, because of his size—or lack thereof—at the time (though he would hardly be "bitty" in high school). His father, Henry King, was often simply a voice heard beneath Leon's bedroom door. Henry worked two jobs, gone most mornings before young Leon was out of bed and returning well after the children's bedtime. He first reported for janitorial work at the Majestic Theater in downtown Dallas. Once done there, he headed toward the opposite end of downtown, near the banks of the Trinity River, to work at the train terminal until 10 p.m. Sunday nights provided a rare opportunity for Leon to see his father. Sunday night was not only face time with Dad, but also his father's bath time. Henry was a loyal consumer of Mennen aftershave, which Leon took a liking to. Leon first shaved at age fourteen, primarily so he would have a reason for using Mennen.

Henry's hours dictated that Leon's mother, Jesse Mae, ran daily operations of the home. She grew up in the central Texas town of Calvert, located between Waco and Bryan-College Station, and was forced to leave school after the fifth grade to work. Jesse Mae worked downtown at the H.L. Green department store, where young Leon first encountered segregated water fountains. His mother dearly hoped all five of her children would graduate from high school ... *and* from college. And almost all of them did. The exception was Charles, the oldest son and second in line to Vivian. Charles, ironically, was the only King sibling who attended a private high school (St. Peter's Academy) rather than the neighborhood public school. After graduation, he immediately found work to help support the family, and eventually helped his four siblings attend college. While at St. Peter's, Charles got involved in athletics. And whatever Charles did, Leon—four years his junior—wanted to do, too. That was Leon's first exposure to sports. Charles played football, so Leon wanted to play football. Charles played end on the football team, so Leon wanted to play end on the football team. Luckily for Leon, he grew into the position while in high school.

For the King brothers—Charles, Leon, James, and Chauncey—each was expected to look after any younger brothers. Charles worked as a supervisor at American Wine and Importing Company. Leon worked summers at Classified Parking and sometimes caddied at Cedar Crest Golf Course, which provided him the initial opportunity to interact with white people. The two older brothers bought Chauncey a Western Flyer bike complete with lights and a horn. Chauncey then became something of a one-person security patrol when his mother walked to St. Paul Baptist Church on Tuesday, Wednesday, and Friday nights a few blocks away on Lamar Street. St. Paul was founded in 1952, though its flock initially didn't have a sanctuary to call its own. The members met at other neighborhood churches, which graciously welcomed them until a church was built at the corner of Lamar and Pear.

Once King moved up from Harllee Elementary School to Lincoln High and added track to his football schedule, he and his Tiger track teammates worked out at P.C. Cobb Stadium at the same time as the track team members from Dallas's white Sunset High. That included Sunset's star sprinter, Eddie Southern, who would compete in the 1956 Melbourne Olympics. The two schools' relay teams sometimes raced against each other and politely shook hands afterward.

As a Lincoln freshman, Haynes reluctantly complied with his father's requirement that he continue his participation in the church choir. That precluded him from trying out for the football team, a yearning of his since he'd begun to play the game informally in Denton with his "partners." King's free time after school was similarly occupied by his membership in the school's celebrated Harry T. Burleigh choir, whose schedule of performances across Dallas included racially mixed events. Such developments kept what appeared to be excellent athletes off the Tigers' roster and prompted football coach Farley Lewis to moan that some of the best football players at Lincoln weren't on the team because they were harmonizing.

As the school year continued, the lure of the purple-and-gold Lincoln letterman's jacket proved simply too great for Haynes to deny. The fact that he was a preacher's son sometimes was enough to invite taunting and laughter from fellow students, especially those who considered his family's denomination "holy rollers" because of some of their demonstrative practices. Haynes and King had become acquainted soon after the Haynes family moved to Dallas. King was running on the track team that spring and was among those who urged Haynes to join him. Not to mention the Tigers' track coach, Alpheus "A.W." Brashear, who cornered Haynes in a school hallway one day and informed him, "You're my hurdler." Lincoln's track team was held in high esteem among the student body; the Flying Tigers in 1940 won the first state high school track championship conducted by the Texas Interscholastic League of Colored Schools, the forerunner to the Prairie View Interscholastic League (PVIL). Haynes joined the track team, the beginning of his participation in formal athletics.

As a sophomore in autumn 1953, Haynes finally played organized football for the first time. He earned playing time at linebacker on Lincoln's B team and could barely believe it when presented with a uniform before his first game against Kaufman. During a practice against the varsity, Haynes unwittingly created a position for himself on that squad. He and varsity running back Elijah Walker (at 6-foot-3, 225, the junior was four inches taller and almost 50 pounds heavier) met in a violent collision that resulted in Walker leaving the field. The subsequent void in the Lincoln backfield was filled by none other than Haynes. He began to play a position that would be his beyond the middle of the following decade.

When the 1954 Lincoln Tigers dominated Central High of Galveston 27-7 in mid-October, the *Dallas Express* acclaimed the Tigers as giant killers in PVIL football. Haynes was honored by the black weekly as the area's back of the week, thanks in large measure to three touchdown runs, one that was described as a "snorting" 65 yards off right tackle. The *Express* published a photo of Haynes in uniform and helmet, the latter featuring a chin strap, but no faceguard, of course. He was selected for a similar honor by Dallas's Channel 8-WFAA that same season. Haynes was taken to the station one Sunday night by Lewis for an appearance on live television, resplendent in a black-and-white plaid jacket. It was probably about then that Haynes began to think he could play college football. If a kid could be named Dallas's back of the week as a junior, surely he could play college football. The feeling, it turned out, was mutual. Soon after the back of the week bestowal and the live television appearance, Haynes received a letter from the University of Colorado's coach, Dallas Ward. Haynes was star-struck by the correspondence and composed a polite reply that he handed to Lewis to have sent off to Colorado.

The highlight of any Lincoln football season was the annual showdown with Dallas's only other black public high school at the time, Booker T. Washington. Bragging rights between the schools often meant far more than being the best in the city. The PVIL's state football playoffs were started in 1940, and the Booker T. Bulldogs had reached the championship game five times by 1954 and brought home the trophy three times, most recently in 1950. Lincoln had reached one state final, sharing the 1949 title with Port Arthur Lincoln, thanks to a 13-13 tie.

When the Tigers and Bulldogs met in the '54 season finale at Dal Hi Stadium near the Cotton Bowl on Wednesday night, December 1, the *Express* estimated the crowd (for the schools' "gridiron death struggle," as the paper phrased it) at 12,000. There would actually be no death of the football variety involved that night; the rivals fought to a 7-7 tie. Haynes set up the Tigers' touchdown by scooping up a blocked punt to give Lincoln a relatively short field to work with. In the following week's *Express*, he was named to the second team on the paper's All-City squad consisting of players chosen from Lincoln, Washington, and the private St. Peter's Academy.

Neither King's parents nor Haynes's parents attended Lincoln football games, but the two Tigers often had a family cheering section of two to root them on: Neaul Haynes was dating Vivian King. A Lincoln graduate herself, Vivian got a teaching degree from Prairie View and returned to Dallas to begin her career in education. Neaul, it turned out, was the heir to the Haynes ministerial line after graduating from Denton's Fred Moore High as valedictorian and initially seeking a degree in architecture from the University of Denver. Neaul had been preaching occasionally since high school, including at revivals out west while he was in college. He was convinced by one of his professors that his future was in pastoring. Neaul was assigned to the Church of God in Christ location out in the Texas Panhandle, in Pampa, some years after Odus Mitchell had left for Marshall. On one of Neaul's trips back to south Dallas, he was looking for Abner and Leon, and stopped by the Kings' home. There, he met, as he put it, "someone who was much more interesting than Leon." Neaul said he didn't want to appear impolite to Vivian upon learning the boys weren't there, so he engaged in conversation. Neaul resourcefully mentioned that their brothers would be playing in a football game the following Thursday night while he was still in town and asked if she'd like to go. She said yes, took in her first football game, and a romance began to blossom.

Abner Haynes and Leon King became family when Neaul married Vivian in October 1955. The couple had courted for about a year, their relationship often tethered by the U.S. Postal Service as he preached in Pampa and she taught school in Dallas. When their schedules allowed them to actually visit in person, their dates often consisted of going to church and then dropping by a sandwich shop. The growing friendship between their younger brothers also often made its way into church doors. Leon was quite willing to accept an invitation from Abner to attend services and related activities at the Haynes house of worship. Leon would stand with Abner in the choir, chime in when possible, and even clap and bang a tambourine on occasion.

Haynes and King were among the senior mainstays of Lincoln's 1955 football team, Haynes as one of the team captains. At 6-foot-2 and 180 pounds, King was a capable receiver and middle linebacker and an excellent kicker (a straight-on kicker; today's sidewinders were introduced during the 1960s). But while they individually played well, the Tigers stumbled into the regular-season finale on November 24 against favored Booker T. Washington with four losses and a tie on their record. Yet a victory over the Bulldogs would, in addition to claiming city superiority, qualify the Tigers for the PVIL state semi-final playoffs in Class AAA, the largest classification among the state's black schools. Lincoln responded by forcing Booker T. into nine fumbles and six interceptions, stunning the Bulldogs 15-7 before another raucous crowd at Dal Hi Stadium. The Tigers held a tenuous lead of 9-7 with a few minutes to play when Lincoln's Earl Riggs came up with one of the interceptions and returned it 30 yards for a touchdown to close the scoring.

After Lincoln's initial touchdown, King kicked off and watched in near horror as the Bulldogs ran a play similar to the NFL Tennessee Titans' famed "Music City Miracle" of 2000. The returner, just about tackled, heaved the ball across the width of the field to a Booker T. teammate, who took off and appeared to have a clear path to the end zone since most of the Tigers' defenders were on the opposite side of the field. But Lincoln's Billy Wedgeworth managed to somehow make the touchdown-saving tackle. Maybe that inspired the ground-fixated Tigers to attempt similar razzle-dazzle later in the game. "If we threw three passes in a ballgame, that was a record," King said. "I scored one touchdown as a receiver in high school." On that game's play, Haynes took the handoff but threw toward King. "Everybody in the stands probably knew," King said. "I guess he led me a couple or three yards. It hit my fingertips, but everybody said I should have caught the ball. I missed it … but I blamed it on him."

Lincoln continued its unlikely run the following week with a definitive 39-0 thumping of Marshall's Pemberton High to secure a berth in the championship game against Port Arthur Lincoln, its championship opponent from 1949. Haynes set up one of his own touchdown runs with an interception, and later returned a punt 79 yards in advance of another Tiger score. The championship game was played at Port Arthur. A scoreless first half had the savviest fans scrambling to determine the new tie-breakers that would be used in the event of a deadlock after the regulation four quarters, long before overtime was introduced to high school football in the state. The first tie-breaker was first downs (the teams were even), then penetrations—the number of times that each team got inside the opponents' 20-yard line (Lincoln led 3-1).

Such calculations weren't necessary. The host Bumblebees took advantage of six Tigers turnovers against none of their own and defeated the visitors from Dallas 9-6. The Tigers only trailed 7-6 with about three minutes to play when they suffered a bad snap on their 24-yard line that flew into the end zone and was recovered by the host school for a two-point safety. The Bumblebees apparently keyed on Haynes and the running game, forcing the Dallas team to pass whenever possible. The Tigers managed only ten yards rushing, and had three passes intercepted.

By season's end, the state's black college football programs had joined Colorado in making known their interest in Haynes. He was definitely interested in Colorado, but was most keen on the major college program located only a few miles from his home: SMU. The Mustangs were coached by Chalmer "Woody" Woodard, and the athletic director was still Matty Bell, whose efforts led to Penn State's integrated team playing in the 1948 Cotton Bowl Classic. Haynes has said he wrote to Bell asking to play for the Mustangs, but was informed the school didn't accept black students. He has also said he sent a similar letter to Texas Tech, and received a similar courteous renunciation. Haynes visited Prairie View, Texas Southern, Wylie, and Bishop College. But blacks were playing college ball at integrated schools beyond the South, in the Midwest, and West, like Colorado. He hoped it didn't come down to choosing one of Texas's black schools. Prairie View would have presented the best football program among those institutions, and three of his siblings had attended the school. But Fred Jr. was killed in an auto accident on his way to campus, and that greatly contributed to his disinterest in becoming a Panther. Then, Haynes said Colorado's Ward came to Lincoln to talk to Lewis about him and other players. Talk about a rock star; boys were practically hanging out of classroom windows when he pulled up to the school.

Years later, King and Haynes offered differing views on their dealings with Colorado and North Texas. Haynes has said King and he had discussed attending the same school, but that Colorado offered a scholarship only to him. Another factor was the wishes of his brother and ailing father that he attend a college much closer to home than CU. King has said he, too, was offered a scholarship from Colorado (as well as Prairie View) and isn't sure why the two of them turned down those scholarship offers to begin their college football careers as walk-ons at North Texas. King said his parents' main priority was for him to attend a college where he could earn a degree.

According to Haynes, the bishop and Samuel suggested North Texas, given its new policy of admitting black undergraduates. Haynes's sister, Naomi, lived in Denton with her husband and five sons in a three-bedroom house. With on-campus housing not yet an option for Haynes and King, they could share the front room of Naomi's home. Such cozy confines proved to be no issue for King, who grew up in a family of seven in a three-bedroom home. The decision was made; Haynes and King would enroll at North Texas and try out for the football team. Haynes said, "At that time, friendship seemed more important than whatever else we expected to get."

While the decision was that Haynes and King would continue their football careers at North Texas, they really had no idea at that point if they'd be welcomed into the program. Fred Sr., Samuel, or both of them decided the next step was to contact the Eagles' coach and schedule a meeting. Again, the versions of that meeting as described years later by Haynes and King contradict one another. King said he attended the meeting; Haynes said it was he and his brother who made the trip. According to Haynes, Samuel drove Abner up to Denton to meet with Odus Mitchell in his office. During the drive, Samuel prepped Abner on what to say and do and what *not* to say and do—though the general strategy was to let Samuel do virtually all of the talking on behalf of the family. The conversation, Haynes said, went something like this: Samuel: "This is my brother Abner." Mitchell: "Yes, I've heard of Abner." Samuel: "We just thought we'd see if it would be possible for him to enter North Texas." Mitchell: "I don't know. … You want to play up here?" Abner: "Yes, I think I can play up here." Mitchell (after taking a good look at the young man dressed in a white T-shirt and jeans): "You're so little. I don't know if you can play with our big boys." Abner:

"Yeah, I can play." Samuel: "Could he get a scholarship … if he made the team?" Mitchell: "If he made the team, we might give him … I'll have to check on that. But you can come."

Mitchell was apparently cordial but measured. He made it clear there was no promise of scholarships for Haynes and King, and they'd also be on their own regarding housing. They could receive meal money, but the athletic dining hall was for scholarship athletes. It wasn't overtly stated that race played any role in King and Haynes being prohibited from eating in the dining hall. The session lasted about thirty minutes, after which Abner couldn't get out of his head that Mitchell appeared unconvinced that he could make the team. On the trip home, he wished he'd said more in his own defense. But King and he would have their opportunities in a little more than a month to supersede any talk out on the practice field.

CHAPTER 7

"Blacks don't play"

HAD NORTH TEXAS NOT BEEN in the process of changing leagues in the fall of 1956 from the Gulf Coast Conference to the more prestigious Missouri Valley Conference, Haynes, King, and all the other freshmen entering the Eagles' football program would have been eligible to play on the varsity. But North Texas was counting on being accepted in "The Valley," a conference most known for its quality in basketball, and one condition of membership was confining freshmen to their own athletic teams. Official word arrived from a meeting at league headquarters in Kansas City only days before football players were scheduled to hold their first practice on Saturday, September 1 that North Texas and one other aspiring applicant, Cincinnati, had been accepted. The two newcomer schools would be eligible to play for the Missouri Valley's football championship the following year.

The newest of North Texas's three assistant football coaches—Ken Bahnsen, hired a year earlier—was assigned by Odus Mitchell to serve as the head coach of the freshman squad in addition to helping Fred McCain with the varsity backs while Herb Ferrill tutored the linemen. A native of small-town southwest Louisiana, Bahnsen was an Eagles running back for three seasons just a few years earlier and led the Gulf Coast Conference in rushing as a sophomore in 1950. He played in the NFL in 1953, seeing limited action for the San Francisco 49ers, and then coached for one season at McNeese State near his boyhood home before joining Mitchell's staff. Bahnsen's exposure to pro ball also exposed him to his first integrated team, namely sharing a backfield with Joe Perry, the NFL's rushing leader that season.

Bahnsen's two fellow assistants were also former North Texas football players. McCain finished his Eagles playing career under Mitchell, but started it before World War II under Jack Sisco. He was a graduate of Gainesville High School near the Oklahoma line, arriving in Denton in 1941. McCain turned down a scholarship offer from Abilene's Hardin-Simmons and coach Warren Woodson to simply try out for the team at North Texas, where his brothers were enrolled. North Texas competed then in the Lone Star Conference and allowed freshmen to play on varsity; Sisco's method for informing young McCain during the Eagles' opener at SMU that his college quarterbacking career was about to begin was to summon him on the sideline and say, "Sit down and pee in your pants; I'm going to send you in." (McCain was indeed surprised—not enough to prompt urination—but initially thought his coach merely wanted him to get him a drink.) He joined the Marines during World War II, when North Texas's program didn't operate from 1943-'45, then returned to campus and completed his football career. McCain then taught for two years back in Gainesville before answering his college coach's call to join the staff.

By the time the 1956 season arrived, McCain was established as the staff's "bad cop," who would gladly deal with disciplinary issues. He also became the staff's primary recruiter, and gladly handled the business affairs of the program. Ferrill was more of a player's coach, less likely to get in a player's ear and more likely to allow one to camp out at his home with him and wife "Mutt" during a school holiday if the player didn't have a way to get home and back. Ferrill played his high school ball at Grand Prairie, somehow accounting for four of the Gophers' six touchdowns during his senior season despite playing guard and linebacker. He then played a year at the two-year North Texas Agricultural College (now the four-year University of Texas at

Arlington) before joining the Naval Reserves. Following his military discharge in January 1946, Ferrill tried out on a whim for the football team at Oklahoma that spring and was offered a scholarship. But he considered himself too much of a long shot to actually see significant playing time with the Sooners, and instead drove home—straight through Denton, which prompted him to seek a spot on Mitchell's first Eagles team. Ferrill played three seasons at guard, and then served as an assistant coach for one season back at his high school alma mater before Mitchell asked him to join the North Texas staff in 1950, albeit at a slight pay cut. He eventually added duties as the golf coach to those of tutoring the football linemen.

Mitchell was knowledgeable, organized, and unflappable. His daughter, Margaret Cole, says she often wondered how someone who was never gruff or churlish was able to command respect from a squad of ornery football players. Not that Mitchell stomached losing well. "At home, we were *not* supposed to be happy when they lost," Margaret recalls. "I would just be sad. He wouldn't talk when they lost." She adds that her father, while successful, had time for more than business. "I always saw him for breakfast and supper," she says. "I did a lot of athletics, and he was at everything I ever did." Margaret says her father didn't often bring work home with him, so to speak, but did occasionally watch game film in the living room.

Soon after Mitchell met with the contingent from Lincoln, he called in a handful of his veteran players—juniors Garland Warren, Don Smith, and Charlie Cole—to inform them that a couple of black players from Dallas likely would be trying out for the freshman team that fall. Mitchell sought to gauge their opinions. Cole was almost relieved when he learned the reason for the rare invitation to his head coach's office. "I thought maybe he caught me smoking," Cole says with a laugh. He asked Mitchell if he thought they were good enough to make the team. "We think they can," Mitchell replied. "Well," Cole said, "let's find out." Mitchell closed the session by insisting that the three players relay to their teammates to make the black newcomers welcome.

Charlie Cole, a lineman, rejoined the North Texas program in 1955 as a sophomore after four years in the armed forces, and then welcomed his youngest brother to the freshman team in '56. Charlie first arrived at North Texas from nearby Pilot Point as a freshman in 1949. He chose the Eagles over TCU and Southwest Texas State primarily because of the campus's proximity to the Cole farm, located about twenty miles from campus and a few miles south of Pilot Point in the community known as Blue. But he suffered an attack of appendicitis on the first day of practice and couldn't play that season.

Charlie belatedly played as a freshman in 1950 and then joined the Air Force a few weeks after the season ended, along with about a dozen of his friends from back home. He became a crew chief on a bomber in Korea, leaving the service in January 1955. As was the case with many a southern white, his experiences mixing with black peers in the military served to help increase his acceptance of interracial relations. Not that he and the rest of his family weren't previously open to that. When Charlie was a boy, he was taught to treat a neighboring black family, the Washingtons, with respect.

Charlie was the fifth of seven siblings. Vernon Cole, six years his junior, was the youngest, and was Pilot Point's top athlete as a senior in 1955-'56. He had been approached by SMU and TCU, but had long ago decided to follow Charlie's path to North Texas. Vernon was one of a handful of Pilot Point High boys who often drove down to Denton to visit with girls from the "big city." Another was a Pilot Point Bear-cats football player a year behind him in school, G.A. Moore (since he was Gary A. Moore Jr., he went by G.A.). Among the Denton girls whom they'd take to the drive-in or play table tennis with was Margaret Mitchell, daughter of North Texas's coach, and one of her best friends, Carolyn Logan. The Pilot Point football players were practically dumbstruck when they spent time at the coach's home on Scripture Drive, only a few blocks from the north end of campus. And the Denton girls would sometimes make the return trip up to Pilot Point, too.

On one occasion, Margaret borrowed a brother-in-law's red convertible for what was supposed to be a short drive into downtown

Denton to get a soda from Lane's, but she ended up driving to Pilot Point to see the guys. They were dumbstruck by that car, too. On one of the group dates, Carolyn Logan was sitting in G.A. Moore's car when Vernon Cole dropped by to say hello to his friend. That was the first time that Logan had seen Cole, and they were introduced. The next day, she told a friend that she'd just met the man whom she would marry. "The minute I laid eyes on him," Carolyn recalls. "The minute he walked in front of the car. There was just this instant spark."

One of the freshman linemen was another North Texas "football legacy" like the Coles. Amarillo High's Bob Way had a brother, Fred, who played center for North Texas during the 1952-'53 seasons before going into the service. With Fred four years older, it would be possible for them to play together for the Eagles with Fred scheduled to leave the service in 1957. Bob's high school coach wanted him to play for Oklahoma A&M (which became Oklahoma State in 1957). Bob chose North Texas thinking it was closer to Amarillo than OSU, although that actually wasn't the case. His girlfriend, Carolyn Woods, enrolled that fall at Amarillo Junior College with the intent of transferring to North Texas for the following semester.

Way soon discovered that one of his roommates that fall, fellow lineman George Herring, was almost obsessed with tidiness. It seemed that Herring had his bed made each morning before Way had even gotten out of his. Herring graduated from Snyder High, located in west Texas along the highway that connects Lubbock and Sweetwater. He was the middle child of three, and his father was a junior college All-American football player at Texarkana Junior College. The Herrings lived in San Angelo for a few years when George and younger sister Sally were elementary school students, and while their mother worked at the local J.C. Penney's. George and Sally often walked to the store after school and were struck by the signs that delineated the water fountain for whites from the one designated for "coloreds." George was convinced that meant the water that was made available to the blacks tasted different, probably worse. So he ... boldly ... made Sally taste it first to make sure. She reported no real difference.

Raymond Clement, a freshman running back, grew up on a farm near the town of Bowie, located almost sixty miles northwest of Denton up in Montague County. Clement was the star athlete coming out of Bowie High in 1956; he had been built up by the locals to believe he would continue to thrive as a college football player upon his arrival at North Texas. The town of Bowie wasn't terribly accepting of blacks. It was no coincidence that a settlement was established just south of town called Sunset, as in blacks shouldn't let the sun set on them in Bowie. Clement didn't consider himself a racist, figuring a person would have to have had a bad personal experience with one or more blacks to be a racist and he'd never seen a black person by the time he arrived in Denton. The only blacks with whom he was remotely familiar were those he'd heard about on radio, like Jackie Robinson, Don Newcombe, and Roy Campanella playing for the Brooklyn Dodgers.

Farm life was central to the Clements. Raymond's mother, Anna Bell, would sew shirts for her sons from the cloth of feed bags. Fast food sometimes meant Anna Bell going out back, grabbing a chicken, swinging it just so by the neck a few times and bringing the unfortunate bird into the kitchen to be fried. Clement's father wanted Raymond to continue with the family business. "College is a waste of time," he once told the young man.

But Raymond loathed the prospect of becoming a farmer himself. He wanted to attend college and go into coaching. Clement essentially recruited North Texas instead of the other way around, showing off his athletic ability at a high school track meet in Denton in lieu of Eagles coaches watching him play a football game. Whatever he showed them must have been impressive; Odus Mitchell informed Clement by mail that he was welcome to try out for the football team. Clement arrived on campus a few days before that first day of practice with two pairs of blue jeans and two shirts.

Sammy Stanger came from Van in east Texas, where he worked on the family farm. His father worked for Humble Oil, so Stanger landed summer work as a roustabout for $2.75 an hour. He made the Vandals' varsity as a freshman but played sparingly. His sophomore season ended prematurely when he suffered a broken right ankle in a game against Athens. Stanger put together a solid junior season and was looking forward to a standout senior year, which was lost before the opener when his left knee was severely hurt in a pre-season scrimmage. North Texas was recruiting one of his teammates when Stanger's play as a junior caught the Eagles coaches' eye on the film. He arrived in Denton beneath a crop of red hair affixed atop a head that was bigger than most, to the extent that North Texas equipment manager Ira DeFoor couldn't find a helmet big enough to fit him. Stanger was resigned to having someone in Van send his high school helmet to North Texas. He arrived as a fullback, where he and Clement split time.

At nearly 250 pounds, Joe Mack Pryor was probably the closest thing to the modern-day lineman among those who joined the North Texas frosh that year. Pryor actually might have been the largest player in the entire football program, varsity included, yet one of the quietest. He began his high school career at Diamond Hill-Jarvis High in Fort Worth as a fullback before his size dictated he move to tackle. He'd hoped to attend nearby TCU, and actually considered North Texas too far from home before agreeing to enroll. His chances of joining a higher-profile program were probably curtailed when he tore up a leg while working on a roof during the summer after his sophomore year of high school. At one point, there was concern that he would lose the leg.

Before Haynes and King arrived at the practice field by cab that Saturday, many of the white Eagles players discussed what they should do if the two blacks really did show up. "Don't worry; they're not going to be suiting up," one player remarked. "Ain't no way," said another. "Blacks don't play." At the same time that some players expressed doubt that Haynes and King could make the team, there was mention that Haynes wouldn't be coming to North Texas because he was going to play for Colorado.

Charlie Cole recalls: "The taxi pulled up to the practice field. Coach said, 'That's them.' So we walked out there kind of slow. Leon and Abner got out of the cab. They were in uniform. Abner's eyes were real big. Some of our boys from deep in east Texas really looked closely at them. I just walked up to them and said, 'My name is Charlie Cole, and I want to welcome you to North Texas.' They looked at us and got friendly. We walked up with them and introduced them to the team: 'We think they're football players. Give them the opportunity to show us, and we want you boys to cooperate.'"

During that first day's practice, Mitchell conducted a drill for punters. The players fielding the punts were simply supposed to bring the balls back upfield for the punters to kick again and not stage an actual return. Haynes apparently didn't receive the memo and, in the process, provided a preview of what to expect from him in terms of both talent and attitude. Mitchell recalled in a UNT oral history interview conducted during the 1980s: "Abner fielded the ball and ran from sideline to sideline, shifting the ball from hand to hand, avoiding imaginary tacklers. I thought, 'You sure are a put-on.' But that was just the way that he played. He was going to make the team that first day."

After the first practice, at least one of the white players wasn't shy about confronting Haynes to make clear his aversion to the new racial policy for the football program. Mac Reynolds was a junior end who grew up in the small east Texas town of Karnack, playing six-man football, and transferred to North Texas in 1955 following a stay at Tyler Junior College that earned him junior college All-American honors. As per state educational practices, Karnack had separate schools for its white and black students; what set Karnack apart was that almost three quarters of its populace was black. As a young boy, Reynolds often socialized with the town's black kids, getting together for touch football, softball, and fishing. He and his white friends even attended the black high school's football games and were amused—and somewhat dismissive—of the black teams' frenetic, ad-lib offenses. (That was a common occurrence in Texas towns—whites watching the blacks play high school football and disparaging the blacks' seemingly disorganized, freelance playing style.) But while Reynolds and his buddies were willing to watch the blacks play football, it was clear in Karnack, and virtually everywhere in Texas, that the whites and the blacks had separate neighborhoods.

Reynolds approached Haynes that afternoon in the venue that he likely considered to be one of the most egregious for the onslaught of desegregation, the locker room showers. He bluntly informed the newcomer that he had no intention of showering with a black and asked Haynes why King and he enrolled at North Texas when they had their own schools, just like the white students had. Haynes was succinct and measured in his response, which dissipated the tension. Reynolds later complained to teammates that he didn't want to lose his position to a black, though the prospect of King as a sophomore (once varsity eligible) challenging Reynolds as a senior in 1957 seemed improbable.

Beyond confrontations in the showers, there were other ways that North Texas players who were far from enthused over the presence of King and Haynes expressed both their displeasure and their determination that the two wouldn't receive free passes to the freshman roster, which would play its first game three weeks later. There was, of course, a commitment to message-delivering tackles and hits on the practice field. But less overt was offensive players conveniently slipping or falling when blocking, exposing a vulnerable Haynes or King.

After only a few practices, Bahnsen determined Haynes had not been taught the proper backfield stance during his Lincoln days. Haynes's feet were spread far apart instead of tightly supporting his upper body. Bahnsen had a difficult time convincing Haynes that he'd benefit from a more fundamentally sound stance. So Bahnsen, only two years separated from playing in the NFL, informed the freshman that he could beat him running backwards. Since Bahnsen was calling the snap count, he took a slight head start. Plus, Bahnsen wasn't really running backward at all but more backpedaling and looking over his shoulder back at Haynes. But after Bahnsen won a couple of those races, he was able to get Haynes to put his knees beneath his body and provide more push. "Abner won us over right there because he'd catch ol' Bahnsen in a hurry," Clement recalls. "Abner always had a big grin, even his freshman year. While he'd be chasing Bahnsen, you could hear him laughing and cutting up and having fun. And the harder they worked him, the better he seemed to like it."

While Mitchell, the staff, and the upper-class team leaders succeeded in preventing any melees from breaking out on the practice field or elsewhere, there was no forgetting that many of the players came from backgrounds that relegated blacks to second-class citizenship, if they were considered citizens at all. Some of the whites reacted in the heat of practice by using derogatory terms that they'd grown up with. Charlie Cole recalls an episode in which a varsity linebacker from east Texas was upset that Haynes sped past him on a dive play and blurted out, "Stop that coon!" "We had a little get-together with the coach after that," Cole remembers. "He said, 'We don't call our teammates by those names.' We soon found out that Leon and Abner could both play football."

CHAPTER 8

"You will never enroll in this school"

ON THE SAME SATURDAY DURING which Abner Haynes and Leon King pensively made that first walk across the gravel parking lot at Fouts Field toward the gentlemen whom they hoped would accept them as new teammates, the members of a far more combustible inter-racial exchange were smoldering about fifty-five miles to the south in the southern Tarrant County farm town of Mansfield. That episode—having started a few years earlier and which would continue for almost another decade—contained enough vitriol and acrimony to compel the *New York Times* to dispatch a reporter to the scene for a story and photo that would appear on its front page after the threat of violence prompted the government to call in state militia. That act would have a profound effect at another time and place as the battle for civil rights continued to ignite across the South in the years to come.

Mansfield was a town of about 1,450, nearly a quarter of whom were black and lived in and just beyond the northern and western portions of the city limits. The town was informally centered during the 1860s around a gristmill that was owned by Ralph S. Man and Julian Feild and became known of Mansfeild, later changed to today's spelling. Many of the berg's original residents brought with them

African slaves. The flour and cornmeal produced by the mill were soon included among the young state of Texas's contributions to the Civil War. Early in the twentieth century, the establishment of formal education in Mansfield was, of course, structured along segregated lines. The black elementary school children attended classes in Mansfield, but in a building that was far inferior to the town's white school in terms of physical structure (lacking electricity and indoor plumbing) and staffing (one teacher taught grades one through eight). Mansfield's black students in grades nine through twelve were bused for a fee into southeastern Fort Worth, to the secondary facilities for blacks in that part of the city: James Guinn School for ninth graders and I.M. Terrell High School for those in grades ten through twelve. There was one bus driven to both schools, and it didn't stop right at the campuses, only in the general vicinities. For students bused to Terrell, the one-way ride was about twenty miles.

There had been an active presence of the Ku Klux Klan during the 1930s and '40s which was connected to at least one lynching of a black resident. After World War II, Mansfield's black community began to seek new and superior educational opportunities for its children. According to the 1950 U.S. Census, Texas featured the smallest black population of the eleven states that had made up the Confederacy—fewer than 13 percent. An attempt to desegregate schools in north Texas occurred in 1950 in Euless, a town located between Fort Worth and Dallas, just west of today's Dallas/Fort Worth International Airport. The black population of Euless lived in an area called Mosier Valley that included a grade school often maintained in an unkempt condition relative to the town's school for white students.

In August 1949, the Euless superintendent determined it would be cheaper to bus the black students to Fort Worth rather than renovate the school for blacks. The dissatisfied Mosier Valley citizens filed suit in U.S. District Court to block the superintendent's action. In July 1950, a judge ruled in favor of the parents, that Euless's black school should receive funding equivalent to that of the town's school for whites. A subsequent bond issue to enable the funding was easily defeated by the white majority. The Mosier Valley families responded by attempting to enroll thirty-five black elementary school youngsters in Euless's white school on Labor Day in advance of the new school year. That prompted a white crowd estimated at about 150 to quickly congregate at the school and express its repugnance for a desegregated school. The superintendent consulted with school board members, then gathered the black families in the school auditorium to inform them that enforcement of state segregation law superseded any other legal dictum. When repairs were soon begun at the Mosier Valley school, Euless's blacks retreated from their fight.

A Mansfield branch of the National Association for the Advancement of Colored People was formed in 1950. One of the black leaders in town was T.M. Moody, who had experienced the dawning of the new racial era while fighting in World War II and wasn't afraid to speak out regarding the possibilities for Mansfield's future. Moody became the head of the town's NAACP and superintendent of Mansfield's signature black church, Bethlehem Baptist. He established enough credibility in the white community to be designated as the blacks' liaison to the Mansfield board of education.

Facility improvements were indeed made for Mansfield's black school children, but they were far less than what was provided to the town's whites. A new black elementary school included restrooms and was larger; it had four rooms. The staff for teaching the eight grades was expanded from one teacher to two. As for the secondary students, they were still bused to Fort Worth, but families no longer had to pay for that service. At the same time, the Mansfield board passed more expensive renovations and expansions for the white facilities. Moody and the town's other black leaders were frustrated by the board's decisions and, bolstered by the addition of the 1954 *Brown v. Board of Education* decision to the *Sweatt* verdict of a few years earlier, pursued not only educational improvement for Mansfield's black children but educational equality with the town's white youngsters.

Three months after the *Brown* ruling, Moody argued before the board that Mansfield was obligated to follow the new federal law and desegregate its schools. This fell on deaf ears that extended well beyond Mansfield, all the way to the statehouse in Austin. Governor Allan Shivers grew up in segregated east Texas, in the town of Lufkin in the "Piney Woods" region. He had relocated down to Port Arthur, where he both graduated from high school and first worked following his graduation from the University of Texas. Shivers readily acknowledged his opposition to desegregation as he campaigned for re-election via the Democratic primary in July 1954. (In heavily Democratic Texas at the time, the primary amounted to the election itself.) Such was the case when he spoke in the east Texas town of Nacogdoches only days before the primary, stating, "We are going to keep the system that we know is best. No law, no court can wreck what God made. Nobody can pass a law and change it." Speaking that same day in the nearby town of Palestine, Shivers chided his opponent, Ralph Yarborough, considered the more liberal Democratic candidate, for not making known his stance on the controversial issue. "You know where Allan Shivers stands. The decision as to whether or not we continue to operate our Texas public schools on their present segregated basis will be made July 24th, when you cast your ballot in the race for the state's highest office."

Brown v. Board of Education returned to court early in 1955 when some school boards across the country requested exceptions to the ruling. The Supreme Court responded on May 31, declaring that the nation's public schools must desegregate "with all deliberate speed." For the black community in Mansfield, the second ruling from the high court bolstered the pursuit of educational equality. Not that Shivers was prepared to acquiesce. He reacted to the call for "all deliberate speed" by appointing an advisory committee in late July 1955 to study how best to comply with the ruling. And with some of the state's local school districts having voted to desegregate, he warned not to "dash head-long" into complying with the court's decision. "Hasty, ill-advised action could do much harm," Shivers said from Austin as he further urged districts to wait for recommendations from his new committee before making plans. Among the districts that continued ahead and desegregated for the fall term of 1955 (at least in some of their schools, if not the entire system) were Austin, Lubbock, and Brownsville. A handful of black families in Dallas and Fort Worth attempted to enroll at white schools, but were rebuffed without much clamor.

The Mansfield blacks petitioned the school board in July for admittance to the town's white schools beginning with that 1955-'56 school year, but were likewise turned away. A month later they tried again, with black attorney L. Clifford Davis of Fort Worth writing to the school board on their behalf. Mansfield school superintendent R.L. Huffman answered with another rejection. Among those who sought enrollment at Mansfield High was the family of sixteen-year-old Floyd Moody, who had completed his sophomore year at Terrell. Floyd's father, a first cousin to T.M. Moody, was a sharecropper. The Moodys lived in a farmhouse that belonged to his father's boss, Wilburt Seeton. The farm was located about two miles outside Mansfield. Floyd and his brothers often played with the two Seeton boys, Wesley and Charles, with no issue. Floyd Moody recalls a meeting involving Huffman, the black families, and their attorney at the high school before the 1955-'56 school year began: "I already knew Mr. Huffman from when he would come to the Mansfield black school. I thought he was a real nice man. We sat around a conference table. He said, 'You will never enroll in this school.' When he said that, I knew I'd be out of high school before this thing came up again. He was probably afraid they would take his job away [if desegregation was allowed], and you have to go with the folk with the power."

On October 7, 1955, three black families in Mansfield filed suit to have their fifteen-year-old sons attend Mansfield High instead of being bused forty miles round-trip to Terrell High in Fort Worth. Listed as plaintiffs were Nathaniel Jackson, Charles Moody, and Floyd Moody. (Floyd's father and Charles' mother were first cousins.) The primary attorney who represented the families, Davis, requested an immediate hearing and injunction that would allow the three teens to attend Mansfield High. Among the other attorneys listed for the plaintiffs were U. Simpson Tate, who was the regional NAACP attorney, and Thurgood Marshall from the national NAACP office. The presence of Marshall revealed the commitment that the national organization had made to the Mansfield legal challenge. Superintendent Huffman told the *Fort Worth Star-Telegram* that he wasn't even aware of the suit until he heard about it on television. "I can't even say what we'll do," Huffman told the newspaper. "I plan to talk to the president of the trustees [O.C. Rawson], and then we'll know where we stand."

Some Texas towns mobilized to fight desegregation by forming White Citizens Councils. The practice started in Mississippi in 1953, before the first *Brown* ruling amid fear that such a change was coming, and began to spread throughout the Southeast beginning in late 1954. One such council, in the west Texas town of Big Spring, took its efforts to court, arguing that state funds were not meant for integrated schools. That attempt was denied by a federal court and, in mid-October 1955, Texas's Supreme Court affirmed that state funds could be used by desegregated school districts. Mansfield formed its own Citizens Council in the wake of the lawsuit that sought entry for the three black teens. The group met in the town's Memorial Hall on October 25, 1955, elected temporary officers, and began to determine a strategy for maintaining segregated schools in their town. That included expressing support for the board members. Thomas B. "Bud" West, the council's chairman, was quoted in the weekly *Mansfield News* as telling the assembled gathering, estimated at 125 people, that, "We ought to get the monkey off those men's back." He accepted the appointment as chairman to a rousing ovation. The evening's featured speaker was Howard Beard, president of Fort Worth's Citizens Council. Beard charged that the Supreme Court's decision was based on the Swedish book *American Dilemma*, written by experts and scholars with communist backgrounds. He addressed the integration of the races. "Once mixed, they can never be unmixed," Beard said, according to the newspaper, "and this is the surest way to destroy us. If we don't organize, it will be our children who will pay the price in the next two generations for our cowardice." He referenced the NAACP and said the group should more accurately be called the National Association for the *Agitation* of Colored People.

The trial that could desegregate Mansfield's schools began in U.S. district court in Fort Worth under the jurisdiction of Judge Joe E. Estes on November 7, 1955 (one day after the oldest of the three living Confederate Army veterans then—Walter W. Williams of Franklin, Texas—celebrated his 113th birthday). The Mansfield school district was represented by J.A. "Tiny" Gooch of Fort Worth. He told newsmen that his charge for handling the case was only $1 because he knew the school district was financially strapped. Gooch called only one witness, superintendent Huffman, to the stand for the defense. Huffman said the town's black high school-aged students preferred attending Terrell High in Fort Worth "with one or two exceptions." He said he wasn't prepared to make the changes necessary for desegregation: "We can't undo in 60 days what has lasted 100 years." Tate, representing the plaintiffs, pressed Huffman on what specifically had to be done to accommodate the black students. Huffman replied, "Breaking down old traditions. Getting two different types of people ready for something new. Getting people to accept it. It couldn't be done overnight." Gooch called to the stand under cross examination Nathaniel Jackson, one of the three teens affiliated with the lawsuit. Jackson told Gooch that he'd moved from Fort Worth to Mansfield that August and previously attended one of the black junior highs in Fort Worth, Carver, before being bused from his new home to Terrell High. Jackson described his typical morning: catch the bus at 7:30, wait for its stop at Guinn Junior High, and then arrive at Terrell at 8:10 for the class day beginning at 8:30. His typical post-school schedule: The bus left about five minutes after dismissal. If he missed that, he simply walked home and arrived between 5:30-6 p.m. Jackson added that the Mansfield High bus went right past his home and he wouldn't need to leave until 8:30 a.m. Gooch pointed out that those Mansfield High students who play football miss the only afternoon bus and must make do on their way home, too. Estes asked Jackson how he'd feel about transferring from Terrell to Mansfield High in the middle of the academic year; Jackson indicated that he wouldn't want to do that.

After hearing arguments before a courtroom crowded with many residents of Mansfield, white and black, Estes that afternoon denied the plaintiffs' claim. He said he recognized the legality of their case in light of the Supreme Court decision, but sided with the school district's insistence that such change couldn't be accommodated in such a relatively brief period of time. Estes also told the trustees to get started on their plans for desegregation but did so in relatively vague terms: "make a prompt and reasonable effort" as soon as possible when considered practical, while noting that doing so in the middle of a school term was impractical. Gooch replied, "We are ready to meet the issue head on."

Attorney Davis said he would take the blacks' case to the U.S. Court of Appeals, and activity on the defendants' side of the argument continued despite the legal victory. In November 1955, the Mansfield Citizens Council solicited 150 names on a petition that sought to create a national referendum on racial integration. With the school district having announced no efforts toward desegregation for the 1956-'57 school year, the blacks' appeal was assigned to the U.S. Fifth Circuit Court of Appeals in New Orleans in early June 1956. Before the month ended, Chief Judge Joseph C. Hutcheson reversed the decision of Estes's lower court and ordered the school board to allow for the enrollment of blacks throughout Mansfield schools. The tiny farming community in southeastern Tarrant County had earned the distinction of becoming the first school district in the state of Texas ordered to desegregate by dictum of the federal judiciary.

Mansfield's white citizens made known their feelings about racial integration, in schools and beyond, through referendum questions that were appended to the Democratic primary ballot in July 1956. Regarding laws that fought desegregation, they approved by a vote of 407-31. For laws banning inter-racial marriage, they approved 404-26. For laws supporting interposition of states' rights over federal law, they approved 400-26. All three questions were approved by more than 92 percent of the town's citizens, while the entire state concurred on a lesser basis while still a convincing majority: between 77 and 81 percent on the three questions.

In the wake of the latest legal jousting, the *Star-Telegram* published a three-part series in early August 1956 detailing how the small town was dealing with the accompanying attention and with the antici-pated transition to desegregation. Whites and blacks who were inter-viewed agreed that, as one unidentified citizen said, "It just won't work." J.L. Curry, a white man, told the newspaper that the whole mess was caused by pressure from communists. Curry operated a drive-in and dancing spot for teens and placed a sign at his establishment: WE DON'T SERVE NEGROES. One of the black residents who was questioned, Maude Lewis, expressed a preference for leaving the school system segregated. "I believe that is the way God intended it," she said. The *Mansfield News* weighed in with an editorial in mid-August, expressing the news-paper's displeasure with the outcome of the legal wrangling and aligned with the citizens who sought to remedy the situation through a national referendum. Its message essentially was that everyone makes mistakes, even the nine judges of the nation's highest court, and that Congress should step in and render the decision null and void: "We are not against the Negro, but we are against social equality. We think the Negroes are making great strides in improving their race and commend them for it, as long as they stick to their race."

With little more than a week to go before the beginning of Man-sfield's 1956-'57 school year, and only a few days before the two-day registration period, Judge Estes distributed a two-page order on Monday, Aug. 27, 1956, calling for the town's school board to allow blacks to enroll and attend classes. The school board trustees huddled with their attorney, Gooch, and responded with a familiar refrain: the school district doesn't have time to prepare for desegregation to be implemented the following week and seeks a legal delay. They cited finances, that the Mansfield district had already compensated the Fort Worth school district for each black student who would be bused up there for the coming school year to the tune of $75 per pupil. Amid the latest round of community chaos, the *Fort Worth Press* caught up with Jimmie Irene Moody, mother of Charles Moody, one of the plaintiffs. She expressed dismay over the seemingly never-ending decisions and appeals that had gone on for more than a year. "It's just back and forth," she told the *Press*. "I just guess nobody will know for sure until school starts."

It didn't take that long. Anyone who questioned the resolve of the Mansfield whites to hold their ground against federal legal mandate need only have looked up at the effigy that was suspended above Main Street sometime during the night of Tuesday, Aug. 28, 1956. The effigy body was dabbed with red paint, and two signs attached to the feet of the figure duly noted: "THIS NEGRO TRIED TO ENTER WHITE SCHOOL ... THIS WOULD BE A HORRIBLE WAY TO DIE."

Jimmie Irene Moody said the incident wouldn't deter her family from attempting to register Charles that Friday; school district residents who lived within the city limits would register on Thursday, while those living outside the city limits would register on Friday. "It didn't scare him," she told the *Press*. "I'm sure most other Negroes in the community are not afraid, either." Tarrant County sheriff Harlon Wright essentially shrugged at the effigy, saying it wasn't uncommon in Mansfield and assuming most people interpreted it as a practical joke. "If any violence should break out," Wright told the *Star-Telegram*, "we can have men there in a few minutes." Floyd Moody recalls that his father was confronted by his boss, Mr. Seeton, about the desegregation controversy. "The farm owner asked my father if he was going to send me to the Mansfield school, and he said yes. The man said, 'All these white folk in town are mad at you, and they'll be mad at me. You'll have to move.' And we moved where the other black folks lived, out of the man's house, and my dad quit the farm and went to work for Texas Steel."

On Wednesday, August 29, Gooch's petition for a stay of enforcement to delay desegregation yet again was filed in U.S. District Court with Estes scheduling a hearing for the following day, the first day of Mansfield school registration. That night, T.M. Moody reported receiving multiple death threats over the phone. One caller said Moody had twenty minutes to vacate his home before a bomb would go off. Moody left along with his wife and mother-in-law to stay with a neighbor, returning later after nothing had happened. When the school district opened registration on the morning of Thursday, August 30, hundreds of whites had already gathered in front of the high school. Some shops in the town's business district closed that morning in support of the protesters. Another effigy was hung atop the flagpole in front of the high school. Its accompanying message that time: "STAY AWAY NIGGERS."

The protesters were monitored by what the *Press* called a "sizable" force of law enforcement officers. According to the *Star-Telegram*, Sheriff Wright was asked by one man, "Are you going to give them a police escort into school?" The sheriff replied that he was simply there to maintain law and order. The man continued, "We want a yes or a no answer; that's all. Are you gonna escort them in there with guns?" The sheriff said he didn't want the townspeople taking the law into their own hands. The man added, "If you escort them in with guns, we are gonna have to get guns ourselves." Jimmie Moody, while not eligible to register Charles that day, was present and appeared to have at least become unsure of whether to attempt to enroll him on Friday, given what she told a *Press* photographer: "There's such a big stink, I'm going to send my boys to school in Fort Worth." Later that day, she backtracked and stated she would talk to friends that night before deciding what to do.

Later that day, Estes denied the school's district's request for a stay, ruling that he lacked the authority to buck the decision previously made by the Fifth U.S. Circuit Court of Appeals. Estes's voice cracked, according to *The Dallas Morning News*, when he said, "By taking an attitude of prayerful obedience to the law, the school will stand as a proud monument to the patriotism of the people of this land." He suggested to Gooch to either try the Circuit Court of Appeals again or go straight to the U.S. Supreme Court. Gooch immediately sought out Judge John Brown, a member of the Fifth Circuit Court of Appeals in Houston, to arrange for a meeting the next morning to seek a stay. Though the plaintiffs had won their day in court, attorney L. Clifford Davis sent telegrams to Shivers and U.S. attorney general Herbert Brownell, asking for an additional presence of law enforcement given what happened at the school that day, when no blacks even tried to register, and since Sheriff Wright had told Davis that his staff lacked the numbers to quell the expected trouble.

A similar scene played out on the morning of Friday, August 31, the second and final day of registration. Hundreds of whites milled around outside Mansfield High, and no black families attempted to register their students. Davis attempted to circumvent the perceived threat and register the three students by way of telegram to Huffman that morning, but the superintendent stated that any student must enroll in person. *New York Times* reporter Luther A. Huston asked one of the protesters what they'd do to a black if one came on the school grounds. The reply: "You just hang around and see." Some folks who attempted to be peacemakers, an Episcopal priest from Fort Worth and a county assistant attorney general, were run off by the crowd. The threat of violence and the decision by Huffman to lock the school doors at noon was enough for Shivers to change his mind and send in a handful of Texas Rangers peace officers. That decision was accompanied by orders that any blacks who attempted to register at the high school would in essence be inciting mob violence and should instead register at Terrell High in Fort Worth. Shivers used as his precedent the action taken at the University of Alabama during the brief but effective Autherine Lucy protests. Shivers placed the blame for the mob scene at the feet of the NAACP and the federal judiciary: "I hope the U.S. Supreme Court will be given an opportunity to view the effect of its desegregation decision on a typical, law-abiding Texas community."

In that morning's *Star-Telegram*, the registrar at Terrell High reported that five blacks from Mansfield asked to enroll. They included Charles and Floyd Moody. Floyd's mother was quoted in the newspaper as saying, "It would be better if Floyd could go to school in Mansfield because he would be near home. We don't want any trouble, but I want my boy to go to school." State representative Joe Pool of Dallas wired the governor late that night, asking for a special legislative session to convene for the expressed purpose of outlawing the NAACP in Texas.

In Houston that day, Gooch's efforts fell short yet again, rejected by a panel of three judges. He then set his sights on the Supreme Court and, on Saturday, September 1, was granted permission to file an application for a stay. In Mansfield, a man from Dallas offered to remove the two effigies that remained aloft. His offer was declined by the townspeople, whose wishes were expressed by J.L. Curry, whom you might recall posted a sign at his eatery that he didn't serve blacks: "No one had better come out here and take those dummies down." The legal stay was denied by Justice Hugo Black on the next working day after Labor Day, Tuesday, September 4, 1956, which was also the first day of classes in the fall term.

Another mob congregated at Mansfield High first thing in the morning to make sure no blacks tried to enroll. One protester brought a toy monkey that sported a sign reading, "I WANT TO PLAY FOOTBALL FOR MANSFIELD HIGH." Others, including "Bud" West of the Citizens Council, brought bloodhounds meant to discourage any blacks from registering. A photo of the dogs and their owners in the *Star-Telegram* included a caption that, either as a cruel joke or an attempt at absolute specificity, identified the canines as "coon dogs."

Six officers of the Texas Rangers were present to maintain order, and were called upon to defuse a tense situation that developed between the white protesters and a white clergyman from Fort Worth who wanted to help effectuate a peaceful resolution. Instead, the Rev. D.W. Clark only succeeded in making himself a target of Mansfield's resentment toward unwanted intervention. Rev. Clark urged the crowd to "put the Bible's love thy neighbor together with this crowd." A quick, caustic riposte came from the gathering: "This ain't a love-thy-neighbor crowd." When the reverend tried to make a point of man being made in the image of God by using one of the effigies as an example, a man yelled back, "That ain't no image of a man. ... If He wanted 'em to live together, why didn't He make 'em all the same color? You can't cross a mockingbird with a chickadee."

Despite yet another legal victory for Mansfield's black community, the continued threatening presence of a convulsed group combined with the frayed and drained emotional state of the town's blacks was enough for the NAACP to abandon its attempt to desegregate the town for the 1956-'57 school year. When Mansfield schools opened the day following Labor Day, no blacks attempted to register or attend, and attorney Davis that night told *The Dallas Morning News* that the fight was over for at least the time being. "We have concluded we are not going to enroll those students under the circumstances at this time," Davis told the newspaper. "We could not take them in there while that mob is standing there ready to do violence. There will perhaps be some further proceedings in an effort to ease the situation and make it safe for the enrollment of Negro students."

The following day, Wednesday, September 5, 1956, President Dwight Eisenhower addressed desegregation difficulties across the South and, without naming Shivers, appeared to question the Texas governor's decision to send state peace officers into Mansfield. "We'd better be very careful about moving in and exercising police power," Eisenhower told reporters in Washington, D.C. (Shivers would be praised for his actions by the state Democratic executive committee a week later.) A reporter then stated that the attorney for the Mansfield plaintiffs didn't receive help when asking for assistance when they feared violence. The president noted that state authorities had managed to keep the peace before the federal government could take any action. "So the question became unimportant," Eisenhower said. The following day, Thursday, September 6, Shivers told reporters the calm that had returned to Mansfield proved he did the right thing by sending in Texas Rangers: "That order was not issued in defiance of anyone. It was just a state order for law and order."

The editorial page of the *Star-Telegram* that morning called for the state legislature to take up the fight against desegregation as the state's populace had so emphatically called for through the July Democratic referendum. That evening's weekly edition of the *Mansfield News* provided a relatively serene depiction of the opening of the school year, devoid of references to threats or coon dogs, stating it took place "without any trouble whatsoever." "A large crowd lined the sidewalk and gathered in groups to talk. It looked like a gathering of good neighbors for a picnic and talk-fest. Everyone seemed to be in excellent spirits, and the cheery 'hellos' from one group of students to others was, indeed, a welcome sound." In curious contrast, a collage of staff photos accompanying the article showed a "human wall" that protected the high school from the "deteriorating outside factors," locals assuring a visiting assistant district attorney that they aren't a "low class of people" and a group of "sober faces" that revealed the strain of the recent events. The photo caption closed with a nod to the obvious to those who were there: "Yes, the Fall Term 1956 in Mansfield High School will be long remembered."

There actually were some tangible reminders; some locals who feared the white majority might become complacent and let down its guard regarding segregation in the future printed signs that implored "REMEMBER MANSFIELD." That fall term of 1956 at Mansfield High was also remembered formally a few months afterward in a summation published nationally by the Anti-Defamation League of B'nai B'rith. The sixteen-page report's title was "Mansfield, Texas: A Report of the Crisis Situation Resulting from Efforts to Desegregate the School System." One of the co-authors was John Howard Griffin, a popular writer and novelist living in Mansfield. Griffin interviewed both whites and blacks in the town and was troubled by much of what he was told. For one, he came away convinced that any black in Mansfield who was intent on convincing the town to follow the directive of the federal courts would probably be killed. When Griffin asked townspeople for their suggested resolutions to the civic embroilment, recommendations ranged from segregating schools according to intelligence rather than race to secession from the United States.

In early September 1957, almost a year to the day that Texas Rangers officers were called into Mansfield, troops of the Arkansas National Guard were summoned by Gov. Orval Faubus to "assist" nine black students to enter previously all-white Central High School in Little Rock, with desegregation having been mandated by court order. But thousands of white protesters prevented any semblance of orderly assimilation. The subsequent violence reached such a fever pitch that

President Eisenhower reluctantly called in soldiers from the U.S. Army's 101st Airborne Division from Fort Campbell, Kentucky.

The legal battle in Arkansas continued for years, with Faubus closing all of the city's high schools for most of the 1958-'59 school year to avoid integration. F. Ross Peterson, a history professor at Utah State University, compared the actions of the federal government during the episodes in Mansfield and Little Rock in a speech delivered to the Organization of American Historians in 1975 in Boston. Peterson called the Mansfield clash "an important step along the path that led to the famous Little Rock integration battle."

In a Gallup Poll taken late in 1958, Faubus was chosen as one of the nation's ten most admired men.

CHAPTER 9

"Go back to Africa"

ABNER HAYNES AND LEON KING weren't the only members of Lincoln High's class of 1956 to continue their education in the unlikely venue of North Texas State College that September. Another handful of Tigers decided to take advantage of the opportunity that had been laid before them by the enrollment of Irma Sephas seven months earlier, as fourteen black freshmen and two black transfers came on campus. Several had the decision made for them, which was the case for Burlyce Sherrell.

Sherrell was prepared to attend Prairie View A&M, the alma mater of her parents. But only weeks before the fall term was scheduled to begin, she was informed by her folks that they'd prefer she attend North Texas. The primary reason that they cited was Denton being located much closer to the family's south Dallas home than Prairie View, just northwest of Houston. "Hey, they were paying the bills," Sherrell recalls. It also helped that she planned to major in music, and North Texas boasted one of the best music schools in the Southwest, if not in the nation. Any trepidation that she had was also muted when her best friend, fellow Lincoln grad Lurline Bradley, joined the Tiger contingent headed to North Texas. Still, when the Sherrells moved Burlyce into her new off-campus home and began to drive away, she recalls, "I thought I was going to die." Before the hugs and goodbyes, her parents reminded her of the struggles that might lie ahead and urged her not to retaliate.

Sherrell and Bradley were excited when they attended the freshman orientation and listened attentively as a school representative explained various school procedures and opportunities. That excitement quickly dissipated, Sherrell says, when the administrator stated that some of the students were there only because the state mandated that they couldn't be turned away. Sherrell recalls it took only a few seconds before the black students concluded, "It's us!" The administrator went on to say that those students would have no reason to be on campus other than when they were attending classes, but not on nights or weekends. At a faculty meeting held about that same time, school president J.C. Matthews made only a brief comment about the new black students; he warned teachers not to award them sympathy grades.

One weekend early in that semester, Sherrell and four of her new black classmates from Dallas decided they'd test part of the recommendations that had been bluntly delivered to them during freshman orientation. They set off to go on campus, to see what would happen. Their itinerary was random and harmless, simply walking from here to there and not entering buildings, and they took photos along the way for proof of their apparently brazen excursion.

Sherrell, Bradley, and the other black women soon experienced the simple reality that King and Haynes had learned a few weeks earlier during football camp. Living on Denton's east side meant long walks just to reach North Texas's campus. Simple grocery shopping meant an extended walk, since the closest store was relatively small and didn't offer the same variety that they'd enjoyed back in Dallas. It was on one of Sherrell's walks home from the grocery store that a young black man who'd often driven by and seen her finally stopped to offer help on the final leg of her trip. She was happy to accept Raymond Logan's hospitality, and the two began dating soon after.

It was difficult for Sherrell to follow her parents' advice, to not fight back. It was difficult when white students called her and her friends ugly names. It was difficult when people threw rocks at them. It was difficult when they came upon a group of protesters carrying signs that read PIGS BEFORE NIGS and GO BACK TO AFRICA. No, she didn't fight. In fact, she once started laughing. "Go back to Africa—I'd never been to Africa, and I didn't want to go there," she recalls. "It just struck me as funny. I started laughing and couldn't stop, slapping my knee. They [the whites] must have thought I was crazy."

. . . .

The freshman football players often practiced with the varsity since, with all of sixteen members starting out, there weren't enough to regularly merit their own exclusive drills. It was in those sessions against the varsity, during which the newcomers often seemed like helpless targets for the upperclassmen, that Raymond Clement struggled most with his transition from the single wing that he'd run at Bowie High to North Texas's T formation. It felt as though he was always backing up a step after the snap of the ball when playing offense, which all but put him two steps behind almost before the play began. That invited the wrath of assistant coach Fred McCain, who gladly applied pressure to a player who appeared near the breaking point. Some of their encounters simulated scenes straight out of *Gomer Pyle, U.S.M.C.*, with Sgt. Carter constantly in Pyle's ear while the inept private couldn't left-right-left with the rest of the new Marines. McCain kept yelling, and Clement seemingly couldn't keep in step.

After the first week's practice, Clement returned home to Bowie for the weekend and dutifully informed his parents about what he considered the unreasonable rigors of being cannon fodder for the varsity unit. He also proceeded to inform his mother of what might be considered a deal-breaker, resulting in the family ordering him to come home and forget about North Texas. "Now, Daddy ain't gonna want me playing with some niggers, and we've got some niggers on our team. So I'm not going back." Clement's mother looked up at him and replied, "If you want to play football, you play football. If you want to quit because it's too tough for you, you quit. But don't blame it on two colored people."

Clement very much wanted to simply remain in Bowie, or at least attend North Texas without playing football. Instead, he returned to campus that Sunday evening and was back on the practice field the following day.

Clement's early progress was almost imperceptible. The young man was near the breaking point, certain only that he'd never master the fine art of college football, at least not at North Texas, at least not to McCain's liking. With that despairing view of the football world apparently etched on Clement's face, McCain pulled him over one day and said, "I want to tell you something." Clement was sure the end was near, that he was about to receive his dishonorable discharge from McCain's football army. "Clement, as long as I'm chewing on your ass, you're going to get to stay. . . . Cheer up." Which Clement did, suddenly aware that every missed assignment would only help him learn what to do correctly and didn't mean he was an abysmal failure. They *did* want him on the football team, just like that letter from Odus Mitchell said.

Haynes and King made the trek from east Denton to practice for weeks before fall classes began. They were formally welcomed on the practice field but not in the athletic dining hall. The first player who didn't simply accept the stratification of King and Haynes from the rest of North Texas's football players at meal time was one of the players who first greeted them after they cautiously exited the taxi on the first Saturday morning of September. Vernon Cole couldn't really do much about it, but what he *could* do spoke volumes. Haynes and King were prohibited from eating with their teammates in the chow hall, but that didn't mean they couldn't at least eat and drink some of what was available *outside* the building. A carton of milk here, a piece of fruit there. That's what Cole brought out to them whenever he got the chance. It wasn't much, yet it served as a significant memorandum. The freshmen were planning to stick together wherever and however they could.

On Thursday, September 20, the president of the state chapter of the National Association for the Advancement of Colored People compared the persecution of Texas blacks to German Jews under Adolf Hitler. In Washington D.C. that same day, a local high school principal told a House subcommittee that black students in his racially mixed school lagged behind their white counterparts despite coming from similar socio-economic backgrounds. That night, the 1956 North Texas Eaglets opened the football season at Fouts Field against the freshman squad from Hardin-Simmons in Abilene. It was the first of three freshman games that North Texas managed to schedule toward a goal of five. The Eaglets' roster numbered twenty-three, thanks to seven players who joined the team only two days earlier with the beginning of classes, but freshman coach Ken Bahnsen held the new additions out of the opener. Hardin-Simmons's Buttons had the advantage of already beginning their season, though they lost to San Angelo Junior College 19-7. North Texas students were admitted free to designated seating on the east side, as long as they presented a school ID card. Adults were hit up for 75 cents to sit in the west stands, along with any students who were high school age or younger allowed in for 50 cents.

Haynes was a starting halfback and King a starting end; they, of course, also filled similar positions on defense in the era of one-platoon college football rosters. Haynes—the "fleet Negro halfback" as described by *Denton Record-Chronicle* sportswriter Dub Brown—and King were each significant contributors as the Eaglets won 13-9. King accounted for North Texas's first score of the season on a 30-yard pass from Cole. Haynes soon after raced 56 yards into the end zone, only to have the play nullified by an offensive penalty. He followed that with a 30-yard gain and returned an interception 65 yards—all before halftime. His 47-yard run of the second-half kickoff set up the Eaglets' second touchdown, scored by fellow halfback Gordon Salsman, from nearby Lewisville. A new era of collegiate athletics had begun at North Texas and, truly, for the entire state of Texas.

CHAPTER 10

"Is it really worth it?"

THE 1956 EAGLETS' FIRST ROAD game was scheduled for the final Saturday night in September, about a two-hour drive southeast to Corsicana to play Navarro Junior College (now known as Navarro College, though still a two-year institution). Ken Bahnsen doesn't recall when the Navarro game was placed on the schedule, but a story that appeared in the *Corsicana Daily Sun* two days before the September 29 meeting noted the game wasn't included in Navarro's season tickets.

Navarro Junior College opened in 1946 just outside of town on the site of an air base that was abandoned upon the conclusion of World War II. The school was moved in 1951 to the four-acre site west of downtown, where it's located today. The majority of students were commuters from the small towns across the county of the same name and surrounding counties, an area primarily settled decades earlier by people who moved west from Tennessee, Alabama, and Mississippi. They often came from humble households. Most students ate the majority of their meals at the campus cafeteria—Rose's Cantina, or Rosie's. That included the Sunday night meal that consisted of a sandwich and chips in a sack. A series of bus routes fanned out to provide transportation for students who didn't live in the school's limited dorm space and couldn't afford their own cars. The drivers were students looking to earn extra money to help make ends meet. And, of course, Navarro Junior College's enrollment included no black students. Bahnsen says North Texas never overtly informed opponents that season that its freshman team included two blacks. All of the Eaglets' three road games were day trips. Therefore, there was no need to arrange for overnight lodging, which would have become problematic. The advance story in the *Corsicana Daily Sun* didn't mention North Texas bringing any black players, simply that the freshman team from North Texas State Teachers College was highly regarded.

Bahnsen's players loaded onto the bus that was affectionately known as the "green goose" around noon. For the 8 p.m. kickoff, Bahnsen's routine was to find someplace in town to have a pre-game meal. Upon reaching Corsicana, he spotted V's Cafe, just off the main road into town. The North Texas party disembarked, ready to eat. The food apparently wasn't ready, King said, and players killed some time by walking around. King said he walked with Joe Mack Pryor and Eugene Haecker, the latter a tackle from the central Texas town of Seguin, and they drew some stares from the white townspeople. When the team prepared to enter the restaurant a short time later, an employee noticed at least one of the black players. Bahnsen was informed that blacks couldn't eat in the main dining area with the rest of the team; they would have to eat back in the kitchen. At least three of the white players—Pryor, Cole, and George Herring—emphatically informed the eatery staff that the North Texas freshman football team would not be staying. The group was able to pick up food that was suddenly "to go." As the players left, Haecker kicked over his chair.

Navarro played its football games off campus, at Corsicana High's Tiger Field near downtown. Like most high school football facilities of the day, seating consisted of bleachers located on opposite sides of the field's sidelines. North Texas's bus pulled up to the southwest gate, where the visitors' dressing room was located, relatively close to the home stands. It turned out *someone* by then was aware that North Texas was bringing some black players; that afternoon's episode at V's Cafe certainly could have been a tipoff. Bahnsen says the attendant who checked in the bus asked him if he intended to play "those nig-gers," to which he replied yes. "Well, they might die," Bahnsen says he was told.

As for the game itself, Bahnsen's plan was to employ Haynes as a decoy in the early going and give most of the carries to Salsman. As kickoff approached, it became clear the crowd of a couple of thousand—separated from the field by a chain-link fence about chest high—wasn't pleasantly surprised to spot King and Haynes amid the Eaglets warm-ing up. According to multiple members of the North Texas contingent that night, a chant along the lines of "Get them niggers off the field!" rose from the west stands, and some fans threw objects toward the visi-tors' bench. Haynes approached King as pre-game drills continued and asked, "Did you hear that?" "Yeah, I heard it," King answered. Haynes said, "Tell you what. Before we get through here tonight, they're gonna wish they had us off the field." Some of the white North Texas players were getting agitated by the crowd's behavior and began to volley back with comments of their own. But Haynes interceded: "Don't do it. That doesn't bother me at all." Even if it did.

Navarro struck first, scoring soon after North Texas lost a fumble at its 15-yard line. The host Bulldogs increased their lead to 14-0 with two minutes remaining in the opening period before the Eaglets finally came to life. Haynes' number was finally called on a quick pitch, which resulted in a violent collision in which one of his knees connected directly with a linebacker's helmet. That left the defender lying on the field and Haynes dazed enough to be helped to the sideline. King could only wonder what the Navarro faithful thought then, and what it might mean if Haynes couldn't return to play and he was the lone black to play most of the game. But Haynes returned soon after, and North Texas scored three touchdowns within nine minutes, two of them registered by him. A point-after kick by King notched the final point of the half, North Texas heading to its meager halftime accommodations with a 20-14 lead.

During the break, Bahnsen made it clear that he wasn't pleased despite the comeback and six-point lead. "You let them get to you," he growled. "Play some football." The visitors certainly played some football during the second half. They never relinquished their advantage, with Haynes and King counted among the standouts. Haynes scored four of the Eaglets' six touchdowns in the game, and King grabbed two receptions of more than 25 yards, one on a play on which he would have scored a 28-yard touchdown had he not stepped out of bounds. North Texas won 39-21. As the final minutes ticked off the clock, cheers for North Texas's performance could be heard.

Cheers or no cheers, Bahnsen had no intention of allowing his team to stick around for long after the game to gauge the locals' apparent newfound appreciation for the Eaglets. Before the game ended, he had the bus driver grab the players' street clothes from the tiny locker room, put them on the bus, and then back the "green goose" around so it would be ready to pull out.

When the game ended, Bahnsen instructed his players to simply walk straight out to the bus, and not to remove their helmets. The driver was motoring out of town in no time, while the players sat in something of a daze during the first minutes of the ride home, both pleased with the victory but also unsure of what to think of the reception that they'd received in town and at the game. Cole found Haynes on the bus and told him he was embarrassed, that he had no idea the black players would face treatment that hostile. The team became emotional, some in tears. Haynes stood and declared, "Man, we're gonna sing together." And sing they did.

The North Texas freshmen outgained the Navarro lineup of freshmen and sophomores 346 yards to 185, according to statistics compiled by the *Corsicana Daily Sun*. The following day's edition of the *Sun*, with the game story written by sports editor Paul Moore, identified "negro" Haynes as "one of the fastest and best broken field runners to cleat Tiger Field in many moons." Haynes, Moore continued, "was ably assisted by another of his race, Leon King, right end, who guarded his territory well on defense and was a pass-snagging star on the offense as well." King said he woke up that night in cold chills and asked himself, "Is it really worth it?" He thought of A.W. Brashear, his track coach back at Lincoln, who convinced him that any race worth starting was worth finishing.

Bud Osborne played end for Navarro that season and recalls, "Leon played in front of me on defense. I was impressed with him." As for Haynes, Osborne laughs and says, "I can tell you what he looked like from behind." The game summary in the 1956-'57 Navarro yearbook made reference to "the speed and deception" of North Texas's two "Negro stars." A photo of Haynes running in the clear was accompanied by the phrase "Catch Him If You Can." "How many people [back then] would put the black in your annual?" Osborne asks. "And there he is." Osborne and teammate Rudy Carroll, a tackle, say they can't recall any hostilities at the game, though they acknowledge they weren't focusing on the crowd. As for the accepted narrative at North Texas that the crowd was at best unwelcoming to King and Haynes, and at worst threatening, Osborne says, "You can have some people that can ruin the reputation of the town."

North Texas was able to add a game to the schedule for the first Thursday night of October, at Murray State Agricultural College in southern Oklahoma, bringing the season's total of freshman dates to the desired five. Best known then as Murray A&M, the two-year agricultural school in the small town of Tishomingo had opened in 1908, thanks to the efforts of the state's agricultural-minded Speaker of the Oklahoma House of Representatives, "Alfalfa Bill" Murray. The student body was initially made up primarily of Chickasaws and Choctaws; Tishomingo is capital of the Chickasaw Nation. Maybe that's why Bahnsen didn't experience the same difficulties getting his full squad served for a pre-game meal as had been the case at Navarro. ("Alfalfa Bill" didn't prove to be as personally welcoming when it came to blacks. At the 1906 Oklahoma convention that preceded statehood the following year, he said Oklahoma could only be a great state if blacks were kept separated from whites.)

The North Texas team was provided an eating room of its own adjacent to a school cafeteria; it wasn't an actual dining room, but a meeting room where the team would have privacy. Also, it might have been difficult for Murray A&M to take issue with serving the Eaglets' racially mixed roster a pre-game meal, since the host school's payment to North Texas for making the trip *was* the pre-game meal. Instead of agreeing to an amount of money to be paid to the visiting school, Bahnsen says the contract stipulated North Texas be "paid" with chicken-fried steak before kickoff.

For the second trip of the freshman season, Bahnsen took steps to try to prevent a repeat of the apparently abhorrent episode in Corsicana. He enlisted the help of Denton County Judge Jack Gray, a North Texas grad whose resume included time in both the Marines and the FBI. Judge Gray accompanied the freshman team on its two remaining trips that season, and also arranged for law enforcement to be present at each away game. But there was nothing that Bahnsen or Gray could do about what most of the North Texas traveling party considered inadequate lighting at Murray A&M's football field. From midfield, it was difficult to see into the end zones. Bahnsen addressed that issue during his pre-game talk in the visitors' locker room. During his remarks, Bahnsen concluded that Haynes, lounging in the back of the room atop some tackling dummies, wasn't paying attention. So the coach, like a teacher boring in on an inattentive student, halted his spiel and quizzed his star runner on what he'd just said. Haynes, with a shrug, not only repeated Bahnsen's concern about the lights but also tried to alleviate any fears: "Coach, all they're going to see are the whites of my eyes."

The Murray Aggies saw more of Haynes than they probably wanted to—29 carries for 171 yards. Haynes, though, didn't reach the end zone, while King proved to be the scoring star in North Texas's 27-14 victory. King caught scoring passes of 18 and 10 yards to account for the Eaglets' first and last touchdowns, not to mention converting three of four point-after kicks. Cole returned an interception 75 yards for a touchdown, and Clement also picked off an Aggies pass to set up a touchdown. Three starts, three victories for the North Texas frosh.

The following Saturday night, the varsity Eagles opened the home portion of their season following lopsided losses at Mississippi and Arizona State. The Eagles opening their season at Ole Miss was something of a financially necessary evil. North Texas visited the Rebels in 1956 for the fifth consecutive season; the game paid far more than chicken fried steak. Try $20,000, according to Fred McCain, making it the Eagles' most lucrative road date. North Texas also made frequent trips during the early 1950s to play Mississippi State College and Mississippi Southern College for only slightly less money, making those games also very important to North Texas's athletic income.

The visit from the team representing the San Diego Naval Training Center on the first weekend of October marked a rare appearance of a black player on an opposing team at Fouts Field, possibly the first since Nevada's trip to North Texas in 1950. Of greater local interest was the fact that the black player on the naval squad was a graduate of Denton's Fred Moore High. Fullback William "Buddy" Clark had played for the Moore Dragons, Prairie View A&M, and the Canadian Football League's Toronto team before entering the service. Clark and his San Diego Bluejackets teammates were no match for the Eagles. Even with Mitchell emptying his bench early and often, North Texas scored the first 38 points and cruised to a 65-6 victory, losing the shutout in the closing minutes.

The frosh Eaglets then had three weeks off—if you count practicing against the varsity as off—before playing their fourth game, on the road in late October against the freshman team of Abilene Christian College. Abilene Christian's Kittens went into the game winless in three previous outings, and were missing several injured starters. North Texas's pre-game agenda was again altered when a local restaurant refused to serve the full squad. Bahnsen, slightly more prepared, elected to pick up chicken to go and had his team eat at a nearby park. Haynes and King scored three of North Texas's four touchdowns in a 27-6 victory. Haynes found the end zone on a 1-yard run in the first quarter and an 11-yard run in the second quarter. In between, King caught a 32-yard touchdown pass from Cole. Bahnsen used mostly reserves throughout the fourth quarter and still prevented Abilene Christian from scoring a second touchdown. In four games, the undefeated Eaglets had outscored their opponents, 106-50.

North Texas's fifth and final freshman game of the 1956 season was played at home in early November against Paris Junior College, which arrived in Denton with a record of 3-3-1. The Eaglets faced one of their stiffest tests of the season, but were able to cap the first undefeated campaign for a North Texas football squad at any level by beating the Dragons 27-12. Haynes scored on a pair of runs, and King caught a touchdown pass in the fourth quarter that gave North Texas breathing room.

Afterward, the players were congratulated on their way into the field house, with coeds hugging their gridiron heroes. For King, that presented what he considered a perilous situation. It was one thing for whites growing up in segregated communities to accept blacks who would help the football team win or sit in the same classroom; it was another for those whites to tolerate the sight of white females throwing their arms around the necks of the black players. "It frightened me a little," King said. He said he later experienced a similar scenario in a science lab when one of his partners was a white co-ed named Sandra Palmer, who went on to become a star professional golfer. Lab partners shared a microscope and practically nuzzled cheek to cheek while both getting a glimpse of a particular slide. "I immediately moved to let her have it," King said. "No one in the classroom ever thought anything about it. I doubt if anybody in the classroom knew that had happened. But I did, and I moved."

It's doubtful anyone associated with North Texas football could have asked for more from the school's 1956 freshman football team. Five games, five victories, with the first two black members of the school's football program making significant contributions to the success of the squad. Of the team's fifteen offensive touchdowns, Haynes ran for eight of them. King accumulated four TD catches and was one of the team's regular placekickers, converting three of six PATs. At the same time, Vernon Cole established himself as the quiet conscience of the team, firmly in control while saying very little. Said King: "Vernon was the kind of guy that would go into the huddle and call a play and would look at you in such a way that if you didn't block, you wouldn't go back to the huddle."

The North Texas varsity ended its eight-year stay in the Gulf Coast Conference by finishing with an overall record of 7-2-1 and winning at least a share of the league championship for the fifth time. The GCC, left with only three members following the '56 season, elected not to seek a replacement for North Texas and instead disbanded.

On the Tuesday following the freshmen's season finale, the state of Texas threw its support behind the reelection of President Eisenhower over Democratic candidate Adlai Stevenson. Ike was technically a native son of the Lone Star State, having been born in the Grayson County town of Denison, though his family moved to Kansas when he was an infant. His triumph in Texas marked only the fourth time that the Grand Old Party claimed a major race in Texas, the first being Sam Houston's triumph in the gubernatorial race of 1859. In 1956 as in '52, Eisenhower was backed by Democratic governor Shivers, whose conservative devotees were called "Shivercrats."

Exactly one month after Haynes and King completed their season of freshman competition for North Texas's Eaglets, another collegiate athletic color barrier in the state was eliminated in similarly understated fashion. On December 1, 1956, Texas Western College in El Paso began its 1956-'57 varsity basketball season with a relatively routine 73-48 victory at home over New Mexico Western. By all accounts, a black athlete appeared in a varsity competition for the first time for a predominantly white four-year university in Texas, if not in the entire South. The Texas Western Miners' starting lineup included sophomore guard Charlie Brown, a black who transferred from Amarillo Junior College. His nephew, Cecil Brown, also transferred from the same school, was a reserve on the team, and came off the bench during that game. Charlie led Texas Western with 19 points, the only home-team player to score in double figures in a game in which coach George McCarty emptied his bench; Cecil registered one made free throw. The milestone didn't make it to the front page of the *El Paso Times*, but the paper noted "history was made" by Charlie Brown's appearance at the tipoff in the second paragraph of the game report.

Charlie was twenty-three years old, a graduate of Pruitt High School in the small east Texas town of Atlanta, and a three-year veteran of the Air Force before belatedly beginning his college basketball career in Amarillo. He and Cecil arrived at Texas Western for the 1956 summer session, about a year after the school integrated, and initially weren't allowed to live on campus. Through the efforts of McCarty, they were permitted the use of a dorm room only during the day, but would occasionally quietly spend the night. They were permitted to eat with their white teammates at the athletic training table, unlike the arrangements for King and Haynes at North Texas. The black campus community was small and tight knit, and Dallas's Joe Atkins became one of Brown's close friends. Atkins recalls that he and other black students often dropped by the Browns' dorm room on class days to relax or study.

Charlie played three varsity seasons, led the team in scoring each year, and finished his Miners playing days as the school's career scoring leader at that time. Cecil came off the bench throughout his two seasons on the team. Charlie majored in history, graduated in May 1959, and then did graduate work at Texas Western the following year. He was inducted into UTEP's Athletic Hall of Fame in 2008, and had his uniform number retired by the school in 2011.

CHAPTER 11

"They were out to get me"

KEN BAHNSEN ALMOST DIDN'T KNOW what to think. Word was sent that Bahnsen, freshman football coach—and varsity golf coach—at North Texas State, was requested to come down to the Melrose Hotel in downtown Dallas to meet with a couple of college head football coaches who were in town for a meeting during the 1956-'57 winter off-season. One was named Paul, the other Charles, though few fans probably recognized them by their given names. Paul "Bear" Bryant's Texas A&M team had just won the school's first Southwest Conference championship in fifteen years, completed an undefeated season, (9-0-1) and finished fifth in the Associated Press national rankings. For Charles "Bud" Wilkinson, undefeated seasons—perfect *seasons*—were becoming the norm. His 1956 Oklahoma Sooners finished 10-0 to repeat as national champions, and continued an overall winning streak that reached a record forty-seven straight the following season. When whimsically tossing in the 5-0 record of Bahnsen's 1956 Eaglets, a summit of unbeaten football authorities was about to take place.

Bahnsen might not have known all of the won-lost numbers regarding the Texas A&M and Oklahoma teams, but he recognized that two giants of his profession asked for the presence of his company. He made sure he wasn't late for dinner that night at the Melrose, and was thrilled when given permission to order one of the better steaks on the menu. "I was flying high," Bahnsen recalls. He was prepared for Wilkinson and Bryant to pepper him with questions about his blocking scheme at North Texas, or maybe another aspect of his offense or defense. Well, that wasn't what "Bear" and "Bud" had in mind. Bahnsen says they wanted to know how he dealt with the black players: on the field, off the field, everything about assimilating them into what previously was an all-white football squad. "I was so depressed," Bahnsen says.

Wilkinson had actually integrated the Sooners' football program that same autumn with Prentice Gautt, a freshman running back from Oklahoma City. Gautt became an all-conference performer, the most valuable player of the 1959 Orange Bowl, and built a career in collegiate athletics. He died in 2005, six years after OU's academic center was named in his honor. Bryant, who left A&M following the '57 season for alma mater Alabama, was still more than a decade away from coaching a black football player.

....

The living arrangement of Haynes and King sharing the front room in the home of Haynes's sister in east Denton came to an abrupt end during the winter of 1957, when a fire rendered the dwelling unlivable and its contents unusable. King recalled sitting in zoology class when he was informed of what happened, and got across town as quickly as he could. "You could see a portion of this, or a burnt shoe, or a shirt with maybe the sleeves burned off and the rest of it intact," King said. He was able to borrow some clothes from older brother Charles, and also received help from the Baptist church in Denton that he attended. None of Haynes's brothers had clothes that came close to fitting Abner, but the North Texas community and his church family apparently more than replaced his wardrobe; some of Haynes's teammates joked that he was better dressed after the fire.

Haynes went to live with another relative who lived in Denton, while King moved in with James Bowdre, a fellow North Texas freshman from Lincoln. Bowdre had played football in high school with

King and Haynes, didn't try out at North Texas that 1956 season, but was planning to do so as a sophomore. Making ends meet became more difficult for King, and the new rental arrangement with Bowdre only represented a small part of his significant life changes. He and girlfriend Claudia Hooper, whom he'd known since elementary school, eloped that May. They initially told only friends in Denton and not their families back in Dallas, where Claudia continued to live. The couple soon welcomed their first child, which continued the alteration of King's perspective and responsibilities. He had his own car by then, but would mostly walk to class and elsewhere around Denton to ensure that he had enough gasoline to visit Claudia and the baby on weekends.

One of the first tangible effects from the addition of Haynes and King to the North Texas football program took place in the form of a phone call made between the 1956 and '57 seasons to head coach Odus Mitchell from Johnny Vaught, the highly successful football coach at Mississippi who'd attended Fort Worth's Poly High School and TCU. King recalled that he and Haynes were passing Mitchell's office and overheard part of the conversation, in which Mitchell told the Ole Miss coach that he fully expected to have blacks on his 1957 varsity squad, a deal-breaker for Vaught. While Vaught's decision surely came as no surprise to Mitchell, there nevertheless was a certain sting in the realization that North Texas's most financially beneficial football endeavor was scratched from the books. Likewise, similar arrangements with the two other major football schools in Mississippi were at best put on hold indefinitely.

. . . .

Bob Way wouldn't be returning to George Herring's fastidiously organized dorm room in autumn 1957. Way's girlfriend, Carolyn Woods, transferred to North Texas during the winter term following one semester of junior college, and the couple got married over the summer back in Amarillo. He was working there over the summer, and there was no time and few resources for funding a traditional honeymoon. The day after they were married, Way changed jobs, from working at a zinc smelter to a position with the railroad, which his father helped him land. When the newlyweds returned to Denton that fall, they moved into a duplex on Chestnut Street. But even before they married, Carolyn was embraced into the social community of North Texas football wives during her first semester on campus. And wives meant not only wives of other players but wives of the coaches as well. "Those women took us under their wing," she says. "'Mutt' Ferrill. Rowena Mitchell. Mary McCain. We'd go to their houses and play cards, even before we got married."

Odus Mitchell began fall drills in 1957 with something of a pleasant problem. Between the new sophomores coming up from the undefeated freshman team and a handful of talented transfers, it would be difficult to determine where all of these new varsity performers would fit in North Texas's playing scheme. NCAA rules required players to play both offense and defense. As productive as Haynes had been with the Eaglets, North Texas was blessed with other talented running backs, including returning lettermen David Lott, John Darby, Jerry Young, and Don Audas. The same was true for King playing two-way end amid the likes of Mac Reynolds, Jim Braymer, and Jerry Russell. Vernon Cole had quarterbacked the only unbeaten squad in North Texas football history, yet was initially listed well down the depth chart behind '56 regulars Ray Toole and J.N. Wright.

The corps of running backs was further bolstered by three transfers: Bill Groce, who'd played one season at SMU; Theon Thetford from Tarleton State in Stephenville; and Morris Rose from Rice. The line figured to benefit from the addition of tackle Frank Klein from junior college. Another roster bonus wasn't technically a transfer: Fred Way was returning from two years of military service, and most likely would reclaim his starting position at center. Because of that, Mitchell considered shifting Garland Warren, who'd started at center in Way's absence, over to guard. That plan was contingent on the coaching staff being comfortable with the depth at center behind Way, where the candidates included former running backs Raymond Clement and Sammy Stanger. Mitchell needed only four days' practice to decide Stanger and

Clement were good enough to provide quality depth at center, allowing the move of Warren to right tackle.

Two weeks into fall practice, Mitchell tested his varsity against the new Eaglets. The resulting 67-7 varsity victory seemed to confirm that the '57 crop of newcomers wasn't quite the same quality as the previous incoming class. The only freshman to score in that scrimmage was quarterback Robert Duty from Waco. The backfield featured Vernon Cole's close friend from Pilot Point, G.A. Moore. An exasperated Bahnsen said he could identify only four true ballplayers among his group: Duty, fellow quarterback Jerry Pair of Grapevine, a lineman, Joe Oliver, from Waco, and Bill Kirbie of Pampa. Of note, the '57 freshman team included another black player, also from Lincoln High in Dallas, fullback Robert Hines. With James Bowdre coming out for the varsity as a sophomore end, there were four blacks in the North Texas football program, all from Lincoln.

In North Texas's first season playing for the Missouri Valley Conference football championship, the school was unable to arrange a full schedule of league games. The conference designated two of the Eagles' non-conference dates as league games. One was a September home game against Oklahoma State, which had just changed its name from Oklahoma A&M early that year, as it left the MVC while transitioning into the more prestigious Big Seven Conference. The other was a late October game at San Jose State. The Eagles' only true conference games would be played against Drake at home, and Tulsa on the road.

The MVC welcomed another new member in addition to North Texas. Cincinnati's football team was overshadowed by a heavyweight basketball program that appeared to only be getting better. The Bearcats finished third in the 1955 National Invitation Tournament when that competition was nearly equivalent to the NCAA championship tournament. The 1957-'58 MVC basketball season would attract national attention because one of the country's standout high school seniors of the 1955-'56 academic year, guard Oscar Robertson of Indianapolis, would join Cincinnati's varsity as a sophomore. With "The Big O" coming aboard, UC was picked to win the league championship, and was ranked nineteenth nationally in the pre-season Associated Press poll.

As North Texas and Cincinnati were entering the Missouri Valley, Oklahoma State and Detroit were leaving. The departure of OSU, which also changed its athletic nickname that year from Aggies to Cowboys, was celebrated by some other Valley members in the wake of an ugly episode years earlier, one that had all the appearances of being racially motivated. Oklahoma A&M hosted Drake in a league game in September 1951 in which the visiting Bulldogs' star player was a black senior Johnny Bright. On Drake's first play on offense, Bright was walloped in the jaw (remember, no facemasks then) by Aggies defensive lineman Wilbanks Smith, a team co-captain, well after handing off to a teammate.

The dazed Bright struggled to his feet, remained in the game and incredibly delivered a 61-yard touchdown pass on the next snap. He absorbed two more significant hits before he was done for the day in the first quarter, taken to the visitors' dressing room. Oklahoma A&M handed Drake its first loss of the season, 27-14. Photos of the incident appeared in the following day's *Des Moines Register* beneath the headline: "Ever Seen a Jaw Broken?" and soon made their way to *LIFE* magazine. After unsuccessfully seeking some league punishment against Oklahoma A&M, Drake withdrew from the Missouri Valley following the football season and was joined in its departure by Bradley University. The two schools returned to the MVC after Oklahoma State had exited.

A different Oklahoma school, the University of Tulsa, was considered the favorite to win the Missouri Valley football championship in 1957, followed by Cincinnati, North Texas, Houston, and Wichita. The Williamson Rating System, a numerical rating of each team across the country computed by a gentleman named Mitch Williamson, projected the Eagles to finish with an overall record of 7-3. (Williamson dutifully pointed out that, in 1956, seven of the eleven schools that he picked to win conference championships did so, while the other four leagues were won by his projected runners-up.) As North Texas's pre-season drills neared the September 21 opener against Texas Western, the coaching staff grew particularly dissatisfied with the state of the players' effort and commitment one afternoon. Fred McCain verbalized the feelings of the entire coaching staff when he challenged anyone on the varsity to run over one of the larger players on the team. Senior guard Charlie Cole, the oldest player on the team at age twenty-five, gladly replied ... and volunteered another member of the team, a freshman, at that, to take on the challenge: "G.A. Moore is! He's not afraid of anything 'cause he's from Pilot Point!"

Moore had planned for some time during high school to play football for Texas Tech following his graduation from Pilot Point in 1957, but making the twenty-mile move to Denton really made the most sense. He'd played running back for most of his time with the Bearcats. As a senior after Vernon Cole had vacated the quarterback position with his ascension to North Texas, Moore moved into that slot. Moore and Cole grew up only a few miles from each other near Mustang Creek south of town and were close friends going back to grade school days. During one of those North Texas practices when the freshmen were matched against the varsity, Moore was playing defensive back and was positive he'd taken the proper angle by which to cut down Haynes coming around the end for only a short gain, maybe even for a loss. Moore ducked his head in anticipation of a worthy hit and left his feet. He returned to *terra firma* having succeeded only in making a one-point landing just beyond the sideline as Haynes advanced downfield. "I didn't even touch him," Moore recalls with a shrug of resignation. "I realized right then what a real running back could do."

CHAPTER 12

"You shouldn't have any problem trying to pick out which one I am"

THE VARSITY DEBUTS OF ABNER Haynes and Leon King took place on Saturday night, September 21, 1957, in the rather inhospitable location of El Paso, inhospitable in that host Texas Western sought revenge for its only regular-season loss of the 1956 season (a 13-6 North Texas upset). The Miners were again led by speedy halfback Don Maynard, a future Pro Football Hall of Famer who was a threat both running and receiving. A key element of Odus Mitchell's plan beginning the season was to leave the bulk of his talented sophomores together as the team's No. 2 unit, resisting any urge to insert the best of them on the No. 1 squad. The hope was that their cohesion from playing together so successfully as freshmen would carry over.

Maynard's speed and hands indeed proved to be the difference in the outcome. The senior star took advantage of a mix-up in the Eagles' pass defense in the closing minutes and scored on a 65-yard catch that—when followed by the point-after kick—gave Texas Western a 14-13 victory. Since North Texas's 1956 varsity had gone undefeated over the course of the previous season's final eight games, the loss was the Eagles' first in almost an entire calendar year. Before Maynard's heroics, North Texas's 13-7 lead was built on a nine-yard touchdown run in the first quarter by starting quarterback Ray Toole and a 33-yard touchdown pass in the third period to King.

"We made one bad mistake," Garland Warren lamented afterward, referring to the defensive confusion that sprung Maynard loose with less than three minutes to play. "We should have had them by 20-0 at the half," growled Mac Reynolds. Part of Reynolds's argument was a long touchdown run by Haynes in the second quarter that officials called back after it was ruled he'd stepped out of bounds near North Texas's 40-yard line. A number of Eagles insisted Haynes never came close to stepping out of bounds. Further frustrating them was their observation that the whistle wasn't blown until he reached the end zone. Haynes, with 56 yards on fourteen carries, was North Texas's third leading rusher. The touchdown catch was King's only reception of the night, one of only four for the team on eight total pass attempts by Toole and backup quarterback J.N. Wright. Though Mitchell and the other coaches were obviously upset by the defeat, they were pleased with the initial results shown by Haynes, King, and the rest of the sophomore-laden unit—so much so that Mitchell declared days later the No. 2 group would see more time on the field the following week against Oklahoma State.

North Texas's baptism into Missouri Valley Conference play the following Saturday night in front of the largest Fouts Field crowd in three years was even more vexing than the defeat at Texas Western. The Eagles played the Cowboys even, 19-19, until Oklahoma State took possession with about three minutes to play and scored again with only 1:41 showing on the clock. Haynes scored one of North Texas's three touchdowns and made a powerful statement by rushing for 110 yards on eighteen carries. King was held without a catch, and had his only PAT attempt of the game blocked. And, for what it was worth, conference commissioner Norvall Neve—in attendance to help welcome the Eagles to the league—announced during the game that he'd received a letter from the National Collegiate Athletic Bureau confirming that

North Texas was officially recognized as a "major college" football program. Why membership in the MVC wouldn't have made that automatic, who knows? That officially made Abner Haynes one of the backs to keep an eye on in major college football. Having played one Missouri Valley Conference game, Haynes was named the league's back of the week.

That honor didn't ward off a flu bug, one that took down Haynes, Vernon Cole, and more than a dozen other teammates during the week. Haynes played the following Saturday against Drake, but was limited to nine carries for 28 yards as North Texas dropped to 0-3 with a 19-6 loss. The Eagles' lone score came in the fourth quarter on a seven-yard pass from Cole to King. King's extra-point try sailed left, leaving him 0-for-2 during the young season, and led to him being removed from the group of players who attempted kicks for the balance of the season. Mitchell later said he regretted not cancelling the game, given how many Eagle players were sick. For the subsequent October 12 trip to Abilene Christian, he abandoned the idea of keeping sophomores out of the starting unit; they numbered the majority of the five players promoted to the starting squad that week, Haynes among them. King almost made it, ready to spell a hobbled Reynolds, but Reynolds's injured knee improved sufficiently during the week that he didn't sit out. But the Eagles inexplicably came out flat, fell behind by two touchdowns, and gave up 334 yards rushing in a 28-20 loss. Haynes hurt an ankle early and finished with only 23 rushing yards.

The Eagles' only solace going into their October 19 date at Tulsa was that the Golden Hurricane, pre-season favorite to wear the MVC crown, dragged an identical 0-4 record into the game. The *Tulsa World* didn't underestimate the importance of TU finally getting into the win column with the Eagles coming to town: "The Hurricane must win or face the prospect of disaster." Tulsa was established as a seven-point favorite. Maybe that was based in part by Mitchell's midweek announcement that Haynes, still bothered by the bad ankle, wouldn't start. Charlie Cole also wouldn't start because of a hand injury, and would be replaced by sophomore George Herring. The

Eagles nonetheless came away with a 14-12 victory, their first in Missouri Valley competition, by the margin of two PAT kicks executed by Fred Way. Haynes did come off the bench and play, and he tied for the team high with 37 rushing yards. It appeared Tulsa would duplicate the eleventh-hour rallies staged by Texas Western and Oklahoma State, reaching North Texas's 9-yard line in the closing minutes. But the Eagles held firm for three plays and, on fourth down, TU was penalized for delay of game and marched back to the 14. Possibly out of comfortable field-goal range, Tulsa lined up in kicking formation but faked the kick and got off only a weak pass that, in the wake of North Texas's determined rush, fell incomplete. The Eagles finally entered the win column, both overall and in MVC play, even if it took half the season to get there.

North Texas then traveled to the West Coast for the pseudo conference game at San Jose State. The 2-3 Spartans were rebuilding, and pinned hopes for success on the quarterbacking tandem of Marv McKean and Dick Vermeil (of future NFL coaching fame) and speedy receiver Ray Norton ("speedy" as in he would compete in the 1960 Rome Summer Olympics in the 100 and 200 meters). The Eagles were cheered on by a small but enthusiastic collection of supporters, mostly Texas transplants. The group of about 35 sported cowboy boots, cowboy hats … and some of them *brought guns*. OK, the pistols didn't contain bullets. But they did contain blanks, and the guns were fired early on until stadium police halted the overt expression of Lone Star pride that surely unnerved other nearby patrons.

North Texas led 12-6 in the fourth quarter, when what appeared to be a relatively civil game turned somewhat chaotic and eventually ugly. The Spartans were whistled for three consecutive penalties, which was more than San Jose center Ron Earl could bear. Earl's reaction resulted in an ejection for unsportsmanlike conduct. The Spartans had the ball at their 32-yard line with six seconds to play and called time out, holding faint hope of cashing in on one last play that would tie the score and allow them to kick for the win. But Reynolds alertly informed the officials that San Jose had already used its final timeout. The referee started the clock back up while the Spartans were still in their offensive huddle, and time expired before Vermeil could take the snap from center.

Spectators didn't have to wait much longer for an additional helping of unsportsmanlike conduct. A melee between the teams broke out almost immediately after the final whistle and lasted a few minutes, which probably seemed like hours to those participating. Probably to those watching, too. Vernon Cole calmly picked out an opposing player about his size and popped him one in the jaw, which ended the Spartan's contribution to the brawl. Sammy Stanger wanted no part in the extra-curricular activity, walking up the ramp to the visitors' dressing room while the roughhousing continued. Haynes displayed a savvy strategy that resembled a dive bomber; he'd race toward a target, strike, and quickly head out of the pile. Up in the press box, *Record-Chronicle* sports editor Dub Brown was already facing an unreasonable deadline given the two-hour time difference. He'd just about finished dictating the final details upon the game's conclusion when a new storyline was unfolding down below. Brown quickly alerted the office that he'd need to add some more material. And they'd need a new headline, too: "NT Wins Fight and Game Too."

North Texas had put together a winning streak with a pair of victories on the road, both designated conference wins, following the wretched 0-4 start. Maybe that's why King and Haynes revived their practice from the previous year of leading their teammates in song after a win. Of course, the crooning back in 1956 was done on the freshman team's "green goose." The flight back from San Francisco enabled them to commandeer the aircraft's public address system. The song list included a few offerings that Haynes claimed to have written. The closest thing to a formal review of the performance at 25,000 feet came from the flight attendants, who told Mitchell that Haynes and King should give up football and become vocalists. When not singing during the flight home, Haynes offered an informal tutorial to his teammates on how to properly engage in a football fight. His first rule: don't remove your helmet!

With only four games remaining in the season, Vernon Cole had thrown all of eight passes. There was no debating senior Ray Toole's status as the starter; he was leading the Missouri Valley Conference in both passing and total offense. J.N. Wright was the established backup. Cole understood his place on the roster, but was still frustrated by the lack of playing time. In an interview that Fred McCain did for the UNT oral history series in 1984, he said Cole told him back then that he had been thinking of quitting: "I don't remember all the details, but I remember that he was really displeased. We would visit a little bit about it and, you know, 'You've just got to take your time. It's going to happen.'"

On November 2 at Trinity University in San Antonio, North Texas's six-point halftime lead was negated when the host Tigers outscored their guests 19-0 and went on to win 26-13. Mitchell was so unhappy with the officiating that he reviewed the game film with a *Record-Chronicle* reporter a few days later to identify penalties against Trinity players that weren't called. He and the rest of the North Texas squad were able to take out their anger on the schedule's three remaining opponents, all visiting Fouts Field: Tennessee-Chattanooga (12-0), Youngstown (68-13), and McMurry (14-7). Haynes set a personal rushing mark with 127 yards against Chattanooga. In the rout of Youngstown, Vernon Cole enjoyed his best game of the season, completing five of seven passes for 120 yards. A few days later, the *Record-Chronicle's* Brown declared Cole the starter for 1958 who would extend the Eagles' recent string of excellent quarterbacks. Between the Chattanooga and Youngstown victories, Mac Reynolds withdrew from school. The *Denton Record-Chronicle* reported that Reynolds's wife had recently given birth, and "the lanky wingman said he couldn't support his family and remain in school."

After the 0-2 start in conference play, North Texas finished 2-2, good for second place behind repeat champion Houston. The overall 5-5 finish could have been considered acceptable only when viewed through the prism of the 0-4 beginning. Haynes led the Missouri Valley Conference with 639 rushing yards; King led the conference with

131 receiving yards on his five catches—Haynes's eleven receptions led the team—and was a backup end behind Joe Mack Pryor, whose protective relationship with King included tips on the field. "He taught me a lot on how to size a guy up and influence him to make him play the way you want him to play," King said.

And the Eagles' representatives to the All-Missouri Valley Conference first team as chosen by the league head coaches were … well, no one. The fact that North Texas didn't play Houston, Cincinnati, or Wichita apparently resulted in not enough coaching votes for Eagles players to make the first team. Haynes, quarterback Toole, and junior guard Jim Sherburn were named to the second team. If coaches were familiar enough with Haynes's production to name him to the second team, it would seem that his league-leading rushing total would have convinced them to place him on the first team. Not so. And Robert Hines was the second leading rusher on the freshman team, which lost all five of its games.

King said that sometime during the 1957 season he convinced his mother to come watch him play football for the first time. Jesse Mae didn't relish the prospect of seeing any of her sons participate in such a rough activity. During King's "recruiting" of his mother to make the trip to Fouts Field, he couldn't resist telling her, "You shouldn't have any problem trying to pick out which one I am."

CHAPTER 13

"You're not like what our parents said"

BURLYCE SHERRELL AND A COUPLE of her black friends were able to move into the Chilton Hall dorm on the North Texas campus for the 1957-'58 academic year. The initial reception from the white women, she says, was well beyond cool: "The white girls were mean and indifferent." That changed, thanks to Johnny Mathis—indirectly. Sherrell had been dating Raymond Logan for months by the time her sophomore year began. He bought her a record player, on which she often listened to her favorite single, Mathis's popular *The Twelfth of Never.* Well, what do you know; the white girls started coming around, asking to borrow the record player.

Relations between the handful of black women and the whites who filled most of the rooms further improved when many of the white residents came down with a stubborn, draining virus. The black women pitched right in to help care for the sick, and a bond was formed. As if a spell had been broken, Sherrell says some of the whites made apologetic statements to the blacks such as, "You're not like what our parents said. They said you were dirty, foul."

While life at Chilton Hall was looking up, Sherrell's school life went in the other direction. She says she stayed up two nights finishing an English paper that she was confident would earn an above-average grade, only to be given an F. When she asked the reason for the failure, she says she was told she misspelled a word. And when Sherrell asked to see the paper, she says she was told doing so would be against the law. She and Logan were married in January 1958 and soon had a child on the way, which eventually made it more challenging to fit into her desk in class. Some white women at school considered that funny, she says, and taunted her about it regularly.

Sherrell and other blacks shared stories of snide comments, or worse. A male acquaintance was excited when one of his professors invited him to his home one weekend when a speaker related to the class would be presenting a talk; the excitement vanished upon arrival, when the black student was handed a white coat and an apron. He was invited to listen to the talk from near the kitchen. If only all of her school experiences could have equaled the piano class that she so enjoyed. It was like a different world, one that she hoped she could enter full-time after graduation. But pregnant, her academic record in shambles, and continually facing racial insults, Sherrell withdrew from North Texas after her second year. The young Logan couple packed up and moved west.

North Texas athletics fans had watched blacks play both for and against Eagles teams on the football field, the players' faces all but hidden by helmets and faceguards. They had yet to experience racially mixed competition in the more intimate environment of a basketball gym, with the players much closer to the seating area—eye contact was possible for some patrons—and with easily distinguishable features. That first took place at North Texas on December 20, 1957, when Pete Shands' varsity Eagles played host to a Missouri Valley Conference opponent for the first time. And what an opponent: Cincinnati, 4-0 and ranked fourth in the country.

UC's primary weapon was guard Oscar Robertson, who incredibly outperformed the era's version of extraordinary advance billing. He would be named national player of the year as a sophomore, junior, and senior. "The Big O" went off for 37 points that night as the Bearcats welcomed North Texas basketball to the big leagues, 94-53. Since the game was played with the student body dismissed for the Christmas break, North Texas's men's gym wasn't even half filled.

A number of late 1950s North Texas football figures—Haynes, other players, and members of the coaching staff—have said that Robertson socialized with Haynes and other North Texas blacks on his trips to Denton. In Fred McCain's interview for UNT's oral history collection, he recalled that black athletes on visiting teams would be housed on Denton's east side in the home of a black couple—"Chick" Miller, who worked at Denton's Texas Woman's University, and his wife, Pillie, a cook at a restaurant in downtown Denton. When Robertson was approached for this book to reflect on his experiences at North Texas on and off the court, his personal spokesman relayed that he declined.

A few weeks after Robertson's hardwood symphony, North Texas fans witnessed the talents of the MVC's other basketball powerhouse that season, the eleventh-ranked Bradley Braves. A gathering of 2,700 watched a team that featured three blacks overwhelm the Eagles, racing to a 14-2 lead and winning 73-53. Dub Brown's coverage of the game in the *Denton Record-Chronicle* began by describing Bradley's hero that night, Shellie McMillon, as a "gangling, loose-limbed 6-5 Negro." One North Texas official years later said that when the players from the two teams mingled after the game, one of the black Bradley players told an Eagles player that he thought the Braves' white players alone could beat North Texas.

One of Bradley's other black players that night was a junior from Houston. Joe Billy McDade's only contribution to the scoring column was two converted free throws. Before the Braves played in Denton, they came through McDade's hometown and faced the UH Cougars. He recalls the disappointment of having the local fans there jeer, call the players racially insulting names, and even spit in their direction. McDade says McMillon was attacked, with his Bradley teammates having to come to his defense. "That was the first time that my grandmother got to see me play," McDade says. "Horrible experience. It was a very bitter experience." He remained in Bradley's hometown of

Peoria, Illinois, following graduation to pursue a career in law, and was appointed a U.S. federal judge by President George H.W. Bush in the district court located there in 1991. Asked if he recalls any distasteful aspects of that first Bradley basketball trip to Denton, McDade says, "My memory might be failing, but I don't remember an unfortunate incident at North Texas State. In fact, I have a pleasant memory from Denton. That's where I was introduced to chess pie. It's like pecan pie without the pecans."

CHAPTER 14

"I won't be surprised if you beat any team on our schedule"

SPRING FOOTBALL PRACTICE AT NORTH Texas in 1958 provided an opportunity for possibly the most talented transfer into the football program to get acclimated to his new gridiron surroundings. Guard Bill Carrico certainly knew his way around campus well before leaving the University of Texas following his two seasons there. Carrico was a 1955 Denton High School graduate whose father was a North Texas chemistry professor. Bill started for the Longhorns as a sophomore in 1956, when coach Ed Price's team finished 1-9 (which remains Texas's worst record), and predictably resulted in Price's dismissal. While Carrico was encouraged by his initial impressions of the Longhorns' new coach, Darrell Royal, he decided to transfer to North Texas for multiple reasons. Carrico and girlfriend Deanna were ready to get married, he was sure he'd enjoy playing for Odus Mitchell, and he was intrigued by the prospect of playing with the Eagles' backfield star, Abner Haynes.

Houston was picked to win its third consecutive Missouri Valley Conference football championship in the *Street and Smith's* national pre-season preview magazine. North Texas was picked to finish fourth, behind the Cougars, Cincinnati Bearcats, and Tulsa Golden Hurricane. "There is confidence in the Eagle roost that this year's team will improve

Left: Leon King's family attended St. Paul Baptist Church in Dallas, and he played end on a Lincoln High football team that rarely passed. (North Texas State College, *Yucca*. Denton, Texas: North Texas State College, 1958)

Above, right: Abner Haynes was the son of a bishop in the Church of God in Christ, sometimes called "holy rollers" by others. He was on Lincoln's B team as a sophomore before he accidentally injured the running back ahead of him on the depth chart in practice and then filled that player's starting position. (North Texas State College, *Yucca*. Denton, Texas: North Texas State College, 1957)

Right: Mac Reynolds, an end from east Texas, asked Abner Haynes early on why Haynes and Leon King didn't enroll at a black college. (North Texas State College, *Yucca*. Denton, Texas: North Texas State College, 1957)

Above, left: Lincoln High '56 graduate Burlyce Sherrell planned to enroll at Prairie View A&M near Houston, but complied with her parents' wishes and instead enrolled at North Texas. (North Texas State College, *Yucca*. Denton, Texas: North Texas State College, 1957)

Abner Haynes [far right in white uniform] chased down a Hardin-Simmons ball carrier while Leon King [No. 81] followed the play in the first game of the North Texas freshman team's season, a 13-9 victory at home on Sept. 20. (North Texas State College, *Yucca*. Denton, Texas: North Texas State College, 1957)

Left: Abner Haynes ran for yardage in the freshman Eaglets' game against Navarro Junior College in Corsicana, the team's first road game. Haynes scored four touchdowns in North Texas' 39-21 victory. (Navarro College photo)

Right: Vernon Cole was approached by SMU and TCU after quarterbacking Pilot Point High but decided to follow older brother Charlie just down the road to North Texas in 1956. (North Texas State College, *Yucca*. Denton, Texas: North Texas State College, 1959)

Left: Lineman George Herring grew up in west Texas. He and younger sister Sally were baffled by the segregated drinking fountains at the Penney's where their mother worked in San Angelo. (North Texas State College, *Yucca*. Denton, Texas: North Texas State College, 1959)

Above: The 1956 North Texas football coaching staff [from left]: Ken Bahnsen, Fred McCain, Herb Ferrill and head coach Odus Mitchell. (North Texas State College, *Yucca*. Denton, Texas: North Texas State College, 1957)

Right: Louisiana native Ken Bahnsen was only a year removed from his first experience with a black football teammate—Joe Perry of the San Francisco 49ers—when his assignment to lead the 1956 North Texas freshmen included coaching Leon King and Abner Haynes. (North Texas State College, *Yucca*. Denton, Texas: North Texas State College, 1959)

Left: Tarrant County sheriff Harlon Wright examined an effigy that was hung across Main Street in Mansfield as white residents expressed their revulsion at the attempt by a handful of black families to integrate the town's public school system days before the 1956-57 school year began. (University of Texas at Arlington Library Special Collections)

Right: J.C. Matthews first arrived at North Texas as a freshman in 1920 and was named as the school's president in September 1951. As the state's curriculum director during the 1930s, Matthews gained first-hand knowledge of the academic challenges faced by Texas's black students. (North Texas State College, *Yucca*. Denton, Texas: North Texas State College, 1957)

The team photo of the 1957 North Texas football team showed 29 white players and three blacks, all three of whom were sophomores and graduates of Dallas' Lincoln High: Abner Haynes [No. 28], James Bowdre [No. 83] and Leon King [to the right of Bowdre]. (North Texas State College, *Yucca*. Denton, Texas: North Texas State College, 1958)

Left: Abner Haynes was tackled by a Texas Western defender in the 1957 season opener, a 14-13 victory for the host Miners. The game, played on Sept. 21 at El Paso, marked the North Texas varsity debuts of Haynes and King. (North Texas State College, *Yucca*. Denton, Texas: North Texas State College, 1958)

Right: Leon King grabbed a pass during North Texas' 14-7 victory at home against McMurry to close the 1957 season, the Eagles' first in the Missouri Valley Conference, with a 5-5 record. King caught five passes that season for 131 yards, which led the league. (North Texas State College, *Yucca*. Denton, Texas: North Texas State College, 1958)

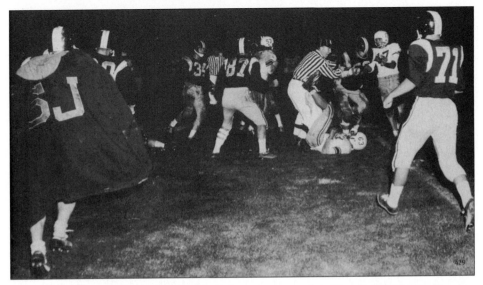

Boys will be boys. After North Texas held on to win at San Jose State 12-6 in October 1957, the two sides continued to battle after the final whistle. Among the Eagles engaged at this particular moment were Fred Way [No. 53], Jim Sherburn [No. 63] and Ray Toole [No. 17]. The headline in the following morning's *Denton Record-Chronicle* read, "NT Given Clear-Cut Game, Fight Decision" (North Texas State College, *Yucca*. Denton, Texas: North Texas State College, 1958)

Lineman Bill Carrico, a Denton High graduate in 1955, transferred to North Texas after playing one season for the University of Texas. Carrico was quite familiar with the campus; his father was a North Texas chemistry professor. (North Texas State College, *Yucca*. Denton, Texas: North Texas State College, 1959)

Leon King, Abner Haynes, and a third North Texas student performed in the school's Union Building "howdy room." King and Haynes often entertained teammates with their singing talents, including on bus and plane trips to and from games. (North Texas State College, *Yucca*. Denton, Texas: North Texas State College, 1958)

Lest anyone forget that college football during the late 1950s was a one-platoon game, here was defensive back Abner Haynes [No. 28] making a tackle during North Texas' game at Oklahoma State in 1958. (North Texas State College, *Yucca*. Denton, Texas: North Texas State College, 1959)

Left: No place like home for the Geezles, a social fraternity exclusive to North Texas that included many of the school's athletes. (North Texas State College, *Yucca*. Denton, Texas: North Texas State College, 1958)

Right: Guard Oscar Miller became North Texas' first black basketball player during the 1958-59 school year and led the freshman Eaglets in scoring. Miller, from Fort Worth, also became the program's first black varsity player in 1960-61. (North Texas State College, *Yucca*. Denton, Texas: North Texas State College, 1959)

Left: John Howard Griffin, a writer who lived in Mansfield, was so appalled by his hometown's violent response to possible integration of the school system that he dyed his skin and posed as a black man for a tour of the South to write a series of articles that ran in the magazine *Sepia*. The series wasn't well received at home, and he later expanded his writing of the experience into a 1961 book entitled *Black Like Me*. (University of Texas at Arlington Library Special Collections)

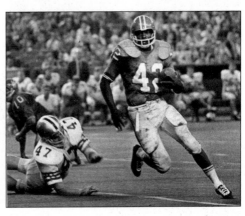

Right: When San Antonio's Warren McVea signed with the University of Houston in July 1964, he had a much greater public profile than when Abner Haynes and Leon King walked on at North Texas in 1956. McVea rushed for 648 yards as a junior and 699 as a senior. (University of Houston photo)

Left: Jerry LeVias became the first black football player to be awarded a Southwest Conference athletic scholarship when he signed with SMU on May 22, 1965. A talented runner and receiver, he was used primarily as a pass catcher with the Mustangs and was named an All-American as a senior in 1968. (SMU athletics photo)

Right: John Westbrook became the first black to play varsity football in the Southwest Conference in 1966. His Baylor team opened its season on Sept. 10 at home against Syracuse, the only major college game played that day as a special national telecast on ABC-TV. Jerry LeVias and SMU started their season a week later at home against Illinois. (Baylor University photo)

Seven gentlemen who were part of North Texas' 1956 freshman football team posed at Fouts Field in spring 2004. Top row from left: Gordon Salsman, Frank Klein, Abner Haynes and Raymond Clement; Bottom row from left: Bob Way, coach Ken Bahnsen and Leon King. (UNT photo)

Burlyce Sherrell withdrew from North Texas in 1958 after two academic years, in part because of the demeaning treatment that she received. Burlyce Sherrell Logan returned to campus more than fifty years later and, in May 2011, walked in her commencement ceremony. (UNT Photo/Gary Payne)

markedly on last year's 5-5 record," the magazine stated. "Helping with all this cheer is a No. 1 backfield that includes Abner Haynes, halfback, and Bill Groce, fullback, two of the nation's top ground-gainers." One national tweak to college football that season was the adoption of two points awarded for a run or pass following a touchdown.

The North Texas team reconvened in the fall, beginning with a barbecue beneath the stands at Fouts Field as a school-record eighty-three players reported, nearly half being freshmen. Odus Mitchell greeted them with a typical, no-nonsense suggestion: "If you're not in good shape, see that you get that way ... by tomorrow." His assessment of pre-season predictions was equally as terse and somewhat piqued. "Those who think we're going to be pushovers this fall are in for a big surprise when they run up against us," Mitchell told his team. "I won't be surprised if you beat any team on our schedule. You are capable of taking any of them." A common opinion was that the Eagles—with the core of the talented 1956 freshman team going into its junior year— were building toward a standout season in 1959.

One of the experiments of early fall drills was moving Leon King, who'd led the conference in receiving yards the previous season, to halfback. That appeared to be a curious move given King's build (6-foot-2, 180 pounds). The trial run didn't last long when King suffered a knee injury during the first week of practice, taking a blow while playing defense. King hoped he'd be held out that season and return to the squad in 1959 as a junior, but that didn't happen. He said he kept getting hit, the knee never fully healed, and he was unable to contribute to the team.

Ken Bahnsen liked the look of his new freshman group following the winless season of the previous year. It included three blacks: half-back Billy Joe Christle from Corsicana, fullback Arthur Perkins from Fort Worth, and quarterback James Price from Denton. Christle helped Corsicana's Jackson High School win PVIL Class AA state titles as a junior and senior, each time shutting out Price and the Fred Moore Dragons of Denton in the championship game. He was spotted in the 1957 championship game by North Texas's Herb Ferrill, who attended the game to scout Price. Perkins's coach at Dunbar High steered him toward North Texas instead of the state's black schools, and Perkins was eager to follow in the footsteps of black running backs excelling at predominantly white schools, like Jim Brown at Syracuse and Abner Haynes at North Texas.

Not that Perkins had seriously considered the ramifications of being one of the few blacks on the North Texas campus. (Of the 6,779 students enrolled for the fall '58 semester, 203 were identified as black.) When Bahnsen and Fred McCain made their recruiting visit, Perkins felt surprisingly at ease. The coaches told him that he'd been chosen because he wouldn't anger quickly or be provoked to fight. He'd be called awful names, they said, sometimes by his teammates. "They warned that I'd face challenges," Perkins recalls. "I knew right away that I wanted to do that." At Dunbar, Perkins's impending move to North Texas was considered a point of pride. "Some of our teachers were taking classes at North Texas then," he says. "They gave me advice. My coach and principal talked to me: 'We know this is something that you can do.'"

At North Texas's fall camp, Perkins was relieved that the new black freshmen weren't called out in front of the entire squad in any fashion. While the veteran white Eagles players had by then become used to having black teammates, it was a new experience for most of the white freshmen. "If I knocked a white pass rusher on his butt, he might say 'Nigger' without even knowing it," Perkins says. "They're finding out I'm like everybody else, and I'm finding out they're like everybody else. Guys came to me and said they wanted to apologize for their actions. They would say, 'I've never been around black people, and my parents told me things about blacks that aren't true.' Things were smooth."

Since Price came from Denton, he simply returned home after each day of pre-season practice, while Perkins and Christle remained on campus and were allowed to stay in the dorm. That's where the fullback from Fort Worth and the halfback from Corsicana truly met. "The atmosphere was nice, other than being segregated," Christle says. "When Perkins was going out for a pass, one of the linemen told the quarterback to just throw it to the white teeth." Says Perkins, "Billy was really quiet. I could hardly get two words out of him. I communicated more with Price then with Billy." When it came time to decide where to live during the school year, Perkins says Christle and he were advised by Haynes to decline what wasn't made available in 1956 to Haynes and King—a room in the athletic dorm. Haynes convinced them to live over on the black side of town. Perkins was fine with that, glad to avoid any hazing that he'd heard about, with the biggest drawback being the walking distance.

With ample time to arrange a season's worth of games, North Texas was able to schedule all four of the other Missouri Valley schools that were competing for the football championship: Cincinnati, Houston, Tulsa, and Wichita. Bradley and Drake were overall league members, but not yet prepared to rejoin conference football play despite Oklahoma State's exit. And the Eagles' four MVC games would be played consecutively, starting the second half of the season followed by a closing trip to Louisville. Drake was actually one of the non-conference games, along with the last game in the two-year contract with Oklahoma State, the annual meeting with Texas Western, and a late add of New Mexico A&M to replace Trinity.

The New Mexico A&M Aggies were led by new coach Warren Woodson, a Fort Worth native who began his playing career at Texarkana Junior College playing for W.G. Herring—father of North Texas's George Herring. Woodson had coached for years in Texas, most recently at Hardin-Simmons. In an era in which defense was stressed, Woodson was interested primarily in offense—passing in particular, with a goal of throwing at least twenty times per game. He was credited with developing a T formation that included a wingback attack. Asked upon his hiring how long it would take him to build a winning team, Woodson replied, "When do we play our first game?"

North Texas came through the first five non-conference games with a 4-1 record, a seven-point loss at Oklahoma State representing the lone blemish. Carrico started immediately at guard and showed why he'd been a sophomore starter in the Southwest Conference for the Texas Longhorns. King moved up to the second team for the OSU game in the wake of an injury to starting end Frank Klein, but moved back down the depth chart when Klein returned the following week. The 43-12 victory over New Mexico A&M featured a melee in the fourth quarter, which, possibly when considered in concert with the fracas at San Jose State the year before, rankled Mitchell.

North Texas's conference slate was set up with visits from Tulsa and Cincinnati, followed by a trip to Wichita and a home game against pre-season favorite Houston. When the Eagles prepared to host the Golden Hurricane, the two teams were the last two in the MVC to begin conference play. Cincinnati and Wichita, each at 0-1-1, were already long shots for title contention. Houston was 2-0 with an overall record of 3-1, including a victory over the SWC's Texas A&M. Tulsa's own 4-1 non-conference record included wins over a couple of big boys, Arkansas and Oklahoma State, somehow combined with a shutout loss to Hardin-Simmons. The Hurricane was very similar to North Texas, with a punishing one-two rushing punch and an effective quarterback.

There was reason for the Denton campus to be excited for Tulsa's October 25 visit, and the fandom responded with North Texas's largest home crowd ever—about 14,000. The Eagles sent them home happy—thrilled, probably—with an 8-7 victory. The teams fought through three scoreless quarters before Tulsa scored a touchdown and added the extra-point kick with 7:26 to play. But the Eagles immediately answered with a scoring drive of their own, Bill Groce running a draw play through the left side of the line and rumbling 39 yards for the touchdown with 2:20 left. Mitchell elected to go for two points, quite a gamble at that late stage of the game. He lined up end Klein far to the right, with halfbacks Haynes and Theon Thetford behind him. Vernon Cole pitched to Haynes, who followed his escorts into the end zone to give North Texas a one-point lead. What must have been particularly galling to Tulsa coach Bobby Dobbs, who just that week had expressed his dislike for the new two-point rule, is that the North Texas coaching staff had designed the play only the previous day after spotting a similar formation that week while reviewing film of the Hurricane.

But North Texas suffered a significant personnel loss in the victory. Junior Joe Mack Pryor, the back-up to George Herring at right tackle, suffered a season-ending leg injury. While Pryor didn't ascend to the starting unit in '58 like so many of the other juniors on the squad, he was one of the stalwarts who continued North Texas's luxury of fielding a quality second unit. He'd been specifically praised by Mitchell following the wins over Texas Western and New Mexico A&M that season. In the 12-6 victory at BYU in mid-October, Pryor blocked the Cougars' PAT attempt seconds into the fourth quarter, leaving the home team a touchdown behind and somewhat deflated after finally getting on the scoreboard. He was replaced on the second team by Joe Oliver.

The Eagles' November 1 home game against Cincinnati was eerily similar, but for one small but significant deviation. The Bearcats successfully went for two points after scoring the game's first touchdown; the Eagles could only subsequently match that with their lone score, which came with 5:05 to play. The result was an 8-8 tie that left the Fouts Field gathering somewhat deflated. Mitchell was again aggressive, following North Texas's tying score with an onside kick that the Eagles recovered. But North Texas failed to capitalize then or later, after Haynes gave them one last shot with an interception. Those last two drives were directed by second-string quarterback Robert Duty, because Vernon Cole hurt a knee on the two-point play. The offensive struggles obviously miffed Mitchell. "This has to be remedied or we'll never win another ballgame," he told the *Record-Chronicle*. Of brighter news for North Texas was the fact that Tulsa upset Houston that day, which put the Eagles in first place in the conference at 1-0-1, ahead of the 2-1 Cougars.

Cole's status for North Texas's upcoming trip to Wichita was iffy at best. His best friend, sophomore back G.A. Moore, saw his season end during practice that week. Moore was going through drills for the dive play and was popped by, ironically, senior lineman Charlie Cole. Moore suffered a broken left wrist, and added a cast to his wardrobe for the better part of the next thirteen months. Haynes, too, was hurting, but was expected to be ready by the following Saturday. Cole indeed was unable to start against the 1-4-1 Wheatshockers, who'd only claimed their first victory of the season the previous week against lightly regarded Villanova. The Eagles' string of fortunate finishes—rallying to win by one against Tulsa, rallying to tie Cincinnati—came to an abrupt halt when Wichita stunned North Texas, 15-13. Haynes was limited to 53 yards, and Cole only entered the game late when the Eagles sought a spark after falling behind yet again. Notably frustrating for North Texas was Groce fumbling into the end zone with the Eagles trailing 9-6 in the third quarter, and Wichita immediately capitalizing with an 80-yard touchdown pass. "Something like that wouldn't happen again in 100 years," Mitchell lamented.

North Texas, 1-1-1 in MVC play, could still win the league championship, but that required beating Houston the following Saturday at Fouts Field. The Cougars would clinch their third consecutive championship with a win or a tie. Dan Shults of the *Houston Chronicle* noted that UH was an eight-point favorite to win on the road following three consecutive losses, the most recent being a 56-7 non-conference pasting at the hands of Mississippi. Handling the play-by-play from Denton back to Houston for KTRH radio would be a young reporter named Dan Rather.

The Eagles' offense produced only one touchdown for the third consecutive week, but North Texas mustered just enough to scratch out a 10-6 victory on a drizzly afternoon on November 15. The victory clinched at least half of the Missouri Valley Conference championship for the Eagles in only their second season as a football playing member; North Texas would share the title with Wichita if the Shockers upset Tulsa on Thanksgiving Day. Cole returned to the starting lineup against UH and directed both North Texas scoring drives. The first resulted in a 14-yard field goal kicked by Morris Rose midway through the opening period for the game's first points. Cole threw a six-yard touchdown pass to Klein late in the third quarter, with Rose's kick increasing the Eagles' lead to 10-0. Houston's only score came with 2:51 to play. Haynes still wasn't up to his usual rushing standards, gaining 40 yards on eight carries, but had enough left in the tank to celebrate the victory by dancing a little jig on the field.

North Texas closed its season on November 22 by winning a non-league game at Louisville, 21-10, then waited for the result of the Tulsa-Wichita game on Thanksgiving, and for any calls from bowl directors looking for a 7-2-1 team to participate in their game. There had been speculation that the Sun Bowl in El Paso and the Tangerine Bowl in Orlando, Florida, were considering the Eagles. Tulsa beat Wichita 25-6, which made North Texas champion of the Valley. But no bowl calls were made to Denton. The *Record-Chronicle*, in an editorial, argued North Texas would make a worthy at-large opponent both on the field and at the turnstiles in the Cotton Bowl to play the host school from the Southwest Conference on New Year's Day. "It doesn't seem illogical to think that NTSC students, alumni and Denton residents could easily fill half of the Cotton Bowl." The Dallas stadium's capacity then was about 75,000.

Haynes finished fourth in the Missouri Valley with 495 rushing yards, a drop-off of 144 yards from the previous season on about the same number of carries, yet he still was North Texas's leading rusher *and* receiver (the latter whether the measure was by catches or yardage). He was one of four North Texas players named to the All-MVC first team, and to the Associated Press's All-American team as honorable mention selections. The others were Cole at quarterback, Carrico at guard, and Bob Way at center. North Texas finished thirtieth in the Williamson ratings. According to Williamson, the Missouri Valley was the fourth-best major college conference behind the Big Ten, the Southeastern Conference, and the SWC. That was ahead of the Big Eight (eight with the addition of Oklahoma State), the Pacific Coast Conference, and the Atlantic Coast Conference.

Ken Bahnsen's 1958 freshmen didn't go 5-0 like his '56 squad, but they didn't go 0-5 like his '57 team. The Eaglets finished 2-3, with two of the losses coming against Texas Tech and TCU squads that were at least double the size of a North Texas team that topped out with 22 players. Perkins and Christle displayed particular promise among the backs, each averaging almost 50 rushing yards per game. Price, played as a running back, was one of the reserves. "There aren't many of them, but all of them are good ballplayers," Bahnsen said. "Usually, we consider it a good year if we can use one-third of the freshmen on the varsity. At least 75 percent of these boys will play varsity ball."

Vernon Cole continued dating Carolyn Logan, who had graduated from Denton High the previous summer. A few weeks after North Texas's season ended, they bought marriage licenses up in Gainesville on the Red River, because they were too young to do so in Denton. They then drove to Fort Worth, where his sister, Mandy Richardson, lived. The three of them headed over to the home of Mandy's minister, where Vernon and Carolyn were married. It was something that they'd informally planned for months, but had told only immediate family when the time came. As Cole continued his football and academic careers, his new bride worked at Chester Morris Chevrolet a few blocks from their home as a cashier, and also helped out with the switchboard.

In December 1958, the Kings' second son was born. That prompted King to drop out of school to focus his efforts on supporting his family, returning to his old job parking cars in Dallas, and hopefully returning to school in another year or two. That same month, North Texas welcomed the first black to its basketball program in 5-11½ freshman guard Oscar Miller from Fort Worth. Nicknamed "Little O" in comparison to Oscar Robertson, Miller averaged more than 21 points per game that year, and then played his first varsity season in 1960-'61, when John Savage, a black freshman forward from the little northeast Texas town of Detroit, joined the program. Miller started on the varsity for three seasons, and Savage developed into one of North Texas's best basketball players ever. As a sophomore, Savage became the first North Texas player named to the Missouri Valley Conference's all-league first team; he repeated the honor as a junior and senior before being drafted by the Los Angeles Lakers.

CHAPTER 15

"Just soon beat them by one as 72"

THE 1959 NORTH TEXAS FOOTBALL Eagles lost only a handful of lettermen from the '58 squad, primarily linemen Fred Way, Ed Gray, and Jim Sherburn, plus reserve halfback John Darby. With so many talented players, coach Odus Mitchell considered forming three entire units instead of two as a way to wear down opponents. It's possible that idea came from the ever-popular coaching copycat book. LSU won the 1958 national championship with a three-pronged attack that featured the now-famous lineup of the White team, the Go team, and the Chinese Bandits. But cutting time for the Eagles' first unit would have been a difficult decision to make. Quarterback Vernon Cole, halfbacks Abner Haynes and Morris Rose, and fullback Bill Groce accounted for 1,945 total yards and 126 points during the previous season.

Street and Smith's picked North Texas to repeat as Missouri Valley Conference champions. If that didn't occur, the magazine wrote, "... it won't be because of lack of experience. Of the 25 lettermen in 1958, 18 will be returning, including eight first stringers." The magazine tabbed Houston to finish second, followed by Cincinnati, Tulsa, and Wichita. Mitch Williamson's pre-season ranking of the 60 best teams in major college football placed North Texas at No. 32; consider some of the schools that were slotted below the Eagles: Southern Cal, Alabama, Texas A&M. Mitchell opened fall drills with double sessions each day. "You'll find out it's tough being the champs," Mitchell told the team. One of the challenges was that North Texas's four-game MVC schedule would include three road games instead of three home games. The Eagles' non-conference slate again featured Texas Western and Drake, along with the return of Hardin-Simmons, plus Mitchell's alma mater, West Texas State. To complete the schedule, a game with the team from the naval station in Pensacola, Florida., was added. Leon King's name no longer appeared on the North Texas football roster. In fact, he left school to devote all his energies to supporting his growing family. "The kiddos started popping out, and I had to drop out for a little while because I just wasn't making enough to do what I wanted to do and go to school," he said. "I felt that was my responsibility to do it. So after my junior year, since it didn't pan out as well as I thought it could have or should have, I dropped out."

G.A. Moore finally returned to the field, having suffered the broken wrist the previous November. He was prepared to compete for playing time at quarterback, most likely vying with junior Robert Duty for the backup spot to Vernon Cole. While cleared to return to football activities, Moore wore a brace with a hinge to provide protection with some flexibility. But the wrist popped back out of place during an early fall drill. It just wouldn't heal correctly. Moore realized his football career was all but over. Football was the primary reason that he attended college. Heck, it was probably the primary reason that he even finished high school. Formal schooling wasn't really considered essential for a life on the farm. Moore drifted away from the team and lost all interest in academics. It wasn't long before he formally withdrew from North Texas.

The Eagles aced their three-week test against Border Conference competition to open the season, beginning with a 46-24 romp at Hardin-Simmons in Abilene on a Thursday night. Mitchell professed to be worried before the game, noting the Cowboys had upset Tulsa each of the previous two seasons. North Texas forced a fumble on

Hardin-Simmons's first offensive play and never looked back. Haynes scored three touchdowns, one on a 58-yard interception. After a Cowboys linebacker yelled, "Get that nigger!," senior guard Bill Carrico looked up at the linebacker and said, "Hey, don't say that anymore." The linebacker actually knew Carrico by name and replied, "Bill, I didn't say it." To which Carrico responded, "When I hit you this next time, you tell whoever said that how much that hurt. And he won't say it anymore." Mitchell practically apologized afterward to Cowboys coach Sam Baugh, the former TCU All-American and NFL star. Baugh actually thanked Mitchell for substituting liberally. "If you hadn't put that tennis-shoe team in there," Baugh told Mitchell, "you'd have beat us a hundred to nothing."

The following week, North Texas made it two consecutive victories in the heated series with Texas Western, bolting from a 7-7 halftime tie to cruise 31-7 in El Paso. Haynes gobbled up 157 rushing yards on only eight carries, scoring on an 81-yard run and a 31-yard reception. Sophomore fullback Art Perkins scored on a 96-yard run, and the *Record-Chronicle* glowingly reported the following week that Perkins was "already being compared to professional great Jimmy Brown." North Texas's home opener on October 3 against West Texas was played in a downpour and mud bath, but the Eagles slogged their way to 383 rushing yards while throwing only four passes (no completions … or interceptions) in winning 28-6. Water seeped into the stadium's electrical system and knocked out some of the lights before kickoff. The end zones were essentially in darkness. ("So there," they probably thought up at Murray A&M.)

North Texas opened conference play on October 10 at Cincinnati, the Bearcats already somewhat desperate since they had lost to Houston. UC boasted the league passing leader in senior Jacky Lee, who was the first-team All-MVC quarterback in 1958. Cincinnati also statistically owned the best defense in the conference. While the pre-game chatter at Nippert Stadium defined the matchup as North Texas's running against Cincinnati's passing, the unit that determined the outcome was the Eagles' defense. North Texas smothered Lee and the Cincinnati offense, seized its league opener 21-6, and improved its overall record to 4-0. North Texas held Cincinnati to 46 yards of total offense and nine first downs. One writer in the press box remarked that George Herring should be listed among the players in Cincinnati's backfield since he spent so much time there while playing defense, though he did injure a knee that would bother him for weeks. Gene Williams of the *Record-Chronicle* exhibited minimal restraint in stating that the Eagles' defensive achievement "could well be the greatest defensive effort in modern football history." Haynes led the way with 95 rushing yards and suffered a cracked tooth. The No. 2 backfield of Perkins, halfback Billy Joe Christle, and quarterback Robert Duty also sparkled again.

On November 17, North Texas welcomed a Pensacola Naval team that featured forty-three players with college football experience. One was former North Texas halfback David Lott, the Eagles' leading rusher in 1957 as a senior. Mitchell planned to empty his bench and minimize the chance of injuries only a week before traveling to Houston. Key players were rested early and often as the Eagles won 43-0, but Perkins suffered a groin injury.

When North Texas traveled to Houston for a game on October 24, the Cougars had played only one conference game to date, the victory over Cincinnati, and had lost all of their non-conference efforts—to Mississippi, Alabama, Texas A&M, and Oklahoma State. UH sports publicist Jack Scott told the *Houston Chronicle* that the only football team in the state better than North Texas was Texas, unbeaten and ranked third in the nation. Houston had initially designated North Texas's October 24 visit as its homecoming game before the season began. Apparently thinking better of it as the Eagles kept winning games, the Cougars made a hasty switch at some point and rescheduled homecoming for their only other remaining home game, over Thanksgiving weekend against Washington State.

Scheduling the game at cavernous Rice Stadium, capacity 70,000, provided an opportunity for any Eagles fan to find a seat for the 8 p.m. kickoff. So, North Texas officials did everything they could to make the trip to Houston, the Eagles' first since 1950, as easy as possible. . . such as a chartered train followed by charter bus service from a nearby hotel to the stadium. A round-trip ticket on the train for students, faculty members, and their families—plus transportation on the bus *and* a ticket to the game–cost $11.25. The train could accommodate 565 passengers (including the 100-piece North Texas marching band, making a rare road appearance); it left the Santa Fe station in Denton at 8:30 on the morning of the game for a journey that would take almost eight hours. For those Eagles fans who roughed it, driving from Denton to Houston and then having to seek out parking, the school staked out designated lots that would be patrolled by Denton police. The postgame train would leave Houston at 11:30 p.m. and roll back into Denton with the roosters at 6:45 on Sunday morning.

As the Eagles began preparations for the game, George Herring was still limping from a knee injury that he suffered against Cincinnati. Duty wasn't fully recovered from his ankle sprain, but was expected to be back to full strength by kickoff. And Perkins was still hampered by the groin injury.

Hal Lahar's Houston offense, like Cincinnati's, pinned much of its hopes on its passing game out of a T formation. Quarterback Lonnie Holland's favorite target was Errol "the Peril" Linden, the conference's third leading receiver. Halfback Pat Studstill was scheduled to return after missing the previous game because of injury. Saturday morning's game advance in the *Houston Chronicle* identified Haynes as the Eagles' "Ebony Flash," and matter-of-factly mentioned that the North Texas team not only was arriving in town by train, but "will return to the Pullmans for the night." Huh?

Fred McCain, who handled travel arrangements for football trips, couldn't find a hotel in Houston that would accommodate all of the Eagles—namely Haynes and the other black players. McCain mentioned his problem in conversation on the phone with Santa Fe while scheduling the team's train travel. The railroad representative informed him that the station in Houston wasn't a "through" station; it would be possible to provide North Texas with Pullman cars—sleepers—that could be parked at the station. Lodging on the rails. With no better option available, McCain took him up on the offer.

On the morning of the game, North Texas players trudged from their sleeping quarters near Union Station and ate breakfast at the nearby Ben Milam Hotel. The trip's itinerary, handwritten by one of the North Texas members with mimeographed copies handed out to each player, contained the following inspirational message printed in capital letters—THIS IS THE BIG ONE. The 1,000 or so North Texas fans in the gathering of approximately 12,000 that night at Rice Stadium couldn't be faulted if they expected a second consecutive Eagles rout following the first possession of the game. North Texas drove from its 40-yard line and scored barely five and a half minutes after kickoff. Cole did the honors on a two-yard quarterback sneak following a serpentine, 22-yard gain by Haynes. Morris Rose added the extra point. But UH wasn't about to be intimidated. The Cougars replied with a 65-yard march, surprising in both keeping pace with North Texas, and by doing so on the ground. Fullback Charlie Rieves did much of the heavy lifting, and halfback Ken Bolin punctuated the drive with a three-yard touchdown run late in the opening period. But on the point after to tie the score, holder Holland struggled to grab a high snap in place for kicker Eddie Michamore. The kick sailed wide, leaving the Cougars a point behind.

Houston had three periods in which to make up that smallest of margins, but couldn't. Neither team scored over the final forty-five minutes, and North Texas escaped with the 7-6 triumph. Both teams threatened to get in the end zone again a couple of times, UH's marches surprisingly keyed by 213 rushing yards. North Texas had three subsequent possessions end at Houston's 18, 8, and 7, while the Cougars never advanced beyond the visitors' 33. In the final minute of the half, the Eagles' Terry Parks recovered a Cougars fumble in mid-air near UH's 30, and headed toward the end zone along with four teammates and only one Cougar standing in front of him. But one of the Houston players who was already on the ground managed to trip Parks soon after his recovery. Duty attempted a "Hail Mary" pass heaved in the general direction of Christle and Dick Hamilton in the end zone.

The Eagles received a pair of standout defensive plays from Cole: an interception in North Texas territory, and a deflected pass in the final minutes that snuffed out a Houston drive. He was also North Texas's second leading rusher, with 76 yards to Haynes's 98. That pushed Haynes over the 500-yard rushing mark for the season, and gave him more ground yardage than he'd amassed throughout his entire junior season. Appropriately, Haynes and Cole were the top two rushers in the Missouri Valley Conference for a ground attack that would statistically take the lead in all of major college football. While seemingly everyone associated with the Eagles was drained by the slim victory, Haynes expressed his joy by dancing in circles in the visitors' locker room. "We beat 'em; that's all that counts," he said told reporters. "Just soon beat them by one as 72."

Rose begrudgingly accepted his role as the unlikely hero; he accounted for one point, the one that separated the two teams. "I had no idea it would win the game," he said. Mitchell was relieved to secure the victory, pleased that his defense limited Houston to 19 passing yards, but shaken by the number of Cougar ground yards. "We drilled on pass defense all week," he said. "I didn't think they had those kinds of runners. Man, they surprised us. I never thought they could do it, but they really fooled us."

The majority of Houston-based sports journalists in the press box that night concluded that the Cougars played their best game of the season, but UH's one-point loss (dropping the team's record to 1-5) apparently didn't satisfy at least one member of the team's fan base. The following morning, an effigy of Houston coach Hal Lahar was hung from the top of the campus's student activities building. Polar-opposite sentiments were expressed toward North Texas's team in Sunday morning's *Record-Chronicle*. It featured a story stripped across the top of the front page, written by Chuck Green, detailing Saturday's experience for the approximately 1,000 Eagles fans in attendance. Green closed by writing that the visiting fans, upon leaving Houston, "recognized no better team in the country."

. . . .

By late October 1959, John Howard Griffin—the Mansfield writer who had co-authored the nationally published necropsy of his hometown's attempts to racially desegregate its schools—was unable to purge his mind and heart of the events that he had witnessed in 1956, and the venom that he had experienced coming from those who lived around him. Griffin approached a friend who published the Fort Worth-based monthly magazine for blacks called *Sepia*, and pitched an idea that he readily acknowledged was at best edgy and possibly unacceptable to both whites *and* blacks. He would disguise himself as a black man and travel the Deep South for a period of weeks, experiencing first-hand life on the other side of the racial chasm for later publication in a series of articles for Sepia. Publisher George Levitan was skeptical yet intrigued; he also recognized that his friend was intent on going through with his potentially dangerous experiment, and agreed to fund the project and publish the account.

Griffin soon after went through a series of medical treatments that dyed his skin black, shaved his head and set out on his treacherous foray beginning in New Orleans. He traveled six weeks through Louisiana, Mississippi, Alabama, and Georgia, suffering indignities that were simply part of everyday existence for a black man in the South. When Griffin sought work beyond the black sections of cities and towns, he was summarily rejected for even the most menial of jobs and told they didn't hire "you people." He obediently sat in the back of the buses. He found temporary lodging in the only accommodations available to blacks, usually in decrepit slums. Maybe worse than the squalid conditions and degrading mores that blacks were forced to accept was the feeling of utter contempt and aversion that accompanied mere eye contact with most whites. "Sick at heart before such unmasked hatred," as Griffin later described it.

The six-episode account of Griffin's journey across the South's racial breach was called "Journey into Shame," and appeared in *Sepia* from April 1960 through September. The series led to the highly acclaimed book, *Black Like Me*, published in 1961. Soon after the initial installment was published in *Sepia* - and Griffin's subsequent publicity appearances on network television—someone in Mansfield expressed his indignation with Griffin's prose by hanging an effigy of him—half-white, half-black—late one night from a traffic signal on Main Street, similar to the one hung at the school in 1956. "All they can accuse me of is pleading for the truth," Griffin told the *Fort Worth Star-Telegram*. "… If people would read what I've been writing, they couldn't help but feel compassion for one another. … My purpose is not to hurt people but to get out the pus. And I sure wish somebody smarter than I am had done it. But nobody else did."

CHAPTER 16

Disappointment and Delight

NORTH TEXAS'S OCTOBER 31 GAME against Wichita was the Eagles' only home conference game of the season. It was a revenge game, given North Texas's surprising loss in Kansas the previous year, and it was homecoming. The Wheatshockers traveled to Denton with a better record than they did a year earlier, 3-1-1, the only defeat coming the previous week at Oklahoma State. The week began on a pair of ominous notes for North Texas. On Monday afternoon, Bill Carrico was unable to practice because of a back injury suffered at Houston.

That night in Wichita, the freshman Eaglets suffered the first defeat by either squad representing North Texas that fall, 35-8, on a surprisingly wintry late October night in central Kansas. Matters only got worse for the Eagles that Wednesday when Haynes suffered an ankle sprain. He remained hobbled on Thursday, and Carrico's back had not sufficiently improved to ensure he'd play. Mitchell ended the day prepared to substitute for two of his best players with a pair of third teamers, leaving the second unit intact. But Wichita was dealing with the potential absence of its most productive player, senior halfback/punter Ted Dean, troubled by nagging injuries suffered over the previous two games.

Saturday in Denton began wet and overcast. Homecoming events started with a mile-long parade that morning from Avenue E to the town square. The procession included cars carrying school president J.C. Matthews, other university officials, and the five finalists for homecoming queen. Among the many floats and marching contingents was a Confederate horse brigade featuring thirty riders.

The weather held down the game crowd that afternoon to 14,000 instead of the expected 15,000 to 20,000. On yet another sloppy track, the Eagles managed just enough offense to claim a 12-0 victory over Wichita. Coupled with Houston's win over Tulsa that day, the Eagles had already clinched at least a tie for their second consecutive Missouri Valley Conference championship, with a game at Tulsa remaining on their league schedule. Haynes started despite his precarious ankle. And while he gained only 38 yards and ceded top rushing honors to Billy Joe Christle (70 yards), North Texas's standout senior was responsible for all of the scoring. His two touchdown runs came on the Eagles' first possession and late in the third quarter.

Carrico played, and so did Wichita's Dean, who got loose on a 31-yard run in the first quarter and nearly enabled the Shockers to tie the score early. But Wichita was thwarted by three interceptions, and didn't present much of a threat as field conditions worsened in the second half. "Maybe we'll get a dry field one of these days," Vernon Cole mused after the game, "We couldn't do anything but run straight ahead." The win gave North Texas an overall nine-game winning streak dating back to the final two games of the previous season, tying the school record. The Eagles' program had not pieced together nine consecutive victories since the 1932-'33 seasons.

Louisville was headed to Denton for a November 7 non-conference game that would precede the Eagles' date in Tulsa the following Saturday. While a non-league game might have led to some subconscious thoughts of a letdown, North Texas's overall record of 7-0 lent itself to dreams of a perfect season. There had not been one of those in any of the forty-three previous seasons. Not even in 1913, when the school's original football squad had a 50 percent shot at one, losing its only game, to

TCU. But before the Eagles could continue pursuit of that North Texas first, another milepost in program history took place early that week. On Tuesday morning, November 2, the release of the weekly Associated Press media poll of the nation's twenty best college football teams featured North Texas at No. 20. With twenty voting points accumulated from the national panel of 202 sportswriters and broadcasters who were asked to choose their ten favorite teams—ten points awarded for a first-place vote and so on down to one point for a tenth-place vote—the Eagles stood five points behind No. 19 Georgia Tech.

If Eagles players or fans dared not speak of what finishing in the Top 20 and completing a perfect season would mean, the *Record-Chronicle* fearlessly performed that task in an un-bylined story published only hours after the poll was distributed: "... then, of course, is the possibility of a bowl bid. Such a bid naturally hinges on many factors, but a perfect season would certainly put the Eagles in contention." Later in the week, the AP's lead sportswriter based in Dallas, Harold V. Ratliff, speculated on North Texas's bowl possibilities:

> *North Texas State appears to be in the peculiar situation of being too good and big for a minor bowl and not well enough known for a major. But North Texas State has a team that would go in any bowl and do a good job. North Texas appears certain to finish the season undefeated and untied and have a 12-game winning streak. The Bluebonnet Bowl at Houston would do well to get North Texas State. The Cotton Bowl won't invite North Texas State [to face the host team, the champion of the Southwest Conference] because of its policy of matching intersectional opponents, but the Bluebonnet doesn't have a host team since it has no tie-up with a conference and can choose some team in the area to be the host outfit.*

If a game of such importance to North Texas football history should have featured breathtaking drama, any nail-biting against Louisville didn't last beyond the early minutes of the second period. The Eagles broke open a tight game well before halftime on a chilly early November night that kept the Fouts Field assemblage down to about 5,000 and cruised to a 39-7 victory over the Cardinals. Haynes rushed for 121 yards and two scores on only fifteen carries. His 667 yards for the season surpassed his previous North Texas high of 639, amassed as a sophomore. The 8-0 Eagles set a school record with their tenth consecutive victory. With three unbeaten teams losing that same day (No. 1 LSU, No. 2 Northwestern, and No. 7 Penn State), North Texas was joined by only three other schools in the exclusive clubs of the unbeaten No. 3 Texas, No. 4 Syracuse, and No. 6 Southern Cal.

Poll watching became a new sport in and around Denton, though. Without ESPN, the Internet, or social media, many didn't learn the details of the AP poll that was released on Monday afternoon, November 9 until they read their Tuesday morning newspaper. North Texas moved up to No. 17, passing Air Force (which lost), TCU (which had an off week), and Arkansas (which won, but by only four points over a poor Rice team). One MVC opponent stood between North Texas and the outright league championship, and that was Tulsa. A second opponent stood between North Texas and an unbeaten season if the Eagles won at Tulsa. That was Drake, at Fouts Field.

There was still the possibility of a three-way tie for first place in the five-team Missouri Valley Conference. If Tulsa brought down the unbeaten Eagles that Saturday, it would mean North Texas would share the title with at least Houston—*Houston, where coach Hal Lahar was hung in effigy only a few weeks earlier?*—and possibly Tulsa, too. So the Golden Hurricane also had a lot riding on its matchup with North Texas.

Cold, rainy weather descended upon Denton on Tuesday and Wednesday, affecting North Texas's practice schedule. (No indoor facilities in those days.) By dawn on Friday, a cold front abruptly ushered in Denton's first freeze of the season. An accompanying fog forced the closure of Dallas's Love Field airport for six hours early that day. Motorist warnings were posted for Oklahoma, where temperatures were expected to plummet on Friday night.

George Herring's older brother, Bill Tom, often drove from his home in Illinois to watch North Texas when possible, and the Tulsa game was circled on his calendar. The treacherous weather in Oklahoma didn't dissuade him, though there were portions of the trip during which the slick roads had Bill Tom's car moving sideways without him turning the steering wheel. In Denton, six of the North Texas players' wives piled into Carolyn Way's two-door 1954 Chevy Bel Air bound for Tulsa. Their greatest issue wasn't the inhospitable weather but the dearth of available gas stations along their route. Betty Rice, wife of senior guard Ronnie Rice, was the primary worrier among the travel party. As something of a public service, Betty often kept a wary eye on the gas gauge and announced how much petrol was (or wasn't) left in the tank. Filling up often required each woman to scramble through her purse.

The Eagles arrived at the Sands Motor Hotel in Tulsa just fine—plenty of gas and no struggles to remain on the roadway—but the weather reduced their workout on Friday afternoon to simply limbering up and running only a handful of drills, instead of running anything that resembled a game plan. Given the weather and the Saturday forecast of temperatures no higher than freezing, Mitchell dispatched a couple of members of the traveling party to buy long johns for every player. When the Eagles returned to Skelly Stadium early Saturday, they were greeted by twenty-seven telegrams from encouraging fans and twenty-five degrees on the thermometer, even with the sun shining. The combination of previously damp conditions followed by freezing cold molded a playing surface that was hard and irregular. The inspirational theme that was scrawled on the Tulsa itinerary was: WHAT A VICTORY THIS WOULD BE.

North Texas was shut out in the first half for the first time all season and fell behind, 10-0. The Eagles managed only 25 yards in the half, only *two* on the ground by the nation's No. 2 rushing offense. Among those occupying the visitors' sideline was Bill Tom Herring, perplexed by the Eagles' struggles and not one to keep his frustration to himself. Bill Tom couldn't fathom why George and the other North Texas defensive linemen weren't rushing the passer. He observed that they instead followed the snap by holding their positions along the line of scrimmage. Bill Tom was compelled to convey that critique to George, essentially urging him to ignore any previous instructions and get his rear end after Tulsa's talented junior quarterback, Jerry Keeling. George's first sack of the afternoon came soon after Bill Tom's "suggestion." George kept right on running after making the play, circling out of the Tulsa backfield toward the North Texas sideline straight for Bill Tom. In a brief exchange that typified behavior of younger brothers everywhere, George sort of "thanked" Bill Tom at a rather high volume: *"Did that suit you?"*

In the stands, Carolyn Way's traveling party was numbed by the Eagles' inability to score, and they were terribly cold, too. The ladies sat in front of Bill Carrico's parents, who benevolently did all they could to keep the women as warm as possible. That included the Carricos tucking them inside their legs. Down on the field, North Texas remained ineffective after intermission. Cole hurt an ankle in the third quarter, and Robert Duty took his place on the first unit. The Golden Hurricane extended its lead to 17-0 before the Eagles began to show some offensive spark early in the fourth quarter. Duty and Haynes hooked up on a 65-yard touchdown pass that was hauled in at Tulsa's 25. The Eagles lost 17-6, barely avoiding their first shutout since the 1956 opener at Ole Miss. Haynes finished with a scant 13 rushing yards, the lowest total of his three-year North Texas varsity career, on eleven attempts. On the Eagles' only two trips inside Tulsa's 40-yard line, he lost fumbles. An offense that was averaging 379.6 yards per game was limited to only 177. Tulsa's primary hero was Keeling, whose two-way play had him on the field for 55 minutes and 56 seconds. His assessment of the Eagles afterward wasn't terribly complimentary, maybe not a surprise given North Texas' atypically ineffective performance: "They had a good club, but didn't seem any better than Houston."

Over on the visitors' side of the stadium, Odus Mitchell wasn't interested in comparisons; he was completely stunned that his team was rendered almost helpless in the cold. "I don't see how in the world so many boys could have a bad day at the same time," Mitchell said. "It must have been my fault and our preparation for the game. Undoubtedly, we were worrying more about keeping comfortable than about winning the game." Decades later, Duty and Way recall the frigid weather indeed playing a role in North Texas's struggles that day. "You don't make the kind of decisions that you should when you're freezing to death," Duty says, adding, "The field got mushy and refroze. Our runners couldn't cut." Says Way: "We left our game in the locker room."

Eight weeks of stellar play, sometimes dominant, had been followed by a resounding thud. The Eagles suddenly lost the opportunity to claim the Missouri Valley championship outright. They closed their league schedule tied with Houston. Tulsa could also share in the championship if the Hurricane won over Wichita on Thanksgiving as expected. Gene Williams wrote in the following morning's *Record-Chronicle*: "Seriously hurt also was the possibility of individual honors for a number of the players on the conference level, and at least one, Abner Haynes, on the national level. And probably gone, too, is the chance to play in a post-season bowl game." *The Denton Record-Chronicle* referred to the loss as "humiliating."

X-rays taken the following day showed that Cole didn't suffer a broken ankle, but it was assumed he couldn't play in the regular-season finale at home against Drake on November 21. Most North Texas football followers probably assumed that would be the only real positive news for the rest of that week, but the pall that fell over the program following that frigid Saturday in northeastern Oklahoma incredibly lifted on Monday afternoon in Denton. North Texas was invited to play in El Paso's Sun Bowl on New Year's Eve afternoon. The opponent would be New Mexico State, the former New Mexico A&M, which was on its way to a 7-3 finish to claim its first winning season since 1943. The invitation to the Sun Bowl represented North Texas's high-water mark in post-season football play, a significant step above the 1946 Optimist Bowl and '47 Salad Bowl.

The loss did result in North Texas's immediate discharge from the AP poll. In the Williamson ratings, the Eagles plummeted from No. 20 to No. 44—still two slots ahead of Notre Dame, for what it was worth. But at least North Texas's 12 seniors—Haynes, Cole, Carrico, Way, Herring, Rice, Frank Klein, Eugene Haecker, Norman Denney, Sammy Stanger, Morris Rose, and Bill Groce—knew they would be playing beyond the following Saturday against Drake. The combined won-lost records for most of the group from three years of varsity competition to date, plus the 1956 freshman schedule, was 25-8-1.

The Eagles took out their considerable frustrations on an over-matched opponent. They smothered Drake 62-2, limiting the Bulldogs to five first downs, four yards passing, and 58 total yards. The visitors avoided a shutout only by harassing Duty into an intentional grounding call while throwing out of his end zone. He otherwise was more than adequate in substituting for the injured Cole; the Eagles punted only once. Haynes was one of three North Texas players to score two touchdowns; he gained another 50 rushing yards to finish the season with 730, and also nabbed another interception. The Fouts Field crowd of 5,000 had little to fret over as the Eagles closed their regular season at 9-1, and there still was a home winning streak intact at twelve games. North Texas boasted the second-ranked rushing offense in major college football, and defensively didn't allow a touchdown pass all season.

Haynes reclaimed the MVC's rushing championship after a year's absence, leading North Texas not only in rushing attempts and yards for the second consecutive season, but also repeating as the team leader in catches and receiving yards. He amassed 1,328 total yards, a staggering total for that era of college football, by rushing, receiving, punt, and kickoff returns and interceptions. Haynes, Carrico, and Herring were selected for the first-team all-conference squad. Three more Eagles made the second team: Cole, end Hal Byrd, and guard Bob Way. Klein, Stanger, Groce, Christle, and Duty were among those named as honorable mention. As for the shared conference championship, Tulsa was surprisingly unable to join in the fun. On Thanksgiving, Wichita stunned the visiting Golden Hurricane, 26-21. That left North Texas retaining partial ownership of a second consecutive crown with Houston, which that night lost its homecoming game to Washington State, 32-18, to finish the season at a dismal 3-7. If Houston had scored two more points against North Texas, the Cougars would have been the league's outright champion with an overall record of 4-6.

While the entire North Texas squad would soon begin preparations for the Sun Bowl, a handful of Eagles seniors learned in late November of their options for pursuing careers in pro ball. Two players were drafted by NFL teams: Haynes by the Pittsburgh Steelers in the fifth round, and Stanger by the Los Angeles Rams in the fourteenth round (there were twenty rounds of the NFL draft that year). The draft of the new American Football League lasted longer than fifty rounds, with four North Texas players chosen: Haynes by Minneapolis (which became the Oakland Raiders before play began), Carrico by the Denver Broncos, Herring by the Houston Oilers, and Cole by the Dallas Texans.

Haynes, the only North Texas player selected by teams in both leagues, was about to experience the type of bizarre recruiting tactics that would occasionally define the player war between the two pro leagues moving into the mid-1960s. One day in early December, he awoke at his house in Denton to discover a Steelers representative sitting on his porch, ready to offer him a contract. Weeks later in Dallas, Pittsburgh's hard sell took the form of veteran Steelers quarterback Bobby Layne. The Dallas native who had starred at Texas played hard on and off the field in the NFL, and lived in his hometown during the off-season. Layne made a recruiting house call … at about two in the morning. Meanwhile, Haynes's AFL rights were acquired by his hometown Texans. The team's young millionaire owner, Lamar Hunt (also the new league's founder), was intent on signing an area talent after star SMU quarterback Don Meredith jilted him by covertly signing with Dallas's new NFL expansion team even before the end of his college season, technically against eligibility rules. Hunt couldn't be outbid or outfoxed with Haynes and, using a more traditional business style than Layne's moonlight serenade, appealed to Bishop Haynes. Haynes would sign with Hunt after the Sun Bowl game right on the field.

CHAPTER 17

"Maybe we just weren't ready"

New Mexico A&M boasted lots of Texas talent in 1959, hardly surprising given the proximity to its neighboring state, and coach Warren Woodson being a native Texan. The most valuable Lone Star export on the squad was junior quarterback Charley Johnson, a big-armed passer from the small west Texas town of Big Spring. Surprisingly, Johnson didn't attract attention from any four-year football program coming out of high school. He opted to start his college career at two-year Schreiner Institute in the Texas Hill Country town of Kerrville, playing football in the fall, basketball in the winter, and golf in the spring. Johnson planned to spend a second year at Schreiner, but sought other options after the school announced it would drop football following his freshman season. His fortunes improved while playing basketball in his hometown, in the Howard College holiday tournament. A representative of New Mexico A&M's basketball team watched him; OK, one of Johnson's uncles practically forced the guy to watch the game. The Aggies soon signed Johnson to a basketball scholarship while letting him walk on in football, with Woodson setting up shop. Johnson quickly won the quarterbacking job and was joined in the backfield by junior fullback Louis Kelley from Abilene, and freshman halfback Richard Cohee from Wichita Falls.

The Woodson scoring machine added some significant parts for 1959. Johnson was still firing away as a senior, among the national leaders in passing yardage, but was blessed with a pair of skilled runners who'd both transferred from junior colleges in California: juniors Pervis "Afterburner" Atkins and Bill Gaiters. Atkins, who actually had to be convinced to follow Gaiters to Las Cruces, led the nation in rushing that season and was among the national leaders in scoring. The Aggies provided their fans with a year to remember only two weeks into the season. They beat arch-rival New Mexico for the first time in nineteen years and did so *at* New Mexico. They averaged 33.2 points per game, and Johnson led the country with 18 touchdown passes. He threw for 1,635 yards on 199 passes, compared to 106 attempts for the North Texas tandem of Cole and Duty.

The North Texas traveling party left Fort Worth by train on Saturday evening, December 26, and arrived in El Paso early the next afternoon for a game scheduled for Thursday afternoon. The group checked in at a Ramada Inn, with the rest of the day allegedly allotted for rest and relaxation before returning to the practice field on Monday for three final days of preparation before kickoff at 2 p.m. on New Year's Eve. But that "R&R" included a team trip across the border for a bullfight in Juarez soon after getting settled. The Sun Carnival *corrida*, intended as a casual outing, turned into anything but, according to Duty. "They had a bullfighter who was a bigger coward than me," he recalls. "We were yelling for the bull. We were ignorant. We didn't know that was a religion over there." Duty says the locals were quite displeased with what they considered disrespectful behavior from their guests.

A Mexican bullfight wasn't much of a novelty to North Texas's opponents, located only about an hour's drive north of El Paso. The Aggies would go to no bullfight during Sun Bowl week. Nor would they take advantage of local nightlife like the Eagles because they didn't spend a night that week in El Paso, which would have been the norm for a Sun Bowl invitee. Woodson took advantage of the short commute, and maintained normalcy for his team as much as possible during that week without shunning the bowl hosts altogether. While the Aggies attended the Touchdown Club luncheon on Monday at the Hilton Hotel and the Sheriff's Posse breakfast on Wednesday at Cowboy Park, their buses were pointed right back to Las Cruces after each event so the players could practice and be "at home" similar to any other game week. "Coach Woodson wanted to make sure that we just kept our heads and kept doing what we were doing," Charley Johnson recalls. "We didn't go anywhere."

The Monday luncheon was a popular affair for local fans, hosted by the El Paso Touchdown Club and attended by almost 500. Every player was introduced and presented with a Sun Bowl watch, and both head coaches were asked to speak. Mitchell certainly played to the locals by winding his way through a sequence of comparative game scores from the season that added up to New Mexico A&M being 32 points better than the nation's No. 1 team, Cotton Bowl-invitee Syracuse, and 10 points better than North Texas. Woodson would have none of that, citing a different set of numbers: Texas Western beat New Mexico A&M by five and lost to North Texas by 24, both games played at the Miners' Kidd Field, site of the Sun Bowl.

Gene Williams's game-day advance in the *Record-Chronicle* declared, "It is undoubtedly NTSC's most important appearance in the school's long football history. The Eagles stand on the threshold of gridiron greatness, and a victory over the highly touted Aggies would send them soaring toward the status that they deserve." In a matchup of two of the nation's offensive heavyweights, Haynes certainly exuded confidence the day before the game in stating that North Texas's defensive prowess could determine the outcome: "I don't think those boys have been hit the way we can hit 'em."

Painfully for the Eagles, New Mexico A&M did the most hitting. North Texas was dominated at the line of scrimmage for the first time all year, fumbled eight times and lost six, four inside the Aggies' 25-yard line. A North Texas defense that didn't allow a touchdown pass during the season allowed two in the first half. New Mexico A&M breezed to a 28-8 victory during which the Eagles' only touchdown was scored on a 51-yard punt return by Billy Joe Christle on the final play of the third period. By then, North Texas was desperate to crawl out of a three-touchdown hole. A crowd of 14,000 saw North Texas give its second sub-par performance within three games. Those who weren't there, some apparently with financial interest in the outcome, must have had a difficult time accepting the news. Unbelieving football followers phoned the *El Paso Times* switchboard to seek confirmation, a fair number of those inquiries coming from the state of Nevada. After the game, a perplexed Mitchell was at a loss to explain the deflating defeat: "Maybe we just weren't ready. Maybe we should have scrimmaged more. But you just don't figure a senior ball team to fumble that much. We must have fumbled more times out there today than we have in the past two years."

The highly anticipated offensive duel between Haynes and "Afterburner" Atkins never materialized. Atkins, with all of three carries for 15 yards, yielded to backfield mate Gaiters, who romped for 123 yards on twenty carries. Atkins did inflict serious damage to the Eagles when he hauled in a 57-yard pass for the game's first score in the final minute of the first quarter. New Mexico A&M doubled its advantage on North Texas's first play following the kickoff, on a pinball of a play. Duty was intercepted by Bob Kelly around the Eagles' 30-yard line. Kelly's attempt to score ended at the 5, where he was hit hard and fumbled. The ball bounced into the end zone, with members of both teams in heated pursuit like five-year-olds at an Easter egg hunt. When the pile of players was carefully peeled away, Aggies tackle Billy Ray Locklin was in possession for the second New Mexico A&M touchdown.

The early deficit steered the Eagles into an offensive game plan that strayed far from what they'd concentrated on throughout the season. North Texas attempted thirty-one passes; it averaged eleven attempts in its nine victories, the only other "pass happy" game being the similar uphill battle at Tulsa that ended with the Eagles throwing twenty-one times. Cole didn't appear affected by the ankle that he'd hurt weeks earlier. After the game, he fumed in frustration: "We played three teams better than them. Houston, Tulsa, and Cincinnati were all better than this bunch." Haynes's offensive contribution was solid, 73 rushing yards and 50 receiving yards, but no other Eagle rushed for more than 22 yards or caught more than two passes.

Many 1959 Eagles have subsequently rued their team's collective entertainment schedule during their time in El Paso leading up to the Sun Bowl. Charley Johnson's thoughts on North Texas having partied its way to defeat? "That's sounds like what we would have said if we'd gotten beat 28-8," he says with a laugh. "North Texas had a great quarterback. They had a *really* great running back. And our defense was just running crazy and doing the best they could. It was a marvelous game to watch." Johnson adds that Woodson repeated the cloistered strategy a year later, when New Mexico State (A&M's name was officially changed in 1960) followed a 10-0 regular season by returning to the Sun Bowl and beating Merlin Olsen and Utah State.

CHAPTER 18

"A chance to exploit prejudice where prejudice exists"

MONTHS BEFORE NORTH TEXAS'S TRIP to El Paso, the University of Texas's dean of student services, Henry McCown, asked the school's head coaches in football, basketball, track, and baseball for their opinions regarding racial integration of their teams. Darrell Royal was going into his third season as head football coach at UT. His previous two coaching stops, the University of Washington and the Canadian Football League's Edmonton Eskimos, featured racially-mixed rosters. At Washington, Royal was hired following a revolt of the Huskies' black players against his predecessor. He was a student at the University of Oklahoma when the school first integrated by admitting Ada Sipuel to its law school following legal challenge.

In a follow-up two-page memo sent to UT president Logan Wilson on November 10, 1959, McCown stated Royal "has coached Negro students, but says they create problems. White players particularly resented Negro boys coming in their room and lounging on their beds. Darrell was quite pronounced in not wanting any Negroes on his team until other Southwest Conference teams admit them and until the housing problem is solved or conditions change."

McCown's memo to Wilson continued, "The coaches wouldn't want to have their players housed in different places. On the other hand, it would be unthinkable to assign a Negro and white student as roommates. If we were the only Southwest Conference team with Negroes it would be ruinous in recruiting. We would be labelled Negro lovers and competing coaches would tell a prospect: 'If you go to Texas, you will have to room with a Negro.' No East Texas boy would come here." He added that UT athletic director Ed Olle didn't think the SWC had yet formally discussed allowing blacks to play sports at member schools. McCown's suggestion was to raise the issue at the league's May 1960 meeting and, in the meantime, "continue our delaying tactics. In my opinion, we are not ready for integration in Intercollegiate Athletics at the present time. Neither is our public."

On New Year's Day 1960, top-ranked Syracuse's 23-14 victory over No. 4 Texas in the twenty-fourth annual Cotton Bowl Classic featured a mid-game melee that included racial strife. The brawl later gained greater visibility through the 2008 film *The Express: The Ernie Davis Story*, which celebrated Davis, the Orangemen's starting halfback, becoming the first black Heisman Trophy winner in 1961. Syracuse offensive tackle John Brown, one of three blacks on the team, was quoted in a post-game issue of *LIFE* magazine as saying that Texas's Larry Stephens repeatedly called him a "big, black, dirty nigger." Brown said he warned Stephens not to say that again and, when Stephens failed to comply, swung at him. An accompanying photo showed Brown with his right fist cocked. But Brown also told *LIFE* that Stephens apologized to him, so he gave Stephens something of a pass on the incident. "That Texas boy was just excited," Brown told the magazine. "Let's just forget about it." A story in *The Dallas Morning News* stated that Stephens denied using racial slurs; he died in 1998. Brown, asked about the fight more than sixty years later, now says little. "I'm not going to disparage anyone," he says. "I remember remarks from two or three different players in the heat of battle ... we were 18, 19 years old, not 25 or 30."

Segregated athletics continued in the Southwest Conference for another couple of years. But on a rainy Saturday afternoon in Austin, Texas, on November 9, 1963, the Longhorn athletic program became the first in the conference opened to blacks when the school's board of regents voted to integrate all school activities (save for occupation of female dormitories, the status of which was being dealt with in court). The regents' action came two years after the school's student body voted in favor of integrating the Longhorns' sports teams. UT's student body had been desegregated in 1956 and, in the fall of 1963, had a black enrollment of 175. Three of the SWC's eight member schools still didn't allow blacks to become students at that time—SMU and TCU by choice, and Rice by stipulation of the school's endowment trust.

"Just how soon the backfield will be integrated depends now on athletic director Darrell Royal," education editor Anita Brewer wrote in the *Austin American-Statesman*. Royal was somewhat busy that day across campus, coaching the top-ranked, undefeated Longhorns to a 7-0 victory over once-beaten Baylor. Royal had little to say after the game about the board's action, "I'll have to meet with the athletic council before I can say anything," he remarked. "I wasn't told about it until just before the game, although I knew they were going to take it up." The *Statesman's* sports editor, Lou Maysel, wrote a column that in part echoed the UT memo from 1959. Maysel speculated that integration of the football team would actually cause some top-notch white high school players to *not* become Longhorns, particularly those who lived east of the north-south corridor that ran from Dallas-Fort Worth through Waco and Austin to San Antonio. "A chance to exploit prejudice where prejudice exists," Maysel wrote.

When Royal next met with reporters the following Monday, he said any student who meets the university's academic requirements and can make the team could play for Texas. Asked if he was interested right then in black high school prospects, Royal's answer was, "No." Other Southwest Conference schools soon followed Texas's lead in officially allowing for integrated athletic teams, probably more to keep up with the Joneses than experiencing racial enlightenment. Baylor was second to join the ranks, later that month and only three weeks after voting to integrate the general student population. The school's president, Abner V. McCall, called the declaration a "clarification of policy" in light of inquiries about black athletics following the regents' general integration vote.

Texas athletic director Royal, and first-year track coach Jack Patterson received little recognition or commendation for welcoming the first black athletes in Southwest Conference history only months after the UT regents' decision. On February 29, 1964, junior Oliver Patterson competed for the Longhorns' varsity track team in the outdoor team's opening meet, a triangular affair at Texas A&M that included Rice. That same day, freshman James Means competed with UT's freshman squad at the Southwestern Recreational meet in Fort Worth. Both were walk-ons then; Means was awarded an athletic scholarship for the 1964-'65 school year, making him the first black on athletic scholarship in the SWC.

Blacks first appeared on Southwest Conference freshman football teams in 1965 for SMU, Baylor, and Arkansas. Texas was among the last in the conference to integrate its football program. A handful of blacks attempted to join the Longhorn football team from 1954 into the late '60s before Leon O'Neal of Killeen became UT's first black scholarship football player in 1968. O'Neal left school before becoming eligible to join the varsity. That distinction went to James Whittier of San Antonio upon his ascension from the freshman team to the varsity in 1970.

The Texas football program, which produced the final all-white consensus national championship team in 1969, acquired the reputation of being unwelcoming to blacks. Bill Little, long-time publicity director for the Longhorns' athletic department, said that stigma contributed to Royal retiring from coaching after the 1976 season at age fifty-two.

Critics contended Royal had the power to counter any administrative pressure to continue a segregated football team, far more visible than the school's track and field team. His 1963 football team won the national championship, and he was awarded tenure in 1964. Not coincidentally, that was when Oklahoma looked south when searching for a replacement for Royal's old coach, the legendary Bud Wilkinson. Decades later, Royal addressed integration of the Longhorn football program with John Wheat, the head of sound archives at Texas's Center for American History: "We should have done it a lot sooner, but it wasn't done in this section of the country."

In mid-November 1963, a five-part series written by two Associated Press writers based in Texas alleged Royal and his football program were hostile toward blacks. One of Royal's staunchest defenders in the media was Dan Cook, a powerful figure in state sports reporting and perception given his dual role as columnist/sports editor of the *San Antonio Express-News* and main sports anchor for the city's KENS television station. Cook refused to run the AP series in the morning *Express* or evening *News*, calling it "one of the most factless character assassinations in modern journalism history."

But the competing *San Antonio Light* ran the series, and Cook then presented an impassioned rebuttal in his Sunday paper. He stated that a local county commissioner, a white man who played for Royal in Edmonton, saw his coach lambast some white Eskimos players for their treatment of the team's few blacks. Cook also cited a little-known story that Royal gave $500 to the family of a black Killeen high school football player who'd been badly injured in a game. In 1976, one of the co-writers of the AP series, Robert Heard, authored a book about Royal that was markedly different in tone from the critical series. It was a collection of the coach's most amusing quotes.

CHAPTER 19

"I'll be here four years from now. Will you?"

DURING THAT AUTUMN OF 1963, Darrell Royal was among dozens of collegiate head football coaches across the country who were intrigued by a seemingly unstoppable wisp of a black high school running back in San Antonio. Warren McVea was a 5-foot-9, 170-pound senior who attended integrated Brackenridge High School. McVea's high school football resume was impressive—rushing for 1,332 yards on 127 carries as a senior (an average of 10.5 yards per attempt)—but his performance in one particular playoff game that year attracted even more attention. Circumstances forced "Wondrous Warren" to play quarterback for the first time in his high school career when unbeaten Brackenridge was matched against unbeaten Lee High School, another San Antonio school. McVea rushed for 215 yards on twenty-one carries, scored six touchdowns—including scoring runs of 45, 48, and 54 yards—and also kicked two extra points. That, incredibly, wasn't enough for Brackenridge to advance, as Lee won 55-48 in a game that is still hailed as one of the best in the state of Texas's storied history of high school football.

McVea has said he would have followed his magnificent senior season and signed with the national champion Longhorns if that were possible then. But off-field issues, reportedly regarding academics and attitude, played into the situation. Much as Branch Rickey was extremely particular in choosing Jackie Robinson in October 1945 for the eventual integration of his Brooklyn Dodgers and all of major league baseball, Royal—and apparently every other head football coach in the Southwest Conference—wasn't willing to entrust the same prestige and responsibility to McVea.

The college that probably featured the best college football in the state outside of the SWC at the time was Houston. UH had left the Missouri Valley Conference following the 1959 season to go independent, and began efforts to join the Southwest Conference that would finally succeed in the mid-1970s. When McVea was eligible to sign a college letter of intent early in 1964, Houston had recently integrated its athletic program with the signing of two high-profile black basketball players from Louisiana: Elvin Hayes and Don Chaney. The path had been cleared for football coach Bill Yeoman, which actually put immense pressure on him to land McVea, since no SWC coach enjoyed such a lead block from his basketball coach. Christmas figuratively came for Yeoman and UH football on Saturday afternoon, July 11, 1964, when McVea signed with Houston in the presence of his mother, Mattie, school sports publicist Ted Nance, and two representatives from the *San Antonio Express-News* (proudly pointed out high up in the *Express-News* account the following day).

The story, written by Dan Cook, stated that McVea had also seriously considered Southern Cal, Nebraska, Missouri, Kansas, Kansas State, and Navy, but wanted to stay as close to home as possible. McVea told the *Houston Post* that he chose UH for its proximity to San Antonio, its outstanding scholastic and athletic programs, and for the opportunities that it afforded following graduation. The *Houston Chronicle* noted that written accounts of McVea's football accomplishments in recent months had nearly been equaled by tales of his "off-field activity." Yeoman addressed that, saying: "All I know is that he behaved in exemplary fashion while he was in Houston. I'm sure there will be 900 million stories started about him." A day after the San Antonio exclusive appeared in the *Express-News*, the rival *Light* published a scathing story that stated UH was McVea's only real option, and the NCAA would be investigating Houston's recruitment of him. In September 1964, the NCAA informed UH that its football program was under investigation for unspecified practices related to recruiting and financial assistance.

McVea's final appearance as a high schooler set a record, thanks to his popularity. It came at the annual state all-star game, before he and other college freshmen joined their new programs. The game was played at TCU's Amon Carter Stadium and attracted a crowd of 39,233, breaking the event's attendance record by more than a staggering 16,000—and resulting in traffic jams in western Fort Worth that had fans still cascading in during the second quarter. His South team lost 23-14, but McVea was selected as the game's most valuable player. He finished with 31 rushing yards on eight attempts, three catches for 51 yards, and a 72-yard kickoff return in the closing minutes that gave the South a chance to win.

McVea made his long-awaited UH debut in the freshman team's opener at home on Thursday night, October 29 against North Texas State. The estimated 4,800 spectators who somehow shoehorned into a facility with a seating capacity of 2,500 were disheartened when head freshman coach Carroll Schultz sat McVea two minutes into the second quarter for the balance of the evening after McVea aggravated an injury to his right knee that had previously sidelined him during an intrasquad scrimmage. But what they saw whetted their collective appetite: In the UH Kittens' 21-0 victory, McVea scored the first touchdown on an 18-yard swing pass out of the backfield, and later darted 14 yards to the North Texas 4-yard line, where he was tackled and suffered the injury. After the game, Schultz waved a dollar bill in front of McVea and told him that he'd receive only half of his allotted meal money since he only played in the first half.

McVea's varsity debut in the fall of 1965 just so happened to take place in the Cougars' first home game to be played in the Astrodome, the world's first domed athletic stadium, which had opened that spring. The anticipated show-stopping debut against Tulsa—unique new home stadium, new star varsity player—didn't run according to the script. McVea's performance was horrendous in a 14-0 loss; he lost four fumbles in the first half alone and lost his footing multiple times on a grass field that featured relatively little grass. (The Dome's grass began to die early in the 1965 baseball season after the roof's initially clear tiles were painted because outfielders had difficulty seeing fly balls.)

McVea, after averaging 9.2 yards a carry as a freshman, was held to 21 yards on eleven attempts. After his fourth fumble led to the second Hurricane touchdown in the second quarter (and some booing), McVea was essentially benched for the rest of the game; he came back in with eight seconds to play. The Cougars collectively committed six turnovers, and at least there were only 37,138 spectators to witness their listless debut, instead of the anticipated sellout of 55,000. "I just can't believe that," McVea quietly told reporters afterward. He said his cleats wouldn't dig into the turf, that the field was as hard as rock. Yeoman said that, given McVea's difficulty in finding his footing, he had to use a heavier running back during the second half. When the despondent McVea handed in his gear before leaving the locker room, he said, "I know one thing. There'll never be another day like this."

McVea didn't get much of a chance to redeem himself for more than a month, coming off the bench while the Cougars sputtered to a 2-5 record through October. Provided with a second start when Ole Miss came to the Astrodome on November 6, McVea responded with 201 yards receiving, a school record, including touchdown catches of 80 and 84 yards. The Cougars' 17-3 victory was considered one of the biggest in program history, since it was UH's first win in twelve meetings with the Rebels and improved their record against teams in the Southeastern Conference, considered among the top football leagues in the country, to 3-26. McVea finished the season with a modest 114 yards rushing and 341 receiving, as Houston finished 4-5-1.

Any hopes that an improved McVea would lead UH to a bowl in 1966 ended only weeks after the '65 season ended. On January 10, 1966, the NCAA placed Houston on three years' probation that banned the Cougars from post-season play (and from national television) for the rest of McVea's time with Houston. Jerry Wizig's report in the *Chronicle* stated that none of the rule violations involved the recruitment of McVea. But given what the future held for McVea at UH, would he transfer? "I wouldn't leave now for anything," he told Wizig. "Once I start something, I finish it." Over the balance of McVea's career with Houston, the Cougars went 8-2 in 1966 (the Astrodome outfitted with the nation's first artificial turf), and 7-3 in 1967.

If the victory over Ole Miss was big, the Cougars' stunning 37-7 upset of No. 3 Michigan State in September 1967 early in McVea's senior season was even bigger. Those around the country who'd forgotten about McVea by then were quickly reminded of his talent when he riddled the Spartans' defense for 156 yards rushing. It was a feast-or-famine performance; half of his fourteen carries resulted in no gain or a loss of yards. In the following week's *Sports Illustrated*, celebrated college football writer Dan Jenkins from Fort Worth stated he needed a thesaurus to find words adequate enough to describe McVea. His collegiate career statistics probably didn't approach others' expectations when he first arrived at Houston—and there was no opportunity to take the Cougars to a bowl—but McVea summed up his UH experience to school publicist Ted Nance thusly: "If I had to do it all again, I'd still come to Houston. The only thing about it is, I'm more sure."

....

One Southwest Conference football coach was ready to bring in a black player despite McVea's uneven freshman season in 1964. When Hayden Fry was hired in 1962 by SMU president Willis Tate from Frank Broyles's Arkansas staff, a condition Fry insisted on—one initially met with resistance—was the right to integrate the Mustangs' football program. Fry grew up in west Texas's "Oil Patch," in Odessa. He played with black children and sat with them in the city's segregated movie theaters. He carried the memory of those experiences with him the rest of his life and, when in a position to fight racial intolerance, was determined to do so.

Fry's magnanimous demand for an integrated football program was also pragmatic. SMU was one of four private schools in the SWC whose enrollments were dwarfed by Texas, Texas A&M, Arkansas, and, to a lesser degree, by Texas Tech (the unofficial university of west Texas). The hirings of Royal by Texas in 1957 and Broyles by Arkansas in 1958 began the rise of those programs back to national prominence and superiority in the league. The four SWC privates (SMU, Baylor, Rice, and TCU) faced a daunting task in trying to break up that monopoly. If the likes of Texas and Arkansas weren't going to integrate their rosters, it behooved Fry's new SMU program to embrace that source of football prowess.

His first three Mustang teams (1962-64) all finished in or near the conference cellar. The league had not yet welcomed its first black football player, despite figuratively opening its doors in November 1963 with Texas's policy change. But in autumn '64, Fry identified a black player in southeastern Texas's "Golden Triangle" region whom he thought could alter SMU's football fortunes. The star halfback for Beaumont's Hebert High, one of the city's two black high schools, was a 150-pound flit of a senior named Jerry LeVias. The "Golden Triangle," which also included Port Arthur and Orange, had been a fount of black football talent that spread across the nation collegiately. Defensive lineman Bubba Smith became an All-American at Michigan State. Two of LeVias's cousins, the Farr brothers—Mel a star running back at UCLA, Miller a standout defensive back at Wichita State—followed Smith into the NFL.

LeVias excelled in the classroom as well as on the field and came from a grounded, church-going family. That made him all the more attractive to SMU. But even after Fry made his interest known to LeVias and his family, it wasn't automatic that the young man would agree to take on such a burden when he could play outside the South and be a "regular" football player. UCLA was aware of LeVias through Mel Farr and was keenly interested. LeVias had a sister living in Pullman, Washington, home of Washington State, a downtrodden program that had recently joined what would become known as the Pac-Eight, and the WSU Cougars were very much in pursuit, too. Also interested was Houston, less than ninety miles from Beaumont, but LeVias made it known early on that he wanted no part of a backfield that featured McVea only a year ahead of him.

Fry, with a 1-9 team in 1964, could promise playing time, a private-school education, and life in the city of Dallas; it couldn't have hurt that LeVias had an aunt who lived there. Fry didn't avoid or minimize the significance of the racial struggles that would probably lie ahead. LeVias and his family didn't seem discouraged nor intimidated by the prospect. By late May 1965, Bob St. John of *The Dallas Morning News* reported that Fry and assistant coach Chuck Curtis were scheduled to travel to LeVias's home to sign him to an SWC letter of intent. Publicly, LeVias would only say that he'd narrowed his choices to SMU and Washington State. And, on Saturday, May 22, 1965, the expected took place when he signed with the Mustangs, which both delighted and relieved LeVias and his parents. "I feel better; a lot of pressure is off me," he told St. John by phone. "My parents said if I didn't decide pretty soon, they'd have to get a secretary to answer the phone and handle the mail. I picked SMU because I was very impressed with the kind of football it plays, the school, and the student body."

Sixteen months later, LeVias expounded on his decision in an interview in his dorm room with Jesse Finney, a writer for one of Dallas's black weeklies, *The Post-Tribune*, following his first varsity game: "I got no special treatment. No special preparations were made for me. They just offered me a scholarship . . . and I decided I would come." Said Fry upon LeVias's signing, "I hope this signing will open the door for future Negro student athletes in the Southwest Conference." (Only seven days later, TCU signed basketball player James Cash from Fort Worth's Terrell High. And Fry added at least one black player to SMU's roster each year while LeVias played there.)

Some recruiting drama concerning LeVias continued, since the letter of intent that he signed pertained only to SWC schools. UCLA coach Tommy Prothro wasn't ready to concede defeat and tried to catch up with LeVias at a postseason all-star game in Pennsylvania. By then, SMU's Curtis had become LeVias's unofficial bodyguard and prevented the determined Prothro from getting an audience with the Mustang-to-be. SMU brought LeVias to Dallas for most of that summer to live with his aunt, got him a job arranged for by freshman football coach Herman "Sleepy" Morgan, and LeVias was able to get a slow, steady start on acclimating to his new life. The atmosphere was both accommodating and realistic. LeVias had a brief meeting with Tate, the school president, who bluntly asked him, "I'll be here four years from now. Will you?" LeVias replied, "I'm going to be there."

It only required a few touchdown runs in LeVias's first intra-squad scrimmage with the freshman team to ignite a violent response that can only be conjectured as being racially motivated. A devastating hit resulted in broken ribs, hospitalization, and his presumed absence from the SMU freshman Colts' opener in Texarkana, Texas, against Arkansas's Shoats on Thursday night, October 7, 1965. Doctors had advised Morgan that LeVias shouldn't play, but could be used as a decoy. Yet LeVias came off the bench midway through the fourth quarter and caught two passes on consecutive plays. The plays covered 50 yards, including the go-ahead touchdown in the closing minutes, rallying SMU to a 14-10 victory before an audience of 5,500 that included Fry. "He's great," an elated Morgan told Louis Cox of the *Dallas Times Herald* afterward. "I told you he was." But the pre-season injury limited LeVias's availability for most of the five-game freshman schedule. He carried only twenty times for 83 yards, grabbed just seven passes for 136 yards, and returned eleven kickoffs and punts.

When LeVias was out of uniform, assimilation included distasteful episodes like Fry had warned of months earlier. The parents of his initial roommate demanded that their son be reassigned and housed with a fellow white player. In one of LeVias's classes, in which he was the only black student, the chairs that immediately surrounded his remained vacant. But it wasn't all cold shoulders and icy stares; one teammate sought to melt any tension and asked LeVias to do an impersonation of the "Godfather of Soul," James Brown. LeVias could eventually play the same game, asking for some "white stuff" to smear under his eyes when white teammates were applying glare-reducing eye black before a game.

CHAPTER 20

"I don't believe he will quit"

WHILE JERRY LEVIAS's SMU DEBUT—even in only a freshman game—
attracted considerable and deserved attention, two other black walk-on
frosh attempted to join him in the SWC football ranks that fall. John
Westbrook at Baylor and Darrell Brown at Arkansas had the gumption
to try to break their schools' respective football color barriers without
the financial advantage of university-provided tuition, room, and board.

John Westbrook grew up in multiple towns in northern and central
Texas, graduating from segregated Washington High School in Elgin,
near Austin. His father and grandfather had been Baptist ministers. John
was ordained at age fifteen, and finding a college with a strong religion
major was his top priority. His father had played football at Paul Quinn
College in Waco, and John was likewise interested in playing football
after high school. His performance at running back attracted scholarship offers from Prairie View A&M, Texas Southern, and Southern
University in Baton Rouge, Louisiana. With the state's previously all-
white colleges allowing black students, Westbrook focused his attention on Baylor—with its Baptist emphasis—and thought attending an
integrated university would aid him in subsequently operating in an
integrated world. There appeared to be few if any concerns regarding
Westbrook's character and educational prowess. At Washington High,

he was the only freshman elected to the student council that year; as a sophomore he beat out a senior for student council treasurer, and placed third in a state debate competition.

Westbrook's family would have had difficulty paying for a Baylor education, so he confidently drove from Elgin to the Bears' football office in person during the summer before his senior year—behind the wheel of his trusty '53 Studebaker—for a cold-call visit to gauge the football staff's interest in awarding him an athletic scholarship. In an extensive interview with Baylor's oral history staff years later, Westbrook said he talked to two assistant coaches, Jack Thomas and Clyde Hart, and indicated that Baylor expressed a desire to scout him during the coming season. But Westbrook never heard from Baylor, neither from the football office nor in reply to the enrollment application that he'd submitted, by the time that he graduated as salutatorian. He was set to revise his plans and enroll at North Texas and try out for the football team, when he was encouraged by a friend to get a definitive answer from Baylor before scrapping Plan A.

Westbrook apprehensively paid another visit to Thomas's office, telling the coach that he feared he'd been rejected by the admissions office. But Thomas, who said he remembered Westbrook, called over to admissions and discovered Westbrook had indeed been accepted, and that a postal glitch was the simple reason why he hadn't been informed. Thomas also learned more about Westbrook from the application's related paperwork and encouraged him to try out for the freshman team, even counseling him on the difficulties that he'd likely encounter. What *wasn't* offered was an immediate athletic scholarship, only the opportunity to earn one based on his performance that fall. Westbrook said he was willing to give it a go. He had an initial issue regarding his roommate in the athletic dorm, one oddly different from the one that LeVias encountered at SMU. Westbrook's roommate was black, but bristled at the thought of rooming with another black, thinking an integrated living arrangement would help him assimilate to his new world. Charles Houston was also Catholic, and none too crazy about bunking with a Baptist. Westbrook was floored by Houston's reaction, and was ready to scrap the idea of attending Baylor right then and there.

Like McVea and LeVias, Westbrook faced constant ostracism from his teammates in the form of either racial insults or relative isolation. The walk-ons couldn't eat in the athletic dining hall, and often couldn't make it to the university cafeteria for dinner before it closed. Westbrook received little sympathy—and nothing to eat, either—from his obdurate roommate. Unlike McVea or LeVias, he never got on the field for a single play during his entire freshman season. The head coach of Baylor's freshman Cubs, "Catfish" Smith, wasn't at all hostile or malevolent toward his one black player; to the contrary, Westbrook said Smith often walked back with him from practice when no teammate would, and tried to buoy his spirits. OK, there *was* the time, Westbrook said, that Smith, from east Texas, called him "Sambo." (Smith was elected mayor of Waco in 1976.)

Westbrook never received a playbook and was almost never aware of when team meetings took place. He recalled attending one, before the opener of the Cubs' five-game season, against the Texas Shorthorns. When players stood and could address their teammates for inspiration, Westbrook said, "I know I'm not going to play, but we ought to go out and beat 'em." He got the impression that everyone in the locker room felt sorry for him. (Score it 0-for-1 in pep talks; Texas won 28-7.) The only time that Westbrook was even sent into a huddle came when Smith was out sick for the Cubs' fourth game—against LeVias and SMU.

The acting head coach, Gwinn Corley, had been telling Westbrook all season that he'd try to get him into a game. In the waning seconds of Baylor's 17-13 victory over the SMU Colts, Corley tried to get Westbrook in for the final play, only to have the clock run out before the ball was snapped. Westbrook was more devastated by the near miss than by the games in which he assumed that he wouldn't play. He sat quietly at his locker afterward, and Corley eventually approached him. Corley thought Westbrook was crying and said, "Man, don't quit. We should have played you. I want you to play. Come to spring training."

Corley's pleadings then took a figurative, if inappropriate, turn: "If you don't, I'm going to come looking for you with a double-barrel shotgun." Westbrook assured that he had no plans to quit.

In Fayetteville, Arkansas, Darrell Brown was one of twelve black students to enroll at Arkansas in autumn 1965. The other eleven all considered him unrealistic for walking on to join the freshman football team as a 5-foot-11, 190-pound running back and/or kick returner for the program that was named national champion the previous season by the Football Writers Association of America. Brown grew up in the small southwest Arkansas town of Horatio, and attended a segregated high school that didn't field a football team. He'd put on pads once, during a summer exhibition fund-raiser back home. College football being a decidedly less formal institution in the mid-1960s than it is today, Brown said he simply sauntered up to the Arkansas football equipment window one day before pre-season practice began and asked for a uniform, pads, and a helmet. The stunned equipment rep initially disappeared for about thirty minutes before returning and, in the tradition of "The Great and Powerful Oz," told Brown to come back the next day. That he did, and was presented with a uniform, pads, and helmet, along with instructions to go change in the locker room. Most of the other Arkansas football players dared not say a word to him, but a couple of them asked where he was from and where he'd played. He dutifully reported that he'd played in the town of DeQueen, which technically was true since that was the site of the fund-raiser game.

Brown described practices with the freshman Shoats squad as daily initiations meant to coerce him to quit. Teammates and coaches often used racial slurs. Brown was routinely pummeled physically on top of any emotional testing. After some practices, he was matched against a teammate fifty pounds heavier in a wrestling match. But Brown didn't quit. Two assistant coaches were encouraging at times, but he said he never encountered varsity coach Frank Broyles and was never given any indication of what the head man thought of his performance. Arkansas's sports publicity department reports no record of Brown playing in a freshman game. He says he played against North Texas and Tulsa, the team's last two games.

At season's end, Brown reported back to the equipment room and handed in his uniform, pads, and helmet. He was never contacted during the off-season, never informed of any off-season conditioning or meetings, not invited to be part of spring practice. But when fall drills for 1966 began, he again requested a uniform and everything that went with it. He would try to make the varsity as a sophomore. The Razorbacks were coming off a second consecutive undefeated regular season and second consecutive SWC title, both firsts for the program. They figured to be loaded again, picked fifth in the AP's pre-season poll. They would open at War Memorial Stadium in Little Rock against Oklahoma State. For Brown, everything regarding pre-season drills was discouraging, similar to the previous year. The unreasonable hitting. The vicious taunting. David Hargis, an Arkansas freshman player that season, told Dan Wetzel of *Yahoo! Sports* years later that he could hear chanting from the varsity practice field: "Get the nigger! Get the nigger!" Three weeks into practice, Brown suffered injuries to a thumb and a knee. As he writhed in pain, no trainer attended to him. He finally staggered to his feet and tried to go on, status quo for so many practice days while he wore an Arkansas uniform. But he hurt the knee a second time that day and couldn't continue. Again, no one checked on his injuries or condition. He was left to seek medical attention at the university infirmary, where the physician on duty told him that he should never play football again. He took that advice.

. . . .

John Westbrook participated in Baylor's varsity spring practice of 1966, playing both running back and defensive back. As a defensive back, he came under the tutelage of assistant coach Taylor McNeel. If no one else on the Baylor staff spelled out that Westbrook would have to outperform his teammates just to pull even with them because of the color of his skin, McNeel, a Mississippi native, wasn't reticent about making that fact abundantly clear as a motivational tool. "I hate that, and I know you don't like that, but that's the facts of life," McNeel told him. "I'm gonna be on your butt left and right. I'm not going let up on you. I'm gonna holler and scream at you. I hope you can take it. And any way that I can help you, I'll help you out." McNeel screamed and hollered and never let up, as promised, and head coach John Bridgers would occasionally offer a word of encouragement like "Hang in there" or "You're doin' a good job." Westbrook made the first-team defense that spring, earned an athletic scholarship, and was moved back to running back in the fall.

As a member of the Baylor varsity, Westbrook finally received his own locker with his name on it. Life for Westbrook in the Baylor varsity backfield meant dealing with the Bears' running back coach, Pete McCulley. Westbrook was startled when McCulley chewed him out for a rare late arrival—he had to stay after class to meet with a professor after being named to the English honor fraternity—when white players routinely arrived late and weren't publicly scolded. Then there was the varsity equipment manager who provided him with ill-fitting shoes until coaches asked Westbrook why he was limping.

Baylor's opener finally arrived, a home game against No. 7 Syracuse that was moved up to the exclusive date of September 10 for a national ABC telecast. Just about every other college team began play a week later, including SMU and Jerry LeVias. Westbrook's presence received merely a passing, understated reference low in the game advance story written by Jim Montgomery in that Saturday morning's *Waco Tribune-Herald*, just identifying him as one of the Bears' running backs.

Syracuse's running game was considered one of the nation's best, a thunder-and-lightning combination of bruising Larry Csonka and nimble Floyd Little. The latter was the latest in a series of talented blacks to play the position, beginning with Jim Brown and continuing with Ernie Davis. Moments before kickoff, a Baylor teammate came over to Westbrook and boasted, "I told them our nigger's gonna be better than their nigger today." Just as Westbrook received muted notice in the Waco Saturday paper, his historic debut was hardly trumpeted in the Sunday paper's upbeat account of Baylor's 35-12 upset victory.

A page 1 story that recounted the day's events both on and off the field featured, near the end of the article's "jump" page inside, a small headline "Cheers for Westbrook" and detailed Baylor's final possession, "… then it was time for John Westbrook. As the crowd roared out its delight, Baylor's first Negro football player in history ripped off tackle to the 13, and then to the 11." The *Tribune-Herald's* reporting failed to include one detail that didn't escape the ear of the *Dallas Times Herald's* Bob Galt: "The only thing that marred Westbrook's debut was an abhorrent announcement by Baylor's public address man. He wanted the fans to notice a Baylor first—'color football on color TV.' The fellow's words were greeted with a coldness that was probably felt all the way to Alaska. Only moments before, Westbrook had received a tremendous ovation from the crowd of 31,000." The first black man to play varsity football in the Southwest Conference came off the bench and carried the ball twice for nine yards.

Westbrook continued to get a handful of carries off the bench as Baylor got off to 2-1-1 start and surprised another ranked opponent, blanking fifth-ranked Arkansas in its conference opener up in the hills. But the Bears lost their next three SWC games to squelch any thoughts of their first trip to the Cotton Bowl, and Westbrook suffered an injury to his right knee in late October that limited his ability to be a regular contributor for the rest of his collegiate career. He finished his first varsity season with twenty total carries for 99 yards. Of note, a second black player joined the Baylor program that 1967 season as a freshman, guard Tommy Reaux from Houston.

A week after Baylor's 1966 opener, LeVias and the varsity Mustangs started their season at home at the Cotton Bowl stadium against an Illinois team that had humiliated SMU during the previous season in Champaign, Ill., 42-0. The Mustangs gained a measure of revenge by winning 26-7, and LeVias touched the ball all of three times. "We were basically a run team," LeVias recalls. "The times I touched the ball, it was strictly to loosen up for the run." But the three touches included two fourth-quarter touchdown catches. One was a 60-yarder before which he went into the huddle and insisted that quarterback Mac

White throw deep to him. LeVias was a threat to score whenever he had the ball, and helped make SMU a contender to win its first conference title since 1948. But the achievements came with a price, as he faced scorn not only from opposing players and fans but still from teammates. Before the Mustangs' game at Arkansas in mid-November, LeVias said he received disparaging letters and phone calls; one envelope included a crudely drawn "boat ticket back to Africa," and one call came at 2:30 a.m. A teammate cursed and spat on him. It was common for opposing players to use racial slurs. When the Mustangs took the field at Texas A&M, black cats were waiting for them. When SMU won at home against Baylor on November 19 to pull within one game of clinching the league championship and a Cotton Bowl berth, LeVias sparked the 24-22 victory with a 100-yard kickoff return for a touchdown and a reception for 68 yards. Yet after the game, LeVias wept in the locker room and revealed to Fry examples of the abuse that he'd endured that fall. According to Dallas's black *Post Tribune* weekly, LeVias was particularly upset that Fry had been called a "white nigger." "At times, he didn't believe it was worth it," Fry told the press soon after, "but I don't believe he will quit. I have told him he is a symbol of his race, and if he quits he will handicap the program for other people."

The only thing that stood between the Mustangs and a New Year's Day appointment in the Cotton Bowl Classic was earning a win or tie on November 26 at TCU against a Horned Frogs team that was 2-7. SMU's top-ranked conference offense was matched against a team that had scored all of five touchdowns that season. While the Frogs didn't appear to pose much of a threat on the surface, there was the matter of SMU's history playing at TCU's Amon Carter Stadium; the Mustangs hadn't won there since 1945. LeVias recalls that when the SMU buses arrived that morning at the stadium, Fry told him to get off the bus last and he was accompanied to the locker room by a team of officers. "I thought I was a big star; I had security," LeVias says. Actually, he was the possible target of a threat on his life. Fry had LeVias warm up beneath the stands instead of out on the field with the rest of the team. Only minutes before kickoff did Fry inform LeVias of the situation. The Mustangs cruised to a 21-0 victory with LeVias tallying the first touchdown on a 68-yard reception. "Anytime I came close to the sidelines, the coaches would scatter," LeVias says with a laugh. As LeVias headed back to the team bus after the game, he was escorted by three uniformed patrolmen plus other officers wearing street clothes. The *Fort Worth Star-Telegram* learned of the threat and subsequent security measures for LeVias, and asked Fry about it before the team left for Dallas. "I am going to call his parents in Beaumont and tell them the situation," Fry told the paper. "I don't want them to hear any reports of an assassination attempt because it would be a terrible shock." Curiously, Fort Worth police that Saturday night told *The Dallas Morning News* that they were unaware of any such threat and didn't increase security for LeVias.

Conflicting reports in the two Dallas dailies regarding LeVias and his future with SMU were published on consecutive days in early December as the tenth-ranked Mustangs began preparations for the Cotton Bowl date with No. 4 Georgia. On December 7, the *Times Herald*'s Cox quoted LeVias as saying he was considering transferring. The episode at TCU was the last straw, he said. "After the Cotton Bowl game and during the mid-term vacation, I'm going to talk to my parents in Beaumont about going to another school." The following day, *The Morning News* volleyed back with a non-bylined report in which LeVias stated it was his father who wanted him to leave SMU: "It's not that I said I was going to change schools. It's just that my father is disturbed about the situation here, whether it's good or whether it's bad. I hope he's not disturbed to the extent that I can't talk him out of it." Charles LeVias told *The News* that he was very upset over the TCU episode and would talk to his son about transferring. Said Jerry, "I just want everybody to leave me alone and let me get my education." When league coaches met in Dallas soon after, Fry went public in calling attention to the treatment of LeVias throughout the season, especially by conference opponents. The SWC coaches subsequently released a statement pledging good sportsmanship specifically toward LeVias.

··········

On the first day of Baylor's spring practice in 1967, Westbrook suffered another injury to his right knee that required surgery and all but ended his college football career. He often spent weekends up in Denton, where his girlfriend and future wife, Paulette White, attended North Texas State. While he was able to come back from the knee injury to begin the season, his football year ended only half-way through the schedule when a series of particularly hard hits to the head in practice built on each other to result in a concussion. Because the damage didn't manifest itself in a limp or other tangible sign of injury, Westbrook's desire to play was constantly questioned by team-mates and some coaches, including Jack Thomas, the very man whose initial encouragement had played such a role in Westbrook even being on the Baylor campus. Westbrook was viewed as slacking off by some, and one disgruntled fan made his acrimony known in writing to the Baylor athletic department: "Niggers belong in the cotton fields." The weight of the physical and emotional encumbrances caused the desperate Westbrook to swallow a handful of aspirins in an unsuccessful attempt to end his life.

Westbrook's physical and emotional states improved enough by the fall of '67 for him to rejoin the team as a junior three games into the season. But the same succession of maladies—knee problems followed by a concussion—limited him to three games and 90 total yards. He could only stand by and watch as the Bears gradually sank to a 1-8-1 finish. Maybe it was because Westbrook had time on his hands that he was invited that autumn to speak on local radio about his experience as a black Baylor student. He didn't take the easy, politically correct route; instead, he detailed the loneliness and rage that he'd felt through two and a half years because of his treatment. Early in 1968, he wasn't able to participate full-time in off-season drills, and continued to spend as much as time as possible at North Texas with White.

He then learned his mother had terminal cancer and not long to live. The assassinations of Martin Luther King, Jr. and Robert Kennedy added to his depression—Westbrook said one athletic department staffer noted, "They finally killed that Martin Luther Coon"—and he again contemplated suicide, thinking of driving his car into Lake Waco one night. Westbrook was prepared to quit the football team before his senior year, but reluctantly complied with Bridgers's request to stick out the final season. He and White were married about six weeks before the season began. Westbrook was decidedly heavier and didn't figure much in the Bears' plans that fall, which resulted in a 3-7 record. For all the disappointment of Westbrook's football experience at Baylor, he led the team in average yards per carry in each of his three varsity seasons and never lost a fumble.

During LeVias's final two seasons at SMU, the Mustangs didn't enjoy the same success and didn't again contend for a conference title. The '67 team finished 3-7, and LeVias's worst suffering was physical rather than emotional. In the penultimate game, at Baylor, LeVias was struck in the right eye by a forearm and lay on the field for twenty minutes. He suffered three fractures, and initial concerns were that he'd lose the eye. The '68 SMU squad went into its league opener against TCU with hopes of again being a force in the SWC given its start in non-conference play. The Mustangs had won two of the three games, losing only to an Ohio State team that would go unbeaten and win the national championship. Back at Amon Carter Stadium, where two years earlier there were whispers of a death threat, LeVias endured another dark incident in the fourth quarter of a tie game. One of the TCU defenders told LeVias to "Go home, nigger" and spat in his face. LeVias took himself out of the game, reaching the bench area in tears. He angrily threw his helmet to the ground and growled, "I quit." Fry came over to counsel him, to get him past the latest hurdle of a four-year emotional and psychological obstacle course that was only a few months from completion. When TCU was ready to punt, with LeVias being SMU's main return man, LeVias told Fry that he would run it back for a touchdown. He did just that, 89 yards worth, to give SMU a 21-14 victory.

The '68 Mustangs were improved, but not good enough to win the conference. Their only two league losses were to Texas and Arkansas, the league co-champions. That earned No. 20 SMU a berth in Houston's

Astro-Bluebonnet Bowl against No. 10 Oklahoma, co-champion of the Big Eight. The Mustangs were seven-point underdogs and trailed 14-6 going into the fourth quarter when an 11-yard touchdown catch by LeVias ignited a scoring barrage by both teams. When the smoke cleared, SMU won 28-27 with LeVias grabbing eight passes for 122 yards in his collegiate farewell. He was named a consensus All-American, and there were two other achievements to note. The Kiwanis Club of Fort Worth, of all places, bestowed upon him its annual sportsmanship award for on-field conduct. And, in May 1969, LeVias received his bachelor's degree at SMU's commencement ceremony. Willis Tate handed him his diploma and said, "You kept your promise."

LeVias, like Westbrook, often spent time in Denton whenever he could during his college days. His best friend from high school attended North Texas, and he also got to know a couple of the Eagles' black football players. "There was no social life for me in Dallas," LeVias says. "At North Texas, you had Ron Shanklin and Joe Greene." And with his girlfriend living in Waco, he occasionally crossed paths with John Westbrook. "He and I talked about what was going on and what it was like," LeVias says. "John was a man of great faith. I would say my faith was strong, but his was a little bit stronger than mine. We kind of played off each other. We could cry in our milk together without anyone else knowing what was going on. We could kind of let our frustrations out with each other."

CHAPTER 21

"We will kick to the clock"

ABNER HAYNES MIGHT HAVE SECOND-GUESSED his decision to sign with Dallas's new AFL club when the Texans reported for pre-season practice in the sultry setting of Roswell, New Mexico. If management's intent was to simulate a military environment as the staff determined which players should first represent the club in September, it selected an optimum venue in New Mexico Military Institute.

The school's amenities included two-to-a-room lodging without the hassle of air-conditioning. Each room had a window, though without a screen. What cool breezes provided a semblance of relief also usually ushered in a horde of mosquitoes. An irrigation ditch conveniently located near the practice field served as something of a recreation spot. For entertainment, there was the curious site of team owner Lamar Hunt and his brother, Bunker, holding their own throwing and kicking contests while the team practiced. The quality of the dining hall food was evidenced by the players' penchant for reporting in as required but then skirting the chow line to sneak out a back door and make tracks to a nearby Dairy Queen. Welcome to the big time, boys.

Another member of the 1959 North Texas team participated in that first memorable Texans camp. Lineman Bob Way, six hours short of graduation, thought he'd give pro ball a try and was also personally signed by Hunt. Way was none too fond of the training camp environment and, upon determining his chances of making the opening day roster to be slight, told Haynes that he was leaving camp. "Bobby, don't leave," Haynes pleaded. "You're going to make the team." But Way was gone soon, on a train bound for his native Amarillo.

It was amid those languid conditions that the Texans' roster began to congeal. The quarterbacking chores were handed to Cotton Davidson, who had retired from pro ball in 1958 and spent '59 coaching at his alma mater, Baylor. The starting halfback took a similar path. TCU product Jim Swink had given up the sport to pursue a career in medicine, studying in Dallas. When approached by the Texans, Swink acknowledged he missed football. He decided to give it another go since he could continue with his medical education through night classes. They were joined in the offensive backfield by three rookies—Haynes, TCU's Jack Spikes, and LSU's Johnny Robinson.

About the time the Texans were beginning their maiden season, Way was making his way from Amarillo to Denton to enroll at North Texas and complete his course work toward a bachelor's degree. He left the Panhandle with wife Carolyn, baby daughter Karen, and also Sammy Stanger, who was headed back to Denton after his attempt to play Canadian football fell short of making a roster. Way made the long drive down U.S. 287 through Clarendon, Quanah, Wichita Falls, and Bowie, heading toward Denton. But as the travelers approached Decatur, about thirty miles west of Denton, Way experienced car trouble and recognized they'd need assistance to reach their destination. He walked into Decatur, hitched a ride to Denton and showed up at the Geezles house. Way barely had to explain his quandary before a number of the brothers gathered up available funds, drove Way back to Decatur, and helped him get his car repaired. For all the Geezles' misadventures, they stood arm in arm when need be.

As the Texans broke camp to begin a six-game exhibition schedule, Haynes was relegated to the reserve unit. Dallas was nearly halfway done with pre-season play before a crestfallen Haynes finally succeeded in attracting the coaching staff's attention during his limited playing time. That wasn't enough, though, to earn a starting spot when the Texans—unbeaten in all six pre-season games—opened the season on Saturday night, September 10, on the road against the Los Angeles Chargers.

The Texans-Chargers debut at the cavernous Los Angeles Coliseum was staged one night after the NFL's Rams played before a crowd of 51,398 there for an exhibition game against their California rivals, the San Francisco 49ers. The assemblage that nestled into the Coliseum officially numbered all of 17,724, but they surely were entertained as their Chargers rallied from a 20-7 deficit in the third quarter to win in the final minutes, 21-20. The AFL's style of play would soon be identified as more wide-open and appetizing than the NFL's. It certainly was on display that night at the Coliseum as the teams combined for 83 passes; the NFL average for the 1960 season would be 52. Haynes came off the bench to carry three times, return two kickoffs, and catch seven passes, one for a touchdown.

Haynes remained on the second team for one more week, and then replaced Swink as the starting left halfback opposite Robinson when the Texans played their first regular-season home game at the Cotton Bowl, a rematch with the Chargers. Most of the estimated crowd of 42,000 were jammed into the end zones; that's where the discounted seats were located. Two weeks later, Swink suddenly decided his belated fling with pro football wasn't really for him and he retired. By then, Haynes was the AFL's leading receiver, with 21 catches for 227 yards. He often stood as Dallas's leader in both rushing and receiving in a game, not to mention playing a regular role in the Texans' return game. "We knew all along Abner was a great runner, with good moves and fine hands," Dallas coach Hank Stram said in early November after Haynes earned his second consecutive league player of the week award. "As he gets more acclimated to our offense, he looks better. He's picking his holes and running patterns better all the time. And Abner is a great competitor. He's tough. It's surprising how much punishment a guy his size can take." When Haynes was asked to explain his ascent, he responded, "It's not me. I think the linemen are sharper."

Haynes led the new league in rushing yards (875), average rushing yards per game (62.5), rushing touchdowns (nine), punt-return yards (215), and all-purpose yards (2,100); he finished fifth in catches. He was not only named the AFL's Rookie of the Year, but also its overall Most Valuable Player, which was announced a few days after the Houston Oilers defeated the Chargers to claim the AFL's first championship. Despite having collected a rare double in terms of individual awards, Haynes maintained afterward that his biggest thrill was simply making the Texans squad. He had already by then partaken of his hometown's hospitality, making speaking appearances all over town. "The eating has been real good," he noted, then tried to assure Texans fans that he wouldn't report to camp in 1961 with ample evidence of a generous off-season: "I bought me a set of weights to keep down my stomach. I don't want to play guard next year."

In the early weeks of the 1961 AFL season, the Texans appeared primed to challenge the division-champion Chargers by winning three of their first four games. Haynes dislocated a shoulder in August and wasn't healed until the season's third game. The Chargers had since relocated to San Diego in search of crowds better than the average of 15,665 drawn to the Coliseum. Dallas led the league in rushing, but was no match for the Chargers, who clinched the division in early November.

The Texans set out to bolster their passing game in 1962. That was just one aspect of the team's operations that concerned Hunt heading into the franchise's third year. Two seasons of mediocre football resulted in home crowds that didn't come close to filling the Cotton Bowl despite a constant wave of promotions and discounted admissions. The 1961 Texans averaged 17,571 per game, which was only slightly below the league average. It was no salve that the NFL Cowboys likewise played before mostly empty seats. Entering into the equation of the Texans' financial future was a federal court decision rendered in May 1962 dismissing the AFL's claim that the NFL tried to operate a monopoly. The prospect of badly needed revenue arriving through a court award was no longer a possibility.

A somewhat desperate roll of the dice for the Texans in identifying a new starting quarterback going into the 1962 season worked out marvelously. Stram signed an NFL has-been named Len Dawson, whom he'd recruited to Purdue almost a decade earlier. Written off by the Pittsburgh Steelers and Cleveland Browns, the twenty-seven-year-old Dawson immediately found new football life with Dallas. His impact on the club was such that Haynes—after rushing for 122 yards and scoring four touchdowns in Dallas's 42-28 opening win at home over the Boston Patriots—insisted that the season's first game ball be presented not to the victorious coach but to the winning quarterback.

Haynes shared carries for much of the season with a new running mate, rookie Curtis McClinton from Kansas, but remained one of the league's offensive standouts. With the Chargers dogged by their first mediocre season, the Texans clinched the West title on the first Sunday of December. A week later, they closed the home portion of their schedule hosting San Diego, which meant a visit to Dallas by Chargers owner Barron Hilton. A man who was forced to abandon his franchise's original home after only one season, Hilton frequently commiserated with Hunt over the inability of their two franchises to draw better. Even Dallas's West-winning campaign barely improved the situation at the turnstiles, the Texans averaging 22,201. Hilton and Hunt had once joked about holding a game between their teams and locking the gates beforehand, not allowing any paying spectators in. They broached that topic again before their teams' meeting at the Cotton Bowl in mid-December 1962. The newly crowned division winners attracted a gathering of 18,384.

Haynes was again the epitome of a hometown hero, something that the NFL Cowboys had yet to realize with their local drawing card, Don Meredith. Haynes rushed for a career-high 1,049 yards, second in the league, and led the AFL in total yards from scrimmage and total touchdowns rushing and receiving. The Texans were headed for the AFL's third championship game, matched against the three-time Eastern Division-winning Oilers.

The host Oilers were seven-point favorites to win their third AFL championship in as many tries, according to the Houston and Dallas newspapers. The size of the point spread was mostly attributable to the Texans missing one of their prime offensive weapons, all-league end Chris Burford, who had suffered a knee injury a month earlier. Stram's bold reaction to Burford's absence was to take Haynes, given his ability to catch as well as run, out of the backfield for much of the game and make him a flanker receiver. The backfield would feature both Spikes and McClinton.

The weather forecast called for a front to move in during the game, probably around halftime, resulting in both a drastic drop in temperature and a significant increase in the wind, which blew out of the north at about fifteen miles per hour when the game began. Jeppesen Stadium wasn't an enclosed structure like the majority of today's NFL stadiums. It featured four sets of disconnected bleachers, the seating areas in the north and south end zones small enough that there was little to stop that day's wind. The game was a sellout at 37,981, the largest gathering in the AFL to date.

The first half surprisingly belonged to the Texans. They outgained the Oilers by nearly a 2-to-1 ratio and, with Houston quarterback/ kicker George Blanda throwing two interceptions and missing a field-goal attempt, Dallas charged to a 17-0 lead. The Oilers concentrated their defensive efforts on Haynes at his new position, which opened the running game for Spikes and McClinton. Haynes still contributed one of the two Texans touchdowns by making a catch while running toward the sideline about twenty yards from the end zone, turning the corner, and reaching the goal line unscathed. But during the second half, it inexplicably looked like the teams had traded uniforms at halftime. The Oilers' defense blitzed frequently to apply more pressure to Dawson, while Houston's offense suddenly found traction. The Oilers tied the score at 17-17 with six minutes to play in the fourth quarter and were in position to go ahead in the final minutes on a 42-yard field-goal attempt. But the kick, with the gusting wind at Blanda's back, was blocked by Dallas linebacker Sherrill Headrick. A light rain began to fall as the final seconds of regulation played out, and the teams headed to overtime, known as "sudden death" since the first score would end play.

Overtime in pro football begins with a coin toss identical to the coin toss that precedes the opening kickoff. The visiting team calls the toss: heads or tails. The team that wins the toss can choose one of two variables: 1.) whether to kick off or receive, or 2.) declare which goal that it would like to defend in the upcoming quarter, with that reversing in subsequent periods. After a choice is made, the team that didn't win the toss gets to select from whichever variable remains.

Given the sudden-death format, standard procedure is for the team that wins the coin toss to say it wants to receive the kickoff. But Stram thought otherwise, given certain circumstances. If the Texans won the toss and elected to receive, the kicking Oilers would take the considerable wind, gusting at about 30 miles per hour at that point, at their backs. And if Dallas couldn't initially muster much of an attack, which had been the case during the entire second half—the Texans' yardage total for the third and fourth quarters was *minus-7 yards*—then Houston could conceivably get the ball at midfield and quickly move into position to win with a field goal. Stram was also concerned with how his rookie punter, Eddie Wilson, had also struggled during the second half. So the Dallas coach explained to his captains, offensive captain Haynes and defensive captain E.J. Holub, that, should Dallas win the toss, the Texans' choice would be to select an end of the field to defend: the north goal. The assumption was that the Oilers would then choose to receive the ball, and the Texans would be in position to stop them and have the wind to help them during the fifth period.

Haynes, Holub, and Houston's two captains—Ed Huseman and Al Jamison—met at midfield along with the referee, Red Bourne. Also right there was ABC's field reporter, Jack Buck, known throughout the Midwest as a radio announcer for the St. Louis Cardinals baseball team, with a microphone that carried the coin-toss conversation into living rooms across the country. (By the way, TV ratings for the telecast predictably increased as the game progressed. For many, it was their first exposure to the AFL.)

Bourne explained to the four captains that the overtime coin toss would be conducted identically to the pre-game version, with the visiting team making the call. (The Houston captains initially indicated it would only be fair if *they* got to call the game's second toss.) Haynes stepped forward to make the call for Dallas, called "Heads" with the coin headed earthward, and the coin indeed came up heads. Bourne then presented the options to Haynes thusly: "You have your choice, of course, receiving or kicking." Haynes, leaning into Buck's microphone, replied, "We will kick to the clock." Oops. Having chosen to kick off, the rest of Haynes' declaration—"to the clock"—was rendered moot. The stunned-but-giddy Oilers captains then chose to defend the north goal, meaning they would receive the opening overtime kickoff and have the wind to begin the extra period.

Holub, just beyond the coin-toss conclave, was the first of the Texans to learn of Haynes's misstep. He hopped awkwardly on his way to the sideline as if burned by a hot foot. It's certainly possible Haynes thought he needed to answer in terms that matched Bourne's question and, in doing so, scuttled Dallas's main intent. Stram, to his credit, appeared to accept the fact that Haynes had erred without retching, convulsing, or screaming at his twenty-five-year-old offensive captain. And, as Dan Jenkins reported later in the week in the *Times Herald*, a fair number of people in the Texans' sideline area didn't realize the game would end on the first score and had to be informed that kicking into the wind figured to be the worst of both worlds.

The Oilers fielded the skipping kickoff from Texans rookie kicker Tommy Brooker near the 10-yard line, began scrimmaging at the 33, but failed to gain even one first down. For all the consternation that Haynes's misunderstanding understandably created, it didn't decide the game. Likewise, pro football's only previous overtime game—the Baltimore Colts' victory over the New York Giants in the 1958 NFL Championship Game—didn't end with a score on the first possession. The Oilers, in fact, had the ball three times with the wind during the fifth period, resulting in a punt and Blanda's fourth and fifth interceptions of the day. (He threw 42 during the fourteen-game season, which set the pro mark and remains the record today.) Dallas converted the fifth interception into a 32-yard drive to Houston's 25. Three minutes into the sixth period, after the teams again changed ends, Brooker kicked a field goal with the wind behind him to end the game and crown the Texans as AFL champions. At 77 minutes and 54 seconds, the game remains the longest in pro football history.

In *The Morning News* story the following day entitled "Delirium Grips Victorious Texans," seven members of the Texans' roster or coaching staff were quoted; Haynes wasn't one of them. Stram was, explaining that the instructions to his offensive captain going into overtime were to take the wind if Dallas won the toss. "The players were excited and tugging at Abner; he just didn't understand the option," Stram told reporters. "It was a mistake you don't like to make, but there's no use crying over it." If anyone wanted to ask Haynes about the botched call upon the team's return that night to Love Field, that wasn't the place. He was one of a handful of players who didn't catch the flight back to Dallas.

Upon deplaning, a bedraggled-but-gleeful Hunt stood in shirt sleeves, tie undone and yanked down to about the middle of his chest. He had delivered a pro football championship to his hometown. As Stram and he raised fists in triumph and players donned cowboy hats for the benefit of photographers, Hunt was likely the only person among the revelers who realized the Texans had probably played their last game representing Dallas because of the team's difficulty in drawing fans at home. Within weeks, word leaked that Hunt was moving the franchise to Kansas City.

"It seems like I'm in a shock," Haynes told *The Morning News*. "Everyone wants to be appreciated. When we weren't winning and didn't get it, we didn't know how it would be if we did win. But then we won, and nothing happened. It was a big letdown." Haynes had one year remaining on his contract, and indicated he'd probably stay with the club though eligible to seek a new football home elsewhere following one season in Kansas City. He added that he didn't think the Texans' departure meant success for the city's remaining pro football team. "The Cowboys may not last more than another year or two."

Haynes displayed faith in his transplanted club by signing a new three-year contract. While he was leaving his hometown, an acquaintance from Dallas was preparing to join the club. The Chiefs' draft going into the 1963 season included speedy halfback Stone Johnson, who began his high school career at Lincoln. Johnson suffered from a debilitating back ailment that forced him to spend nearly a year in a cast that extended from his neck to his knees following surgery. Leon King recalled Johnson missing school frequently and classmates who were unaware of his predicament assuming he was "chicken," afraid to compete in sports. Once Johnson was freed from the cast, it was as if he refused to stop running. He transferred as a sophomore in 1956 to new Madison High, where he developed into a star both on the football field and on the track— an amazing feat given his medical history—before graduating in 1959. Haynes recruited Johnson to play football for North Texas and was confident the young speedster was headed to Denton, until Johnson called one day to say he was at Grambling State, the powerhouse of black college football located only a few hours east of Dallas in northern Louisiana. The Tigers' legendary football coach, Eddie Robinson, later said he suspected Grambling's ability to send players into the NFL was Johnson's deciding factor.

But Johnson played little football for Robinson. He instead focused on track. Collie Nicholson, the lyrical Grambling sports publicist who helped bring national attention to Robinson's program during the 1960s, said Johnson was so fast that glass didn't have time to cut him. Johnson earned a spot as a sprinter on the United States team competing at the 1960 Rome Olympics. At the qualifying trials, he set the world record for the 200 meters. Johnson's roommate in the Olympic village was (small world again) Ray Norton, who played football for San Jose State against North Texas in 1957. Johnson finished fifth in the 200. He and Norton were members of a relay team that finished first, but had its gold medal revoked for making an improper baton pass.

Johnson still had a year's football eligibility remaining at Grambling going into the fall of 1962, but he instead left school and returned to Dallas. He often hung around Haynes and the rest of the Texans during what proved to be their championship season, and final campaign, in Dallas, so much so that Haynes referred to him as a "water boy." Johnson, unbeknownst to Stram, befriended young Hanky Stram, often giving him ice cream after practices. The Texans drafted Johnson in the fourteenth round, hardly a gamble and not the first time that a pro football team auditioned an athlete whose skills had previously been considered better suited to a different sport. Norton, a better sprinter than football player at San Jose, had been drafted in 1960 by the nearby San Francisco 49ers before Haynes was selected by the Steelers.

Johnson was still on the Kansas City squad when the exhibition season neared its close, the Chiefs playing at Wichita, Kansas, against the Oilers on the final night of August. Among his duties that night was playing on return teams, sometimes paired with Haynes. On a Houston kickoff late in the first quarter, Johnson rushed upfield to block on a kick that dribbled out of bounds. He jumped into a pile of players and didn't get up; his neck was broken, and he was rushed to a local hospital.

Later that night, as the Chiefs waited to board their flight back to Kansas City, Haynes sat in the airport sobbing uncontrollably. Johnson remained behind, was placed in traction, but had suffered partial paralysis and never made significant progress. Eight nights after jumping into that pile of football players, with Hunt present in the hospital room, Johnson died at the age of twenty-three of complications caused by the fracture. The following morning, Stram telephoned Haynes with the somber news. "Our boy went home to higher glory," Stram told him, and then they cried for a while. Johnson's parents accompanied their son's body back to Dallas by train. The funeral was held at Munger Avenue Baptist Church, which, for at least that day, was filled with both black and white mourners. Haynes was among the pall bearers.

The Chiefs opened their season on the road one night before John-son's death, crushing Denver 59-7, but a year that began on such a funereal note off the field also soon turned sour on the field. A seven-game winless streak stretched from mid-October into early December and crushed the club's chances of repeating as division champion. Haynes's role in the backfield diminished and McClinton took over as the Chiefs' primary ball carrier in 1963.

But Haynes rebounded in 1964 to rank fifth in the league in rushing, claim the AFL's Comeback Player of the Year award from the Associated Press, and earn his third trip to the post-season AFL All-Star Game. For the first time, the game wasn't hosted by one of the league clubs. It instead was scheduled to be played in New Orleans, at Tulane Stadium, home of the annual New Year's Day Sugar Bowl, for what amounted to the latest audition to see if the city was worthy of supporting its own pro franchise. New Orleans, Atlanta, and Miami were vying for pro football expansion teams that appeared to be on the drawing board to be awarded in the next few seasons, hoping to join Dallas and Houston as the sport's southern markets. But Louisiana sported a checkered past, arguably worse than its regional neighbors, when it came to sports events and the state's racial climate. The Sugar Bowl was the last of the major bowls to allow an integrated team to participate: Pitt against Georgia Tech in 1956. State government responded soon after by passing a law that banned interracial sporting events, before that law was struck down in 1959.

Concerns still persisted as Dave Dixon, the New Orleans civic leader leading the effort to land a pro football team, negotiated with AFL commissioner Joe Foss to schedule the league's annual All-Star Game following the 1964 season. Dixon told Foss there would be no problem for integrated all-star teams to play in the city. Dixon said his organizing group had been assured by the city's business elite that the town was eager to show it was ready to embrace big-time pro sports. Foss and the league agreed to play the game there. As it turned out, another racially-mixed Sugar Bowl was played only weeks before the scheduled All-Star Game, with Syracuse facing LSU.

Many of the fifty-eight all-stars began to arrive in New Orleans about a week before the Saturday, January 16, 1965 game. It didn't take long for many of the twenty-one black all-stars to realize they weren't being exactly welcomed. A number of them were unable to hail cabs at the airport to simply get into town, while their white counterparts were getting rides without issue. After one group of black players had been unable to get rides for hours, they were informed by a black porter that they'd have to call a "colored" cab from downtown to come out to get them.

Once in the city, similar problems became all too evident. Ernie Warlick, the Buffalo Bills' tight end, headed out with two white Bills teammates for dinner in the French Quarter. When Warlick attempted to simply follow his companions into a restaurant, he was abruptly told, "Naw, we don't serve your kind." Many of the other black players experienced similar rejection. Back at the hotel, they traded stories regarding the hostility experienced during their brief time in New Orleans. Some suggested leaving town immediately. When the West all-stars were scheduled to board a bus the following morning for their first practice, coach Sid Gillman of the Chargers was startled when he was taking roll. "Bobby Bell." No answer. "Earl Faison." No answer. One of the players on the bus—a white player, of course—came to the astute conclusion: "Hey, all the black guys are missing!"

The black guys were meeting in the hotel, Haynes among those leading the discussion. They considered a proposal from the white players to stay and bring attention to the problem, but ultimately rejected that in favor of a boycott. Warlick, considered more moderate than Haynes and other firebrands, read a statement to the press before the black players left the city. Desperate AFL officials quickly concocted a suitable Plan B, and shifted the game site to the closest league city, Houston. Haynes left New Orleans for Dallas, and recounted some of his experiences in the Crescent City for the *Times Herald*. "The trouble started as soon as we stepped off the plane," he said. "The promoter said two cab companies had agreed to take us anywhere we wanted to go in town and all that jazz. But we said, 'What's the point in making a special effort?' As soon as we leave town, they wouldn't carry ordinary Negro citizens. Our people would think we were nuts." The hastily relocated game in Houston attracted a crowd of only 15,446, but it has been hailed since as a milepost in the stand for racial equality in pro sports.

Four days after the All-Star Game, Haynes was traded to the Denver Broncos for Jim Fraser, a nondescript linebacker-punter, and an undisclosed amount of cash. Haynes publicly greeted the transaction with relief, and told *The Morning News* that he'd asked for a trade as soon as the Chiefs' season ended. "It's obvious by the kind of deal they made for me that they felt they had to get rid of me," he said. "And not just because I wanted to leave Kansas City. There were other reasons." He identified those reasons for the *Times Herald*: his participation in the All-Star boycott. "Jack Steadman [Kansas City's general manager] told me he didn't condone what I did in New Orleans," Haynes said. "I asked him if he'd ever been segregated. Where had he ever been turned away from?" Haynes played three more seasons in the AFL—with Denver, the Miami Dolphins expansion team that was added in 1966, and the New York Jets—but didn't approach his previous level of play; he quietly retired following the 1967 season. Almost fifty years after he last donned the uniform of the Chiefs, he still ranks sixth in rushing yards gained for the Dallas-Kansas City franchise.

CHAPTER 22

Going their separate ways

PART OF LEON KING GREATLY wanted to pursue a career in pro football, though he wasn't drafted and had not played for more than a year. He told a North Texas historian that he was asked to try out for the NFL's St. Louis Cardinals. Had he not suffered the knee injury while at North Texas, he might have thought more seriously about it. But even if that hadn't occurred, playing pro ball likely would have meant extended separation from his wife and children. He never forgot growing up with a father whom he rarely saw because of his dad's need to work two jobs. King didn't want his kids to know him as a voice carried through long-distance telephone lines.

With the death of Jesse Mae King from a stroke in January 1961, Leon soon after returned to school to complete his studies as a way to honor a mother who had so emphasized the value of education. He played football again—sort of, on a team put together by his black fraternity. The ink was barely dry on King's North Texas diploma in August 1962, when he was hired by the Dallas Independent School District, in the junior high program at his old school in south Dallas, Lincoln. Four of the five King siblings built careers in education, beginning with Vivian. After her husband, Neaul Haynes, was brought back from west Texas to Dallas by his father, Vivian was hired in 1960 to teach the fifth grade in the northern suburb of Plano at Fred Douglass School, which accommodated all of the town's black students from elementary grades through high school. The Plano school district's desegregation was done in phases over a five-year period during the 1960s, with Vivian becoming one of three initial black faculty members placed at Meadows Elementary School in 1968. Any fears that she might have had for taking on that assignment were quickly dispelled. "I was treated royally," she says. She taught in Plano for twenty years.

At Lincoln in the autumn of 1962, Leon King taught science and served as a coach for junior high athletics, including the high school's freshman squads. The most notable athlete to come through Lincoln's freshman team during that time was football player Duane Thomas, the free-spirited running back who briefly starred for the Dallas Cowboys on the club's first two Super Bowl qualifiers, but who made more headlines for refusing to talk to reporters—and sometimes teammates and coaches—than for his on-field exploits. Thomas was a freshman during King's first coaching year, 1962-'63, and wanted to confine his athletic participation to track. Older brother Sonny Thomas was a standout hurdler and wanted Duane to also play football. Sonny proposed that he would join the football team if Duane would, too, so that they could increase their time together.

Duane Thomas made the squad as a two-way end and became a Dallas Texans fan, watching the achievements of Haynes at the Cotton Bowl only a few blocks from his home. He scored the touchdown that won the city freshman championship in the game's closing seconds on a long pass play that he said years later was actually named "Far as You Can." Thomas moved to fullback as a senior and led Lincoln to an 8-2 record and the city title; he ran for a staggering 232 yards on twenty-seven carries in a 14-13 Thanksgiving Day victory over Booker T. Washington that some people in south Dallas might still be talking about.

··········

Vernon Cole, in addition to being drafted by the Texans before the 1960 season, was pursued by the Canadian Football League team that was about to seek its third consecutive Grey Cup league title, the Winnipeg Blue Bombers. The Bombers were coached by the stoic Bud Grant, who'd also unsuccessfully tried to woo Abner Haynes north of the border. While part of Cole probably wanted to play only an hour or so from Denton and remain teamed with Haynes, Cole's wife, Carolyn, says her husband was hungry for a change of scenery. "I think he was ready to leave Texas," she says, "wanted to go somewhere else." Cole agreed to sign with Winnipeg, and did, before Lamar Hunt offered him a Texans contract at a year's salary worth $8,500.

Winnipeg was replacing its starting quarterback and turned to backup Kenny Ploen, a two-year Bombers veteran who had led Iowa to a 1957 Rose Bowl victory and primarily played safety as a pro. Ploen led the 1960 Blue Bombers to a league-best record of 10-4, and into the best-of-three Western Conference playoffs against second-place Edmonton. The Canadian pro season starts in August in an attempt to at least minimize the effect of frigid weather late in the season and into the playoffs. The Bombers played their final regular-season game on October 24 and, thanks to a first-round playoff bye for winning their conference, had a break for two and a half weeks before playing their first post-season game. That break was just when Carolyn was expecting the couple's first child.

As Cole and the rest of the Bombers prepared for their playoff series, Carolyn and he agreed that she would return to Denton to have the baby. Carolyn settled in at their house on Center Street and was doted on by Bill Carrico and wife Deanna. Carolyn would often spend the night at the Carrico house and, during the middle of one of those nights, realized it was . . . time! She needed to stop by her house to pick up a suitcase before going to the hospital. As the Carrico car with the three of them aboard approached the Coles' home, it came to a sputtering stop. Bill looked at Deanna: "We're out of gas!" Deanna replied: "We're out of gas!" Carolyn calmly suggested they wake some of the Coles' neighbors and ask them to complete the trip.

They indeed made it to the hospital in time to welcome little Kyle Cole into the world.

The Bombers won the series opener against Edmonton, 22-16, on the road, but Ploen suffered a broken bone in his passing hand during the third quarter. For the balance of the game, Cole went under center for Ploen, who stayed in and moved to safety. That was the lineup for Game 2 two days later (you read that correctly) at Winnipeg. Cole and the Blue Bombers' offense were stifled, the visiting Eskimos evening the series with a 10-5 win. The series finale was played five days later, also in Winnipeg, with Ploen resuming signal calling duties and Cole returning to the bench. Edmonton scored a stunning 4-2 upset to bring an abrupt close to Winnipeg's season. Cole returned to Texas and finally introduced himself to his new son.

Though Cole hadn't seen as much playing time as he wished that season, Carolyn and he enjoyed their experience and planned to return to the Manitoba city if possible after Cole completed a military obligation. Carolyn's scrapbook from her husband's playing career contains letters that they received from Bombers fans welcoming them to Winnipeg. Cole was assigned to the air force base in Smyrna, Tennessee, just south of Nashville. That's where daughter Karen was born, following a fully-fueled trip to the hospital. The Coles indeed returned to Winnipeg, where Ploen had led the Blue Bombers to Grey Cup championships in 1961 and '62. Cole was again the backup in 1963, when Winnipeg plummeted to fourth place in the five-team conference. He was traded after the season to Montreal, and played only one season there for "Jungle Jim" Trimble, whose coaching career in Canada and the NFL didn't match the legacy of helping to invent the single-support goalpost. The Coles had not yet left Quebec before they said *bonjour* to a third child, Jeff.

Cole was done playing football after Montreal, returning to North Texas to get his master's degree. He was soon hired as an assistant football coach and varsity baseball coach by Gene Bahnsen, older brother of the Eagles' Ken Bahnsen, at Wharton Junior College near Houston. The Coles also served as the dorm parents in the only men's dorm, where the majority of students were commuters, while they and their three young children occupied cozy quarters on the ground floor. At least there were some familiar babysitters conveniently living close by: older brother Glen Cole lived in Houston with his family. But during that first football season, one of the Wharton players suffered a broken neck and was left a quadriplegic. "It just devastated Vernon," Carolyn says. "That soured Vernon on football. He never wanted to coach it again."

Fortunately for Cole, he was soon given the opportunity to deal with college athletics that had nothing to do with football. Wharton vice-president Wilbur Ball was hired to start a new community college in Waco in 1966 and brought Cole along as the first athletic director of McLennan Community College. Cole made the athletic teams' colors orange and black, the same as Pilot Point High. In establishing the new school's health and physical education department, he placed the emphasis on "lifetime" sports, and even taught golf and archery himself. Carolyn says he exhibited an artistic side, such as playing the piano by ear, that he believed was squelched in his early years in an environment that emphasized becoming an athlete. "He was perceptive about a lot of things," she says. She notes the occasion soon after they settled in Waco when he told her, "I just feel like Charlie is here today" . . . only to discover that Charlie Cole was driving from Denton to Austin on business that very day, and was indeed passing through Waco about that time. Cole's hunches or premonitions manifested themselves in other ways. "When we first married," Carolyn recalls, "Vernon told me he thought he would die young, and he would die of a brain tumor."

CHAPTER 23

"The Movement"

As THE NUMBER OF BLACK students on the North Texas campus grew during the early 1960s, the issue of their treatment from businesses in Denton became a greater irritant to them. Some students who were frustrated by the lack of acknowledgment and debate over integration and other social issues in the *Campus Chat* student newspaper distributed alternative newsletters called "Antithesis" and "Synthesis" that were mimeographed and dropped off at various campus locations. A racially mixed group of students began to meet regularly with a handful of faculty members, to test the tolerance of selected establishments in an effort to evoke change in Denton's commercial community. The small but fervid assemblage began to refer to itself as "The Movement."

Art Perkins was a member of "The Movement." So was one of his best friends at North Texas, apart from football teammates–a political science student from California named Bert Christian. Born in east Texas, Christian moved with his family to California's Bay Area, but returned with his mother to Texas—Longview, specifically—after his parents separated. Christian graduated from Longview's black high school in 1959, and was accepted to North Texas. He was initially approved for on-campus housing, then received another letter from the housing office asking him to submit a photo of himself. He did so, and was soon informed there was no housing available.

The students associated with "The Movement" met primarily with three faculty members. Jesse Ritter taught creative writing in the English department, having joined the North Texas faculty in 1960. A Navy veteran, Ritter earned his bachelor's degree from Kansas State, a master's degree from Arkansas, and arrived at North Texas after teaching at Eastern Washington. He was president of the Denton County Literacy Council and superintendent of the Unitarian Sunday School. George "Bill" Linden joined the North Texas faculty as a self-professed whiz kid at twenty-six for his first philosophy teaching job, following graduation from the University of Illinois. Pierre Baratelli was a French teacher, a native New Yorker also in his first teaching job after graduating from the University of Colorado.

One or more members of the faculty trio would meet with the students, discuss racial politics, and organize excursions to businesses close to campus in order to test the proprietors' reactions to racially mixed groups seeking service. Baratelli would pile as many students as he could into his Studebaker Lark station wagon for various drop-offs and pickups. Perkins recalls, "We'd have ten whites go in. Then Bert and I would go in. The others would say, 'Hey, Bert! Art! C'mon on and sit down! What do you want?' But we wouldn't get served, and everybody would walk out. Then we'd do the same thing at another place." The faculty members would occasionally participate; Baratelli remembers a black companion having his order taken, but being told to sit in an area away from the white patrons. Christian recalls the most intolerant and unambiguous reception that he received at a small establishment: "A white friend went in, and I followed him in. We ordered. The owner turned away from us and then pulled out a .45 and ordered us out of the place."

The *Campus Chat* published an editorial questioning the goals of "Movement" members, proposing that they "may be losing sight of the best interests of North Texas and the very people they are trying to help." Christian was among three students who, referring to themselves as "spokesmen for the integration movement," responded with a letter to the editor that ran in late November 1961: "We feel that the remedying of any injustices which exist in our campus community is definitely in the best interest of North Texas. ... Maybe this awareness and willingness to act is an indication of this group's ability to accept the responsibility of a democratic nation and one of the first concrete signs of our emergence as a university."

Only weeks after Christian helped defend "The Movement" in print, the group turned its attention to one of the more popular Denton institutions among North Texas students, the Campus Theater, located on the town square. Blacks were required to sit in the balcony, referred to as "nigger heaven," as Baratelli recalls. On Thursday night, December 7, 1961, a white student asked to buy a group of tickets in the main seating area for him and his friends, motioning behind him to the racially mixed group. The ticket seller said that couldn't be done; the blacks would have to buy tickets to sit upstairs. The group left the ticket window peacefully ... and got back in line to go through the exercise again. "The Movement" returned to the Campus Theater for the same drill that Friday, Monday, and Tuesday with the same results. By Wednesday night, December 13, they altered their strategy. About forty white and black students stood outside the theater clapping, chanting, singing, and passing out small cards—about the size of a movie ticket—that read I BELIEVE IN RACIAL EQUALITY. Present across the street was an unsympathetic gathering of about thirty people who jeered their disapproval when not doing singing of their own ("Dixie"). One young man among the counter group asked a reporter from the *Dallas Times Herald*, "What's wrong with being a segregationist?" As Denton police chief I.E. Anderson and city manager Homer Bly watched from a nearby squad car, the discordant expressions of viewpoints never boiled over into violence.

The *Denton Record-Chronicle* had followed the theater integration attempts from the beginning, but didn't report on them until after the area's major dailies detailed the events of December 13. The following afternoon's *Record-Chronicle* included a news story about the protest, and an editorial explaining that the newspaper feared accounting for each of the attempts to desegregate the theater's main seating area could "incite mob action." With the region's attention drawn to Denton and North Texas in a distasteful manner, school president J.C. Matthews took action; Ritter, Linden, and Baratelli were no longer welcome among the North Texas faculty.

Ritter was told by department chairman Ernest Clifton—the two were close friends, even fishing together for a couple of days in Arkansas a few months earlier—that his contract wouldn't be renewed after it expired the following June, and he would be fired immediately if he participated in further desegregation activities. In a *Morning News* story, Matthews said there was more to Ritter's impending departure than his involvement with "The Movement," citing irresponsibility and non-cooperation over a period of a year and a half.

Linden says Matthews's displeasure with him extended beyond his involvement in civil rights activities into what he was teaching, and what efforts he supported on campus. One such endeavor was a publication named *Coexistence Cafe*, named after the Coexistence Coffee Shop in San Francisco. "The president thought it was communist because it had 'coexistence' in the title," Linden says. (One of the publication's co-authors was a transfer from Rice named Larry McMurtry; the famed Western novelist earned an English degree from North Texas in May 1958.) Linden left at the end of the 1961-'62 school year and became chairman of the philosophy department at Southern Illinois's campus at Edwardsville. He wrote in *The Texas Observer* in 1964 about "the sad story" of what he considered North Texas's intellectual demise beginning in 1957, depreciated by a general stifling of creativity and expression. That, Linden wrote, included the administration's immediate retribution against faculty who were involved in the demonstrations at the downtown theater: "Missing was that momentary hesitation which is the mark of rationality."

Baratelli recalls that the chairman of the foreign language department, Philip Smyth, successfully argued to keep him on staff, but urged him not to talk to the growing group of inquisitive reporters. Baratelli says he was subsequently summoned to the president's office. "He said, 'Wouldn't it be nice if you'd spoken to me about this before?' I said, 'Sir, I can't believe that you didn't know what was going on. It was in the student paper.' He just sort of looked at me. 'If this ever comes up again, I hope that you will come and see me first.' He never really told me not to be involved with the group."

When Matthews spoke at the commencement ceremony five weeks later, after the school officially became North Texas State University in 1961, his remarks were much longer than usual and were directed more at the university and its faculty than toward the eager grads. He emphasized the university's commitment to mold students into better citizens upon their departure from campus. "Every time a student majors in social activities or becomes a disciplinary problem to the university or to the community, North Texas State University is the less for it." He stated that, in the future, "the staff will be selected with greater care, expected to do better work, and set better examples by their own manner of living." Those who didn't meet the school's standards would be "a greater liability than the university has any obligation to carry." Baratelli, less comfortable in an environment that he never found terribly comfortable from the start, left North Texas after the next school year.

CHAPTER 24

"Someone just said, 'We're going for two'"

BEFORE NORTH TEXAS'S 1966 FOOTBALL season began, sixty-seven-year-old Odus Mitchell revealed that the season ahead would be his final one as a football coach. He would spend twenty-one years leading the Eagles following twenty-one years as a high school coach—all forty-two seasons as a head coach. He went out on top, winning the school's first Missouri Valley Conference championship since the standout 1959 Sun Bowl squad. Under Mitchell, a man who had played in the first football game that he ever saw, North Texas produced ten conference winners in three leagues and played in three bowl games.

In 1966, no one seemed particularly interested in how many blacks were on the Eagles' football team. There was keen interest in their play, in particular that of a sophomore defensive tackle named Joe Greene, who'd graduated from the black high school in the small central Texas town of Temple. Greene was well on his way to earning the first of three All-MVC selections. The 1966 team was informally called the Mean Green, but the connection to the Eagles' defensive star was merely coincidental. The label was concocted by Sid Graham, the wife of school sports publicist Fred Graham, simply playing off the school's primary color. North Texas would have been known as the Mean Green had its best player been named Joe Browne, but Greene himself landed a nickname that would stick with him for the rest of his career.

Mitchell's swan song took place on November 19, North Texas's homecoming game against Chattanooga. The Mean Green had already closed their Missouri Valley schedule with a record of 3-1, and clinched at least a second-place finish. First-place Tulsa was 2-0 with two league games still to play, at Louisville that same afternoon and at home the following Thursday (Thanksgiving) against lightly-regarded Wichita State. Mitchell predictably insisted he would approach the game against the Moccasins no differently than any other, going back to that maiden 47-0 pasting at Texas A&M to open the 1946 season, or maybe back to his first game at Post High School out in west Texas in 1925. "My only thoughts are to win the game," he told reporters early that week. "I'm not letting myself think about it. It kind of leaves a little pain to realize this is the last one."

With a few months to prepare for Mitchell's farewell, the school contacted as many of his former North Texas players as possible and invited them to attend that final game. Many were gladly able to answer the call, others prevented by circumstances; Abner Haynes, for one, was preparing to play in a Denver Broncos game the following day. Of the regrets that were relayed either in person or in writing, none approached the expression that was sent to Denton from the other side of the globe, specifically from a Marine based in Vietnam located about sixty miles southeast of Da Nang down the coast.

George Herring, lineman from the memorable freshman team in 1956 and the '59 Sun Bowl bunch, was a captain in the Marines, commanding a company at a base in Chu Lai. He'd hoped to continue his football career after North Texas and was drafted by the Houston Oilers. He signed a contract for $6,000, but was placed on waivers the week of the team's first pre-season game. Herring turned his attention to the military, a natural alternative for the former ROTC student. He tried to follow older brother Bill Tom into the Air Force, but couldn't pass the pilot's test because of an issue related to his eyesight. Herring signed on with the Marines, "Because he wanted to be part of an elite unit," says Herring's sister, Sally Venator. (Days later, his Army draft board came looking for him.)

George Kuhl was a twenty-year-old lance corporal when Herring took company command. Kuhl drove his new boss out from battalion headquarters through dangerous territory to meet his men for the first time. A few miles into their drive, Kuhl was stunned when Herring told him to pull over: "You know where the hell we are?" Herring replied, "Well, I'm from Texas, and I've got a big boot. I want to talk out here where nobody can hear us." With .45s as their only protection from attack, Herring tapped Kuhl for information that would allow him to better understand his new charges. Says Kuhl: "He was the best person that I had when I was in the Marine Corps. He just knew how to deal with people and treat 'em. He didn't have to say anything twice."

In November 1966, Herring's company was defending a position known as "Old French Fort Hill." Wedged into a foxhole that didn't quite fit the frame of a college lineman, Herring was writing a letter to Mitchell to make sure his old coach knew that he dearly wanted to attend his final game and recognized how much his leadership had meant to him. "Received news that this is to be your last year of active coaching and was sorry to hear the announcement," Herring wrote.

I understand this homecoming all of your ex-athletes are trying to make this game in your honor. If it were any way possible, I would attend the ball game, just to let you know how much I think of you and what you contributed to making me a man. We've been in the field for 45 days and casualties have been pretty bad. In this constant rain and terrible terrain, leadership is sometimes critical. My company's spirits always remain high and attain our mission of destroying the enemy. I was taught the traits of leadership by the finest man and leader of men that I have ever known, you Coach Mitchell. This is a nasty, dirty war and seeing some of my young 18 and 19 year old Marines wounded and killed takes something out of me. But knowing that people like yourself, Mrs. Mitchell and [daughter] Margaret are at home make it worthwhile. ... I only wish I could express to you what an honor it was and still is to have been one of your boys. I know my folks thank you and all you did for them. I only hope I can have a small fraction of your type influence on my men. A fraction would help them all their lives.

At that point in Herring's writing his company took on hostile fire. According to Bill Tom Herring, George had eschewed taking a less dangerous position in his company's three-pronged alignment in one of the points in the base of the triangle formation, and instead stationed himself at the apex. A grenade exploded in front of Herring, and shrapnel struck him in multiple places, including his right eye. When the fighting died down, he was rushed to a military hospital for emergency surgery, and was then sent home to the United States. But a fellow Marine from Houston named T.J. Reese, who was right beside him in the foxhole, not only discovered the letter—stained with Herring's blood—but took the time to finish it and mail it to Denton.

"I just flew from Chu-lai to Da Nang here with George," Reese wrote. "He has lost his right eye. But he has muscular control of it. Grenade. I have his blood all over me, but he will be all right and he still has one good eye. George was best man at my wedding. Charlene, my wife's matron of honor and my oldest daughter's godmother. We played football together at Quantico and were in the 8th Marines together. We are very close. I love George like a brother. I was captain at Trinity College (Hartford) and All-ECAC for coach Dan Jessee. I know what respect for a football coach is, what love of the game is. Hope to meet you some day. Try to see George." Soon after Herring's departure from Vietnam, his company honored him with an informal reclassification of the local landscape. With scant resources available, they renamed "Old French Fort Hill" by grabbing an old pillow case and wrote the words HERRING HILL on it to serve as their new battle flag.

The *Denton Record-Chronicle* learned of the letter and asked Mitchell about it shortly before the Chattanooga game. If the old coach was succeeding in controlling his emotions in regard to his upcoming vocational finale, he couldn't conceal how Herring's communiqué made its way directly to his heart. "I read the letter with my chest out," he said. "Then I got down to where his friend wrote that he was hurt, and I was just shocked. At North Texas, George was the ideal guy. He was one of the most popular players and respected players among teammates whom I ever coached."

The homecoming game played out just as any North Texas fan, any Odus Mitchell fan, or even Odus Mitchell could have wanted, even before the opening kickoff. On a 60-degree mid-November afternoon, the North Texas band spelled out "MITCH" at the center of the field, which sent the guest of honor into a rare display of tears. The Eagles never trailed, took control early in the second half, and there was then little doubt that North Texas would claim Chattanooga as Mitchell's 122nd collegiate victory and the 287th of his overall head coaching career. Before the third quarter ended, the Fouts Field crowd was informed over the public address system that Tulsa had lost to Louisville, clinching at least a first-place tie for North Texas. The Mean Green settled for that when Tulsa beat Wichita State a week later.

The final Eagles touchdown of the afternoon extended the home team's lead to 40-0 before kicker John Love, who also caught the touchdown pass, trotted out for the PAT conversion. But skullduggery was afoot on the home sideline among some of the players. At least one of them recognized that North Texas was two points shy of scoring a point for every one of Mitchell's years as a football coach. So, they would instead go for two points. The visitors would hopefully understand the significance of North Texas's aberrant action and not be insulted. Of course, there was no way the Mocs wouldn't be surprised, which was the case when sophomore holder Ted Pospisil fielded the snap, pulled up out of his kneeled stance and darted around right end toward the end zone. Pospisil was forced to outrun one determined Chattanooga defender in hot pursuit and evade another at the goal line. The sentimental mission was a success, and North Texas's lead was 42-0. Only those Eagles can say whether Chattanooga's subsequent touchdown that closed the scoring was allowed as some sort of recompense. Nevertheless, the "42" on the scoreboard next to North Texas was all that mattered to the gleeful Eagles.

For the special occasion of Mitchell's final victory, a photographer from the *Campus Chat* was allowed into the Eagles' locker room at halftime, and *Chat* writer Joe Lemming was ushered in after the game before Mitchell addressed his players for the final time. "You know how I feel about you boys," he said. "You're the greatest bunch of guys I've ever been with." With a full complement of reporters later in attendance, Mitchell continued: "I can hardly believe it. The weather was perfect, Louisville beat Tulsa, and we scored 42 points. I don't think I deserve all the nice things that have happened to me this year, but I'm enjoying them like I do." Interrogation of various North Texas players after the game failed to ascertain the identity of the party who hatched the plan for the two-point escapade. Junior end James Russell, pressed for an answer, managed only to say, "Someone just said, 'We're going for two.'" (Pospisil, contacted for this book, says the two-point play was his idea.)

Mitchell's career was technically extended by one more game, his first as an assistant coach, when he was invited to work the East-West All-America Game in Atlanta that summer and join Nebraska's Bob Devaney and USC's John McKay on the West side. He was honored by North Texas with a banquet in March 1967 at Marquis Hall attended by an estimated 150 guests. One of the six former Mitchell players who spoke as part of the festivities was Herring. After undergoing optical surgery, he was fitted with an array of three replacement eyeballs to fit different occasions. One matched his good eye's pupil size during the day, one matched his good eye at night, and a third would never be confused with his good eye day or night; it featured the Marine Corps logo. Since the nerves to the eye socket remained intact, he could move the prosthetic eyeball in tandem with his real eye; at parties, he would entertain guests by asking them to identify which eye was real. It wasn't recorded which replacement that Herring sported the night of Mitchell's banquet, but he repeated many of the praises that he'd piled upon his coach in the famed, blood-stained letter, and also accurately pointed out that Mitchell apparently didn't adequately teach him to keep his head down.

On Memorial Day 1967, Herring was placed on the Marines' permanent disability list, discharging him from the service, at a ceremony in the downtown Dallas recruiting office. Major P.H. Begnaud read the orders, presented him with a certificate identifying him as an honorary Marine recruiter for the Southwest, and closed by saying, "I can't say congratulations because I know you didn't want it this way." Herring said how proud he was of his company in Vietnam, and that he'd begin job hunting for a new way of supporting wife Charlene and young daughter Kristin. "I may be hungry in a couple of weeks," he said.

Herring tried being a Marine recruiter for about a year, but it just wasn't the same as combat. That became obvious to relatives during his first Christmas stateside following his discharge from active duty. During a holiday visit in Houston, it seemed to others that he constantly looked at his watch and mentioned what time it was in Vietnam and what his men were likely doing. Herring was hired by Collins Radio in Richardson, a Dallas suburb that began attracting tech companies like Collins in the early 1950s, and moved his family there from Dallas. He became a supervisor in the cost department, and was about to start work as a project manager in the fall of 1969 when he was killed in an automobile accident. He was honored at North Texas's homecoming game that season and was buried in Fort Worth, where his tombstone reads: HE LOVED AND WAS LOVED IN RETURN. A MARINE'S MARINE.

CHAPTER 25

"My spirit is rejoicing"

THE TIME DEMANDS OF COACHING on top of teaching proved to be one reason why Leon King got out of coaching at the same time that his academic career turned toward administration. He resigned from Lincoln during the middle of the 1969-'70 academic year, and became an administrative intern at Dallas's Oliver Wendell Holmes Junior High. King spent the better part of the next twenty-five years as a principal at various Dallas school district campuses, including a four-year stint at Madison High School in the late 1970s. His initiatives there included starting the Principal's Club, with students helping faculty and staff perform various tasks and generally promoting an attitude of service to others. King's efforts to further bond with the Madison student body included a stint as an honorary head cheerleader (including playing the bass drum at a pep rally before the Trojans football team played— gulp—Lincoln), and performing in the faculty's interpretation of the then-popular daytime TV offering, *The Gong Show*. The adults staged a "womanless wedding." King was the bride, wearing a dress that stopped short of the knee.

King left Madison in 1980 to take over a succession of DISD middle schools. He was visited one day by Pat McLeod, a long-time North Texas faculty member who had taught King in an industrial arts class.

McLeod years later recalled the visit, which began with King's secretary stammering a bit when McLeod asked if the principal was in. McLeod heard a series of loud whacking sounds coming from King's office. "I know where he is," McLeod told her. He opened the door and was facing the principal's back as a handful of boys were taking some hard lessons to their backsides. McLeod, in a low, exaggerated voice, called out to his former student, "Mr. King!" The principal wheeled around and was relieved to see his audience wasn't a father of one of the paddled. "We're improving communication," King calmly explained.

The passing of time has often skewed the events at North Texas in the late 1950s. Two black players bravely showed up in autumn '56 to try out for the football team. Because only one of them was still on the team in 1959 when the Eagles reached the Associated Press Top 20 and played in a bowl game, Abner Haynes has often been singularly recognized for a milestone in state athletic integration. King said he wrestled with that for years. Then, one evening in the mid-1970s, his brother James, a teacher and coach at Dallas's Pinkston High, related a conversation he'd had that afternoon with a college athletic recruiter who visited the school. The recruiter, upon learning that James was Leon's brother, noted that Leon had been the first of the black athletes who enrolled at North Texas in the late '50s to earn his bachelor's degree. From that point on, Leon began viewing his time at North Texas from a new perspective.

....

Seven years after the courts ruled that Joe Atkins could attend North Texas as an undergraduate, he finally set foot on campus as an NT student. Atkins graduated from Texas Western in 1959 and spent the better part of the next three years in the army. He returned to Dallas in March 1962 following his discharge, and discovered that the city provided vocational opportunities for young black men even if the overall racial climate was considered far from welcoming.

While working nights in the supply division of Collins Radio (the same company that Herring would later work for), Atkins enrolled at

North Texas and earned a teaching certificate. He began a teaching career in Dallas at Madison High School, teaching English and journalism, and pursued a master's degree in education from North Texas. Atkins says he was never tempted to drop his own name on campus to any black students, making them aware that it was he and his family that made is possible for blacks to study there as undergrads. He says one of his journalism professors explained to the class some of the details of the school opening its doors to blacks; if the professor had realized that it was *the* Joe Atkins who was sitting in the room, he never mentioned it.

Atkins taught in Dallas schools for almost a decade, at Madison and later at North Dallas High (where Chauncey King was on staff). He then moved into a different area of education and worked for a teachers association until 1997, when he began to work part-time in real estate. Atkins died of heart failure at the age of seventy-nine.

· · · · · · · · · ·

Sammy Stanger tried pro football with the Edmonton Eskimos in 1960, despite being drafted by the Los Angeles Rams. A bizarre injury ended his attempt to make the roster; while some of the players were passing the time playing touch football, someone stepped on Stanger's face and nearly knocked an eye out. He returned to Texas, hitching that ride in Amarillo from Bob Way, and took up coaching and teaching. He still works in education today in the small east Texas town of Overton, despite having officially retired in 2003 following twenty-three years as the high school principal there.

One of his first stops was Farmersville, located in eastern Collin County, hometown of World War II hero Audie Murphy. One of Stanger's Fightin' Farmers was a talented halfback, a two-time all-district selection, who was also in the Christmas play, a baccalaureate usher, and sports editor of the school newspaper as a senior. Charles Watson moved on to North Texas, dropped out during his junior year, and soon succumbed to the lure of California. It was there that he was nicknamed for his home state. In August 1969,

"Tex" Watson and others who'd become fanatical followers of Charles Manson committed seven grisly murders at Manson's command over the course of two nights. Watson was found guilty in 1971 and has been imprisoned ever since.

....

Bill Carrico likewise took a stab at pro football in 1960 with the Eskimos. He was actually eligible to go pro in 1959 since his original graduating class was leaving school that year, but he passed on that opportunity after the Pittsburgh Steelers drafted him late that year in order to be able to play his final season with the Eagles. Carrico likewise left Edmonton early, the circumstance more bizarre than Sammy Stanger's touch-football injury. Carrico suffered burns on his legs from the fertilizer that was used on the field, once it combined with snow and sleet.

Carrico returned to North Texas, earned his degree, and also built a career in education and coaching, almost exclusively in his hometown of Denton. He was an assistant football coach at Denton High in 1968 when the school first accepted black students with the shuttering of Fred Moore High. He became the school district's athletic director in 1976 and held that position until his retirement in 1997. Carrico died in February 2016 at the age of seventy-nine. Before his death, the Denton school district decided to name the athletic complex at new Braswell High, scheduled to open in August 2016, for him.

....

When the undefeated Texas Longhorns faced the undefeated Arkansas Razorbacks on the first Saturday of December 1969 in the so-called Game of the Century, Darrell Brown was still on campus in Fayetteville. He was a first-year law student, serving as a resident advisor in Razorback Hall, living there with his wife. Brown also was a member of "BAD," Black Americans for Democracy, a group that fought racial prejudice on campus. They wanted more black faculty members, increased financial aid for black students, a section of the new student union devoted to black culture, and they had one request directed toward the school's marching band: stop playing "Dixie" in connection with the football team. Whenever the team appeared at a pep rally, took the field or reached the end zone, the band played "Dixie," and Razorback faithful responded with anticipated Pavlovian glee.

The fandom was particularly gleeful during the '69 season that the Razorbacks often reached the end zone, spending the entire season ranked in the top four, and sitting at No. 2 when No. 1 Texas came to town. So many touchdowns, so much "Dixie." The group made its feelings about the song known throughout that fall with no response. "BAD" finally took action before the pep rally that preceded the penultimate home game on November 27 against Texas Tech. "BAD" members, including Brown, sat in the band's seats and also blocked the band's path to those seats. They said they would vacate the seats if assured "Dixie" wouldn't be played; the pep rally was abruptly moved to another location.

ABC's national telecast of the Texas-Arkansas game would provide a unique forum for a protest, not to mention that the sold-out gathering at Razorback Stadium would include the nation's "No. 1 Fan," President Richard Nixon. Anticipation of the game built that week, and so did debate over the song. The student senate voted to recommend that "Dixie" no longer be performed as a part of any university function (outside the meeting, some students waved Confederate flags). A faculty committee curiously proposed to allow "Dixie" to be played during the first half of the game.

Two days before kickoff, with rumors of a game-day protest in the air, the band director announced that the song would no longer be played. But Brown and other members of the protest group planned to meet the night before the game to discuss a plan to rush the field if the band played "Dixie" despite the director's promise. When the band didn't play "Dixie" at the biggest pep rally of the season that same night, an enterprising student brought a record player and provided a surrogate version. Brown didn't make it to the meeting or to the game the next day. While jogging from his dorm to the Friday night planning meeting, he was shot in the left leg. Grazed just above his knee, he was attended to at a local hospital and sent home.

Brown went on to a career in law, practicing in his home state. He was part of the legal team that defended Gov. Jim Guy Tucker, plus James and Susan McDougal, in the Whitewater trial during the mid-1990s. Brown was among those who questioned President Bill Clinton for a videotaped testimony during the trial. His daughter, Dee Dee Brown-Campbell, became an All-American track athlete at Arkansas. During halftime of an Arkansas home football game in 2011, Brown was recognized for his role in integrating the school's football program and presented with both a plaque and a Razorbacks No. 1 jersey. As Brown watched the second half from the stands, people came up to him, some taking pictures with him, some apologizing, some crying.

....

Vernon Cole was an avid jogger who didn't drink or smoke and watched what he ate when, in 1970, he was startled by numbness and tingling in one of his legs. The Coles were shocked when the diagnosis was cerebral multiple sclerosis. They began to prepare for the disease to become progressively worse over an extended period of time by having Carolyn enroll at a nursing school to eventually take over providing the family income when he could no longer work at McLennan Community College. But Cole's condition worsened more quickly than expected and led to an amended diagnosis: a brain tumor.

Carolyn withdrew from nursing school, needing to be home with their three children since her husband would be hospitalized for extended periods. North Texas football players and staffers from the late 1950s and '60s began a steady pilgrimage to Cole's bedside as he went in and out of hospitals in Waco. G.A. Moore was one of the few visitors who qualified as a teammate at both Pilot Point High and North Texas. "He was the first guy I ever told I loved him," Moore remembers. "When we were growing up, we never did that." Fred McCain wanted to visit

Cole, but couldn't bring himself to make the trip. He even struggled simply to phone him. In his UNT oral history interview, McCain said he would tell his wife that he'd call and try not to break down again: "I'd get me a drink or two and try to get fortified." But Cole's deteriorating state was conveyed to McCain over the long-distance line. "I'd just come unglued. … I'd just bawl and apologize. I wanted to talk to him every day but, hell, I couldn't."

Vernon Cole died at the age of thirty-four in a Waco hospital on June 23, 1972. Months of knowing the day would come still couldn't prepare Carolyn for the reality of it. She didn't attend the visitation at the Connally-Compton Funeral Home, staying home with her children who'd also paid the toll of the preceding months, as their mother stayed at her husband's side during his hospitalizations. The funeral was held the day after Cole's death, a Saturday, at Waco's Lake Shore Baptist Church, and Cole was laid to rest in the family plot near Pilot Point. Among the many former North Texas players who attended the funeral was Abner Haynes, saying one last goodbye to a teammate who'd walked over to introduce himself to Haynes, and Leon King before that first practice in September 1956. Carolyn recalls of Haynes, "He just kind of stood in the aisle and stared at the casket."

· · · · · · · · · ·

On September 9, 1980, John Howard Griffin died in a Fort Worth hospital at the age of sixty, of complications caused by diabetes. Maybe unavoidably, rumors spread that the real cause of death was a byproduct of the dye treatments that he underwent decades earlier in preparation for the series of articles he would then write about what it was like to be treated like a black.

· · · · · · · · · ·

John Westbrook graduated from Baylor in four years, mostly glad to put the experience behind him. Much of his post-graduate life was spent in spiritual vocations; he did spend one year back in college athletics, working for John Bridgers, then the athletic director at Florida

State, as an academic advisor. Living back in Texas in 1977, he made a surprising turn into politics, running in the Democratic primary for lieutenant governor against incumbent Bill Hobby while serving as pastor at True Vine Baptist Church in Tyler. Westbrook surprised many by finishing second in the field of four candidates.

By the early 1980s, Westbrook had become pastor of Antioch Baptist Church in Houston; he was almost 100 pounds heavier than his playing weight at Baylor and in poor health. He collapsed on the evening of Saturday, December 10, 1983, and died that night at the age of thirty-five from blood clots in his lungs. His funeral service had to be moved from Antioch to a sanctuary that would accommodate a significantly greater number of mourners than Westbrook's church. Among those who spoke at the service was the governor of Texas, Mark White.

....

Odus Mitchell was inducted into the Texas Sports Hall of Fame in June 1986, the ceremony held in Dallas's Fair Park complex, amid a class that included boxing champion George Foreman, football great Forrest Gregg, and basketball star Elvin Hayes. The only previous state Hall of Famer tied to North Texas football was Joe Greene, inducted a year earlier, five years after retiring from the pro game with four Super Bowl championship rings. On the eve of the honor, Mitchell was practically apologetic for becoming a coach. "After I got out of school," he told the *Denton Record-Chronicle*, "I didn't know there was anything else to do." Mitchell died a little more than three years later on July 5, 1989, nine days after celebrating his ninetieth birthday, of complications following a stroke. He was fittingly hailed not only for raising the profile of North Texas football, but also for overseeing the entrance of Leon King and Abner Haynes into the football program with no fanfare and apparent minimal discord.

....

Irma Sephas died on October 30, 1991, in a Fort Worth hospital, identified simply as a public accountant in the obituary published in the

Fort Worth Star-Telegram four days after her death. It noted that she had attended Huston-Tillotson College and North Texas, but didn't mention her being the latter's first black undergraduate student. Papers the size of the *Star-Telegram* will typically publish a feature obituary for a well-known person if space permits; the feature obit in that day's *Star-Telegram* was for Irwin Allen, the Hollywood producer who became famous for making disaster movies.

....

Burlyce Sherrell Logan returned to Denton in the early 1990s, nearly four decades after she left North Texas in relative resignation and disgust following two years of mistreatment on campus. She and her husband had moved out west, added to their family with two more children, then got divorced; each remarried, each "re-divorced," reconciled at a family reunion, remarried each other, and eventually returned to Denton. At age sixty-seven she re-enrolled at UNT, having to start from square one academically, and pursued a degree in applied arts and sciences. In the English class that she failed during the late 1950s, the teacher having said at the time that it was because she misspelled a word, she now received a B.

....

J.C. Matthews died on November 9, 1996, twenty-eight years after vacating the president's office at North Texas. "If you are going to build a great university," he once said, "finding the right place would be important. But if you truly sought to build a great one, you would first seek skill in the fine art of developing great men." During Matthews's tenure as school president from 1951 to 1968, North Texas's enrollment increased from 4,318 to almost 15,000, and its budget grew from $4 million to $18 million.

....

Abner Haynes's No. 28 jersey number at North Texas was retired during the 1998 season, joining those of Richard Gill's No. 55 (retired soon after he died of a blood clot before his senior season), and Joe Greene's No. 75. Frank Luksa, writing in *The Dallas Morning News*, offered his whimsical explanation for why it took the school almost forty years to do so: "Only now it is safe to assume Haynes can be hemmed in and made to stand still. He is 61 years old."

....

North Texas's black alumni formed the Trailblazers group in 1998 to recognize and share their experiences of the previous forty-plus years. In February 2004, the school began a year-long celebration of the fiftieth anniversary of A. Tennyson Miller's enrollment as a doctoral student. It featured reunions, seminars, and an appearance by noted poet and author Maya Angelou.

That November, UNT regents voted to award honorary doctorate degrees of humane letters to Miller and Joe Atkins; the school now offers the A. Tennyson Miller and Joe L. Atkins Scholarship Award through its Division of Equity & Diversity. The board that night also renamed UNT's Men's Gymnasium, the school's main arena for varsity basketball from 1950 until 1973, for Ken Bahnsen. He retired in 2000 following forty-five full-time years on staff, serving as a varsity football assistant, head coach of the freshman football team until the NCAA allowed frosh to again participate in varsity athletics in 1972, tennis coach, and coordinator of the school's driver's education and safety program. Bahnsen continued working for the university part-time through the fall semester of 2015, and then struggled to clean out his office. "My wife said, 'Don't bring it all home.'" One of the reunion attendees was Bert Christian, class of 1963, who became a lawyer in California.

....

On March 11, 2008, Haynes was inducted into the Texas Sports Hall of Fame in a class that included Pro Football Hall of Fame receiver Michael Irvin of the Dallas Cowboys, former Texas Tech football coach Spike Dykes, and former Dallas Stars hockey hero Mike

Modano. Haynes's family and his North Texas family were both well represented at the ceremony held at the Hall's home in Waco. Some of the latter were unofficially counted among the former, one of whom was Raymond Clement's granddaughter, Emma Bowman. Raymond and wife Deloris often would bring Emma and older sister Brandi to North Texas alumni functions, or get-togethers of former North Texas football players from long ago known as the Bald Eagles. Emma, even as a pre-schooler, formed a bond with Haynes. With the development of social media, they became Facebook friends. Haynes told Emma that he was her godfather; his sons, Abner Jr. and David, would refer to her as their sister. When Emma as a fifth-grader was devastated just before the Christmas break by the death of her thirty-two-year-old teacher from a brain-stem stroke, Haynes solicited a prayer chain through his network of personal and business contacts that resulted in Emma receiving supportive emails from around the globe.

Most of the Hall of Fame honorees' speeches that night were peppered with humor. It was difficult to identify any humor in Haynes's speech, which lasted slightly longer than six minutes. It began with a man verbally fumbling a bit, apparently out of sheer elation: "It's an honor to be here this afternoon … this evening … I'm kind of excited." He expressed the opinion that North Texas was collectively nervous with Leon King and him joining the football team, how the two of them were obviously nervous, and how that trepidation quickly dissipated when the Cole brothers and Garland Warren walked over to them near Fouts Field and made them immediately feel accepted. "When we got there, Odus Mitchell, Fred McCain, Ken Bahnsen, and many players welcomed us. I didn't say *all*. But it was real, and that was enough. … These are the people that were straight shooters with me. I love 'em today. We tried to set roles for all of Texas. Ten years before any of you thought about me, North Texas opened the door for me. My dad called Matty Bell at SMU and tried to get me into SMU. 'No, no, no. We don't take coloreds.' I called the University of Texas. My brothers insisted, 'They don't take coloreds.' *North … Texas … took … coloreds!* Thank you."

The next recipient to speak in the alphabetical listing was Irvin, who told the gathering he attended the banquet despite feeling extremely ill. Whatever remarks that he'd planned in advance were amended to instead open by playing off Haynes's words: "Abner Haynes just left this podium. And we sometimes get kind of uncomfortable when people start talking about race. I appreciate him sharing his history with us. And if we don't focus on where we started, because of Abner Haynes and because of Charlie Cole extending his hand—and in my mind, I see that hand. And because that black and white hand putting together, I'm able to stand here. I am sick, and I'm miserable when I'm sick, but I would not have missed this for anything. My body is aching, but my spirit is rejoicing."

. . . .

Emma Bowman was selected as the freshman princess in Bowie High's homecoming court in fall 2009. The Jackrabbits' football game against Jacksboro increased in importance since it also marked the opening of the school's new stadium. Emma decided she wanted to share the monumental occasion with a special friend, and she invited Haynes to be her guest at the game. Emma's mother, Kami, recalls trying to brace her ninth-grader for the likelihood that Haynes wouldn't be able to attend, a fear that was unfounded. Haynes indeed came, along with both of his sons. If there was concern in the new stadium that night over how the three black gentlemen would be received in Bowie, that, too, was unfounded. Haynes was introduced to the crowd by the stadium public address announcer to rousing applause. Many of the older men in the stands, some of whom had played for Raymond Clement at Bowie High, later approached Haynes like he was a rock star. Were all of that not enough, the Jackrabbits capped the evening with a 29-9 victory.

. . . .

Fifty-five years after initially enrolling at North Texas State College, Burlyce Sherrell Logan completed her course work in applied arts and sciences, and was among the 4,000 or so who walked in the

University of North Texas's commencement ceremony in May 2011. The actual walking was difficult for her because of a left knee that was a constant source of pain and occasionally restricted her mobility. Logan was almost deathly afraid that she wouldn't be able to make it up to the stage in the UNT Coliseum to accept her diploma.

Getting out of her seat might have been enough of a challenge in itself, so her department chairman did what he could to help the situation. He loaned Logan two large pillows on which to sit, decreasing the distance traveled from a sitting position to standing up, but she was still worried. University president V. Lane Rawlins extended his hands to Logan to help her up onto the stage. Everyone up there applauded and then hugged her as she made her way across. Logan cried, both for what she had accomplished and for the feeling that her late parents—who had insisted she attend North Texas—were somehow there right beside her. After she returned to her seat on the coliseum floor, she was asked, like a curtain call for the headline performer, to stand and receive one more round of applause. The knee simply didn't allow that to happen a second time in such a brief time span. Logan figured the best that she could do was wave, so she extended her right arm skyward. In the process, her right hand balled up just as a UNT photographer snapped her picture. To some in the building, it might have appeared to be a raised fist. When Logan first saw the photo, she feared she was making a black-power gesture. Worse yet for her, that was one of the images soon displayed in a collage of school scenes in the student union. "I hate that photo," Logan says, half crying, half laughing. "Looks like a militant."

Logan says she received Facebook congratulations from around the globe, and from a black woman who sat next to her a few semesters earlier in biology class. The woman often complained to Logan about her own misfortune; her husband was abroad, leaving her to care for their nine-year-old child, in addition to going to school. The woman stated that she often wondered why Logan, hobbling into class with a cane or a walker, put herself through that. "Now I understand," the woman wrote.

....

Four years after Vernon Cole's death in 1972, the shock had still not worn off for his widow, Carolyn. But with three children often out and about, doing things with their friends, Carolyn gradually re-entered her world in and around Waco. She eventually developed a relationship with Tillman Rodabaugh, a social psychology professor at Baylor whose specialty was the study of death and dying. They married in 1977, live in Waco, but spend their summers in the much more hospitable climate of northern New Mexico.

Carolyn is among the handful of Denton High friends from the 1950s who gather annually in late spring or early summer in Granbury, Texas, about an hour's drive southwest of Fort Worth, at the home of Odus Mitchell's daughter, Margaret Mitchell Cole (no, she didn't marry into the same Coles of Pilot Point). The group spends a long weekend reminiscing and catching up. Margaret has saved a small museum's worth of memorabilia from her father's coaching career, even some game films. At one of the yearly slumber parties, Margaret mentioned that her collection included the game ball given to her father in connection with the 1959 Sun Bowl, signed by all of the Eagles' players and staff.

Carolyn has likewise saved many remnants from Vernon's playing days, from scrapbooks of his career both in college and pro ball to game programs and pennants from North Texas, to the welcoming letters that were sent to them from the fans in Winnipeg. During the get-together of 2011, Margaret decided the Sun Bowl game ball should be included in Carolyn's collection. It now commands a place of honor in the Rodabaughs' home.

....

The beginning of the 2011 college football season ushered in a new era of North Texas football with the opening of Apogee Stadium, Fouts Field being replaced following fifty-nine seasons. In a way, the opening of the new facility brought new life to a campus organization that technically hasn't existed since the early 1970s—the Geezles. As Greek fraternities nationally experienced pressures to simply maintain their financial viability, the local social fraternity had little backing on which to depend, and so had closed its doors—figuratively and literally, after almost fifty years. But that didn't prevent Geezles alums from continuing to recognize the group and to meet occasionally on an informal basis, such as a handful of members who met regularly for lunch at the Y.O. Ranch restaurant in Dallas.

The construction of Apogee Stadium provided the Geezles with an opportunity to make a contribution to North Texas's new football home. They reminisced about Fouts Field and lamented the fact that their stadium never sported a statue or sculpture of their team mascot, the eagle. They recalled that such a sculpture graced the entrance to the old Geezles house on Hickory Street and assumed it no longer existed. They estimated that creation of a new eagle would cost about $50,000, and set out to try to locate the original Geezles eagle with efforts expanding beyond the lunch group. One member tracked down the eagle to the home of one of the fraternity's sponsors, Dr. Pat McLeod of the industrial arts faculty for almost half a century beginning in 1954. (Yes, the same Dr. McLeod who dropped in on Leon King's paddling persuasion.) McLeod acknowledged once having had custody of the statue, but said he handed it over during the 1990s to one of the former members, whose name he couldn't recall.

So, the Geezles set out to commission the creation of a new eagle sculpture, about twelve feet tall with a wingspan of about ten feet, placed on a ten-foot pedestal. For such a work, though, the initial cost estimate of $50,000 proved to be about $300,000 short. The Geezles solicited help from as many members as could be located, including holding a Geezle Round-up Reunion at North Texas's homecoming game in 2009. The effort raised only about a third of the necessary funding. The Geezles downsized their specs for the sculpture to a four-foot bronze bust of an eagle's head and chest mounted on a ground-level base. When Apogee Stadium first welcomed fans on September 10, 2011, the new Geezles eagle—located along the team's path from the locker room to the field—created a new North Texas football tradition. Similar to customs observed at many college football stadiums,

Mean Green players touch the eagle—named "Spiriki"—on their way to the field for good luck.

....

G.A. Moore woke up one day, when he was a junior in college, and decided he wanted to get an education. He graduated in 1962 and earned a master's in education five years later. Moore, like Odus Mitchell, couldn't identify a better way to earn a living than coaching. Given that Moore began as a high school head football coach in 1971 and was still doing so in 2011, it apparently appealed to him. He became the state's leader in career victories in 2002. His Celina Bobcats won fifty-seven straight games from the middle of the 1998 season through the end of 2001, each of the four years ending with a Class 2A state title. The eight total state championships that his teams won were divided between his alma mater, Pilot Point, and Celina, located all of seven miles from the Moore family farm in the community of Mustang, where he grew up and lives today.

During the middle of Moore's final season, he was selected for membership in the Texas Sports Hall of Fame. When the class of 2011 was inducted a few months later, Moore closed his induction speech by saying, "There's not anybody will ever be up here probably and deserve to be up here less than me. But I'll tell you this: there will never be anybody to be inducted into this thing that will appreciate it and love the privilege as much as I have."

....

Leon King earned a master's degree from North Texas in 1972 while teaching, and added a PhD from Nova University in 1980. He retired after a long and celebrated career in service to the Dallas Independent School District in 2000, his wife Claudia throwing him a huge party downtown. But even in retirement, King continued to answer the call for education, gladly serving whenever and wherever he was needed. He registered with the district as a substitute instructor into the second decade of the twenty-first century.

. . . .

When North Texas unveiled its All-Century football team in spring 2013, Abner Haynes held the unique distinction of making the team twice: as one of the three running backs, and as the kick returner. Two other honorees were part of his same Eagles football teams of the late 1950s: coach Odus Mitchell and guard Bill Carrico.

ACKNOWLEDGMENTS

I'M GRATEFUL FOR THE COOPERATION of Abner Haynes and Leon King in the earliest days of the project, and regret that they chose not to continue to be involved as the book took shape in recent years.

The following people were also gracious with their time, whether it was to answer one question over the phone or agreeing to meet with me in person on multiple occasions: Ken Bahnsen, Bob Way, Charlie Cole, Raymond Clement, G.A. Moore, Sammy Stanger, the late Joe Mack Pryor, the late Herb Ferrill, Carolyn Rodabaugh, Margaret Mitchell Cole, Art Perkins, Billy Joe Christle, the late Bishop Neaul Haynes, Vivian King Haynes, James King, Chauncey King, the late Joe Atkins, Kristin Herring, Bill Tom Herring, Sally Herring Ventor, Kami Bowman, the late Bill Carrico, Robert Duty, Bert Christian, Burlyce Sherrell Logan, Pierre Baratelli, Bill Linden, Charley Johnson, Joe Greene, C. Dan Smith, Dave Clark, Jim Mudd, Willie Davis, Floyd Moody, Bud Osborne, Rudy Carroll, George Kuhl, Joe Billy McDade, Jerry LeVias, Darrell Brown, John Brown, Ger Schwedes, Steve Goodall, Misty Carpenter, and James Burroughs.

Also providing significant assistance were Courtney Jacobs and Perri Hamilton of the archives division of UNT's Willis Library; Lisa Brown and her student staffers in Willis Library's microfilm division; Gary Payne, UNT's assistant manager of photography; UNT athletics' Eric Capper, Stephen Howard, and Bonita White; UNT staffers

Reginald Johnson, Deborah Leilaert, and Kristi Earley; Mike Ball and Jeff Suess of the *Cincinnati Enquirer*, Mike Fannin and Cliff Phillips of the *Kansas City Star*, Kirk Wessler and Joe Bates of the *Peoria Journal Star*, Navarro College's Dr. Tommy Stringer, Cathy Spitzenberger of the University of Texas at Arlington Libraries Special Collections, Vern Raven of the Mansfield Historical Museum and Heritage Center, Jay Black of the Texas Sports Hall of Fame, Liz Cline of Utah State's Special Collections and Archives Manuscript Collection, Norma Adams-Wade of *The Dallas Morning News*, David Barron of the *Houston Chronicle*, SMU's Kent Best and Brad Sutton, Baylor's Amanda Norman and Lauren Phillips Smith, Ana Chavez of the Sun Bowl, Mary Rixon of Murray State College, Marc Carlson of the University of Tulsa, Syracuse University's Susan Cornelius Edson, Doug Mosley of the University of Cincinnati, Bradley University's Bobby Parker, Kevin Trainor and Derek Satterfield of the University of Arkansas, Jeffrey Bechtold of the University of Washington, Chad Hartley of the University of Nevada Reno, David Bassity of the University of Houston, Tyler Clifton of the *Marshall News Messenger*, Diana Stickler of the *San Jose Mercury News*, authors Robyn Ladino, Rus Bradburd, and Christian Messenger; Leticia McGowan of the Dallas Independent School District, Lesley Range-Stanton of the Plano Independent School District, Brad Gee of the Kansas City Chiefs, Oscar Robertson representative Michael O'Daniel, and my technology mentor, Jason Miller.

BIBLIOGRAPHY

Books

Bates, Ed F. *History and Reminiscences of Denton County.* Denton, Texas: McNitzky Printing Company, 1918 and reprint Terrill Wheeler Printing, 1976.

Bonazzi, Robert. *Man in the Mirror: John Howard Griffin and the Story of "Black Like Me."* Maryknoll, N.Y.: Orbis Books, 1997.

Bradburd, Rus. *Forty Minutes of Hell: The Extraordinary Life of Nolan Richardson.* New York: Amistad, 2010.

Demas, Lane. *Integrating the Gridiron: Black Civil Rights and American College Football.* New Brunswick, N.J. and London: Rutgers University Press, 2010.

Eisenberg, John. *Ten-Gallon War: The NFL's Cowboys, the AFL's Texans, and the Feud for Dallas's Pro Football Future.* Boston, New York: Houghton Mifflin Harcourt, 2012.

Egan, Timothy. *The Worst Hard Time.* Boston, New York: Houghton Mifflin, 2006.

Frei, Terry. *Horns, Hogs, and Nixon Coming: Texas vs. Arkansas in Dixie's Last Stand.* New York: Simon & Schuster, 2002.

Fry, Hayden with Wine, George. *Hayden Fry: A High-Porch Picnic*. Champaign, Ill.: Sports Publishing Inc., 1999.

Gilchrist, Cookie and Garbarino, Chris. *The Cookie That Did Not Crumble*. Buffalo, N.Y.: Self-Published, 2011.

Goldstone, Dwonna. *Integrating the 40 Acres: The 50-Year Struggle for Racial Equality at the University of Texas*. Athens, Ga. University of Georgia Press, 2006.

Green, George N. *Hurst, Euless, and Bedford: Heart of the Metroplex; An Illustrated History*. Austin, Texas: Eakin Press, 1995.

Griffin, John Howard. *Black Like Me*. New York: Houghton Mifflin, 1961.

Grundy, Pamela. *Learning to Win: Sports, Education, and Social Change in Twentieth Century North Carolina*. Chapel Hill, N.C.: University of North Carolina Press, 2001.

Kemper, Kurt Edward. *College Football and American Culture in the Cold War Era*. Urbana, Ill., and Chicago: University of Illinois Press, 2009.

Lopez, Katherine. *Cougars of Any Color: The Integration of University of Houston Athletics, 1964-1968*. Jefferson, N.C. and London: McFarland & Company, 2008.

Martin, Charles H. *Benching Jim Crow: The Rise and Fall of The Color Line in Southern College Sports, 1890-1980*. Urbana, Ill., Chicago and Springfield, Ill.: University of Illinois Press, 2010.

McMillen, Neil R. *The Citizens' Council: Organized Resistance to the Second Reconstruction, 1954-64*. Urbana, Ill., Chicago and London: University of Illinois Press, 1971.

Oriard, Michael. *King Football: Sports & Spectacle in the Golden Age of Radio and Newsreels, Movies and Magazines, The Weekly & The Daily Press*. Chapel Hill, N.C.: University of North Carolina Press, 2001.

Payne, Darwin. *Big D: Triumphs and Troubles of an American Supercity in the 20th Century.* Dallas: Three Forks Press, 1994.

Pennington, Bill. *The Heisman: Great American Stories of the Men Who Won.* New York: HarperCollins 10 Regan Books, 2004.

Pennington, Richard. *Breaking the Ice: The Racial Integration of Southwest Conference Football.* Jefferson, N.C. and London: McFarland & Company, 1987.

Pipes, Kasey S. *Ike's Final Battle: The Road to Little Rock and the Challenge of Equality.* Los Angeles: World Ahead Publishing, 2007.

Ragsdale, Kenneth. *The Year America Discovered Texas: Centennial '36.* Bryan-College Station, Texas: Texas A&M University Press, 1987.

Robertson, Oscar. *The Big O: My Life, My Times, My Game.* Emmaus, Pa., and New York: Rodale, 2003.

Rogers, James L. *The Story of North Texas: From Texas Normal College, 1890, to the University of North Texas System, 2001.* Denton, Texas: University of North Texas Press, 2002.

Royal, Darrell with Wheat, John. *Coach Royal: Conversations with a Texas Football Legend.* Austin, Texas: University of Texas Press, 2005.

Stringer, Tommy. *Dreams and Visions: The History of Navarro College.* Waco: Davis Brothers Publishing, 1996.

Thomas, Duane and Zimmerman, Paul. *Duane Thomas and the Fall of America's Team.* New York: Warner Books, 1988.

Walker, Chet with Messenger, Chris. *Long Time Coming: A Black Athlete's Coming-of-Age in America.* New York: Grove Press, 1995.

Watson, Tex as told to Hoekstra, Ray. *Will You Die for Me? The Man Who Killed for Charles Manson Tells His Own Story.* Old Tappan, N.J.: Fleming H. Revell Company, 1978.

Additional sources

Abilene Reporter-News

Arkansas Democrat-Gazette

Atlanta Journal-Constitution

Austin American-Statesman

Baylor University Libraries Athletic Archive

Campus Chat (North Texas)

Cincinnati Enquirer

Corsicana Daily Sun

Dallas Express

Dallas Morning News

Dallas Times Herald

Denton Record-Chronicle

El Paso Times

Fort Worth Press

Fort Worth Star-Telegram

Houston Chronicle

Houston Post

Los Angeles Times

Lubbock Avalanche Journal

New York Times

NT Daily (North Texas)

San Jose Mercury News

San Antonio Express-News

Seattle Post-Intelligencer

Sports Illustrated

Street & Smith's Football

Tulsa Tribune

Tulsa World

Utah State University Special Collections and Manuscript Collection

University of North Texas Oral History Collection

University of North Texas Willis Library Archives and Rare Books

University of Texas Dolph Briscoe Center for American History

University of Texas at El Paso Oral History Collection

Waco Tribune-Herald.

INDEX

C

I, J

K

T